SECRETS OF SUPPLEMENTS

THE GOOD, THE BAD, THE TOTALLY TERRIFIC

FIRST PRINTING 2008

Published by PHYTE MEDIA INC.

Book and cover design by Louise Donahue, www.laillustrator.com

Library and Archives Canada Cataloguing in Publication
Askew, Gloria
Secrets of supplements : the good, the bad, the totally terrific/ Gloria Askew, Jerre Paquette ; editors: Bonnie Benoit & Carole Jeffries.
Includes bibliographical references and index
ISBN 978-0-9784290-0-3

    1. Dietary supplements--Popular works. I. Paquette, Jerre II. Benoit, Bonnie III. Jeffries, Carole IV. Title.

RM258.5.A85 2007   613.2'8   C2007-905165-0

Printed In Canada

DEDICATION

I dedicate this work to my family: daughter Michelle and son-in-law Kevin, our lovely granddaughter Kennedy, my son Brad, and my husband Alf.

They have always believed in me and encouraged me in my passion and my quest to empower people with the knowledge of nutrition so they can all actually thrive and not just survive!

Gloria Askew

My son Jeremy lived the last years of his life searching rigorously for answers from the medical and alternative medicial professions to resolve his considerable health problems. He was not successful, but his determination to stay true to his trust in the best of science and in the spirit of alternative thinking continues to move me to continue his search. I dedicate my work for this book to him and his two children, Yerachmiel and Elisheva Paquette.

Jerre Paquette

ACKNOWLEDGEMENTS

A book starts out as a rather solitary activity. All the risk and the struggle and the anticipation and joy seems yours alone for awhile. Then reality hits—you're just one part of the team required to get a book to press and to the readers. There are those whom you use as sounding boards and moral support; those who help with research and even do some writing along the way; the many who edit, proof, design, photocopy, advise, challenge, disagree, confirm, fix your computer, and those special ones who hug you at just the right moments and constantly admonish you to stay with the dream.

Carole Jeffries, Jerre's wife and the best editor he's ever met, did all those things (except fix the computer). She was a partner to both of us from our book's inception and, frankly, without her we would not have finished this book. We are indebted to her for her selfless and rigorous research and substantive editing at every phase of the book's production.

Beyond Carole, we applaud the work and support of Bonnie Benoit and Louise Donahue for editing and design, Brad Askew and Michelle Askew for help with language and marketing, Carol MacGregor for assistance with software issues, Gordon MacGregor for last minute help with photography and dinner, Dave Reynolds (at Indigo) for help with marketing, Walter Bruno for getting us started in InDesign, Jim Beckel and the folks at Friesens Printing for shepherding us through the printing process, and Wayne Logan at Field LLP for his enthusiastic and caring legal advice.

We are grateful to Wendy Podborski, Bob Harris, Dr. Robert Boschman, and Judy Frame for taking time out of their busy lives to help us focus our business plan.

Special mention has to go to Dr. Tom MacAlister of Mount Royal College who spent a lot of hours working with us on questions of science and biology. Any errors we made in these areas are not of his making— they're Glorias (I wonder whether she'll catch this in the final proof-read).

And we want to especially thank our expert and peek-preview readers— Dr. Edward Gentis, Dr. Dick Lyons, Jim and Sharon Janz, Dr. Elizabeth Thakkar, Dr. Rebecca Sagan, Jeff and Lisa Applebaum. Thank you, all.

Finally, we simply have to acknowledge all of you who over so many years have insisted that Gloria write this book—without your persistance and support and vision, we wouldn't even have started.

TESTIMONIALS

Gloria Askew has been a specialist in the nutrition field for many years. In my estimation, she is one of the most knowledgeable people in North America on the subject. Her knowledge goes far beyond what most nutritionists have because of her hands-on, personal research into the subject.

She has been a trainer for thousands of people in many parts of the world, and each time I hear her present she impresses me more. I always come away with a renewed understanding of what I need to do to stay healthy, "the natural way."

When you read this book, you will get the best and the latest information you can possibly have on the subject of nutrition supplementation and how it applies to your everyday life.

You will want everyone you care about to have a copy.

Jim Janz
President, Janz & Associates

Optimal health does not happen by itself. It needs to be both nurtured and guarded. Much depends on healthy nutritional choices—difficult to make without awareness of principles and some of the science behind them. This book addresses both.

A must-read if you intend to use food supplements.

Edward F. Gentis MD, FRCSC

Secrets of Supplements is not just another book on nutrition. It provides a wealth of knowledge for both the expert and the uninitiated.

It is easy to read and surprisingly humourous!

This book is a good source for quick reference, but best of all it inspires readers to change their dietary habits.

Elizabeth Thakkar
M.B.B.S D.C.H L.R.C.P M.R.C.S L.M.C.C

THE AUTHORS

Gloria Askew, Retired Registered Nurse

Gloria is in demand around the world as a lecturer on nutrition and supplements. She spent most of her Registered Nursing career as Director of a busy Emergency Department and as a teacher of nutrition in medical clinics. Her research focuses on discovering and revealing the secrets of a major nutritional trend—Optimal Supplementation. She believes strongly that everyone needs an advocate when it comes to nutrition.

Jerre Paquette, B.Ed, M.A., Ph.D

Jerre is an award-winning college instructor whose 42 year teaching and research career spans elementary through university. As far back as 1967, he noted the apparent links among learning, energy, behavior, grades, and nutrition. Throughout his career, Jerre has pleaded with the school system to feature nutrition education across all the school years for students and their parents. He remains perplexed why such a need is so slow to gain favor.

WHY WE WROTE THIS BOOK

We wrote this book because it was obvious the demands on Gloria's time and energy exceeded her ability to meet them. Her presentations filled up, follow-up question periods took as long to deal with as the presentations themselves, her e-mail box was usually glutted, and requests for personal consultations were over the top. It appeared the appetite for good nutrition was growing rapidly. All of us knew a book had to emerge and she had to cocoon herself to get it written.

In spite of the large chorus of diverse voices insisting she write a book, none of us, individually or collectively, could convince her to do that—she was too busy working directly with the people who needed information, education, and consultation.

But if the writing was not yet in a book, it was certainly on the wall. Like so many others who had become repeat ticket-holders to her events, my wife Carole and I couldn't keep up with her. Frankly, it was becoming clear from all the new information Gloria kept offering that there would come a time when she couldn't keep up with her own intentions. She wants to educate her audiences about optimal nutrition; more than that, she is determined to become an advocate for those who need information and guidance that seems inaccessible and overwhelming to them.

I couldn't sit in my seat listening to her any longer (while wildly writing down notes I couldn't understand the next day). "Gloria," I pleaded, "let's write your book together." With hardly a blink, she said she'd love to do that. Why hadn't I asked earlier?

So here it is—not a fast read or a little book to give you a quick fix. Sorry about that: You'll have to journey through the material just as we did in spite of our efforts to make things simple. Some things are just not simple.

Our assumption about you is that you are motivated to take charge of your own nutrition and health, so we've written a book we want you to read carefully, not quickly. And we'd like you to share what you learn— that's all we're doing, really.

So read a couple of chapters. Put the book down, reflect on your eating habits and life style, take a critical gander through your fridge and your cupboards, embark on a shopping trip for groceries—but this time read a few labels. Ask yourself questions. Figure out what you know and don't know about good food and good supplements. Then return to the book—it will have answers for many of your questions or get you ready to answer them yourself.

And here's the surprise—while we provide you with the answers we discovered to many secrets about food supplements, our goal was to have you leave our book not with a just a few answers, but with a list of penetrating questions to take to your supplement providers. We think getting these questions in your hands will reveal more secrets than the biggest book in the world could manage.

We have used these questions ourselves to ensure we and our families have the best supplements possible. We are confident, therefore, that the questuins we offer will help you find what you are looking for, especially if you have some understanding of the science behind them.

They come at the very end of the book, in Chapter 13, but don't you dare peek. They work best if you first have an understanding of the science behind them—the content of the first twelve chapters.

And now I can't wait to attend another of Gloria's presentations. Having helped her write her book, I think I'm ready to appreciate more than ever the combination of knowledge and wisdom she brings to all she does.

Jerre Paquette, PhD.
September, 2007

CONTENTS

A **ANECDOTE** Throughout my early emergency room nursing days, I simply didn't question how little emphasis was placed on the dietary habits of ill people. In fact, the exhilaration of a fast-paced Emergency Department attracted me to this kind of specialized nursing. It focused on exciting technological treatments rather than basic nutritional routines. Emergent and urgent cases were quickly and accurately diagnosed and dealt with. The patient was either admitted for further care or went home after appropriate treatment—often with a prescription in hand, but no advice about foods or food supplements that might be helpful.

Even patients with gastrointestinal problems such as stomach-aches, acid reflux, and irritable bowel syndrome were rarely asked about or given advice on their dietary habits. In the high-tech, high-drama world of pharmaceutical and surgical remedies, my colleagues and I pretty much ignored even the most fundamental aspects of human nutrition and their link to human health.

The irony is that, as a child, I was frequently exposed to nutritional concepts and practices. I grew up in rural Saskatchewan where my father raised many animals on our farm. He was always very particular about the food he fed his livestock, and when something was wrong with them, he or the veterinarian almost always related it directly back to their food. As an adult, however, I had lost sight of the link between the diets of human animals and their health.

It wasn't until several years into my career that I realized we were treating the symptoms of disease without considering the causes. I started searching for answers to our patients' most persistent problems. Eventually, I came to understand that a person is a whole being—and that there is a correlation between the foods eaten or not eaten, the nutrients assimilated or not assimilated, and the genetic factors that may create nutritional needs unique to every person. In short, I came to understand that the nutrients you put in your mouth or don't put in your mouth—either as foods or food supplements—really do matter. I determined to learn more about them.

- Gloria

CHAPTER 1
THE FOOD-HEALTH CONNECTION

Decades ago, physicians began warning diabetics away from sugar and sugary foods. More recently, they have raised the alarm about the dangers of eating trans-fats, and they have begun advising people to restrict their intake of certain fish due to the risk of heavy metals contamination. That is, mainstream medicine has made the connection between food and disease—but it has yet to focus on the connection between food and health.

In contrast, sailors and explorers of the "new world" made the food-health connection five hundred years ago. They learned to avoid the horrors of scurvy by eating fresh whole foods. You have likely heard the classic accounts of Christopher Columbus unloading desperately ill sailors to die on a tropical island only to return a few months later to find them not only alive, but thriving. Similarly, when scurvy devastated the crew of French explorer Jacques Cartier in the winter of 1535 – 1536, First Nations peoples taught the sailors to treat the disease with a tea infused with evergreen needles.

These sailors were lucky because illness and death from scurvy is not pretty. Early symptoms include bleeding under the skin and in deep tissue, receding gums and loose teeth, anemia, fatigue, joint pain, and difficulty walking—a condition the *British Royal Navy* viewed as mere laziness and treated with flogging.

The problem, however, was not laziness, but low production of collagen related to low intake of Vitamin C. As the disease progressed, bones began to rub painfully together, making it impossible to walk. Sailors eventually died of cerebral hemorrhage, blood loss, or convulsions.

Most physicians of the day scoffed at the idea that something in food could offer a treatment, maintaining it was the sea air that made the sailors ill. Nevertheless, Dr. John Woodall began treating scurvy with lemon juice and ultimately convinced the East India Company to provide it to their sailors when they were at sea.

In the mid-1700s, James Lind, a surgeon's mate with the *British Royal Navy*, offered different remedies to six pairs of sailors afflicted with scurvy. To Lind's delight and surprise, the pair given a remedy that included a daily ration of two oranges and one lemon recovered. Eventually, the *British Royal Navy* was persuaded to use lime juice to prevent scurvy, but it took over 40 years of coaxing and cost an estimated 100,000 seamen their lives before the change was implemented.

Today, healthcare providers acknowledge that the Vitamin C contained in citrus fruits and other foods offers a treatment for scurvy. Nevertheless, somewhat like its 18th century predecessors, modern mainstream medicine remains slow to make similar connections between dietary nutrients and health. Yes, physicians have made the connection between some nutrients and certain health conditions: iron and anemia, calcium and osteoporosis, and folic acid and neural tube defects, to name just a few. But are other nutritional deficiencies causing, or at least contributing to, a whole range of unexplained maladies in North America today? It may be possible.

According to nutrition researchers at *Arizona State University* (ASU), Vitamin C deficiency is more pronounced in America than iron deficiency—which is reportedly the most prevalent nutrient deficiency. One study at ASU showed that 6% of subjects were deficient in Vitamin C and another 30% were depleted of it; that is, these subjects did not meet the Recommended Daily Allowance (RDA) for Vitamin C. In a paper entitled "A Case for C", researcher Carol Johnson at ASU argues that scurvy is misdiagnosed today as polio or vasculitis simply because no one, physician or patient, is on the lookout for scurvy (Johnson).

What's particularly interesting here is that physicians may be diagnosing polio (a viral cause) or vasculitis (an inflammation) rather than scurvy (a nutrient deficiency). Perhaps this is to be expected for a couple of reasons: First, of course, scurvy is perceived to be a disease of a bygone era, not of our modern age. Second, medical doctors and registered nurses get very little (if any) formal education in nutritional science; their training and profession tend to focus on pharmaceutical and surgical remedies. As a result, it may simply be unreasonable to expect a doctor or nurse trained in Western mainstream medicine to recognize a nutritional deficiency or to offer a nutritional remedy. And even if a doctor undertook extra study in the science of nutrition, medical licensing regulations under which medical doctors work typically discourage them from recommending nutritional remedies.

This focus on pharmaceutical and surgical remedies may not be surprising. After all, a great deal has been achieved in public health in the past hundred years. At the beginning of the 20th century, infections were the leading causes of death. Mainstream medicine used pharmaceutical remedies to win that fight, and it used them again in the fight against pneumonia, diarrhea, and diphtheria. The result was a dramatic reduction in rates of illness and death from these potentially lethal diseases.

As pharmaceutical remedies were proving their worth, nutritional remedies appeared to be losing their value. Soils across the globe were degrading, but in varying degrees. Plants grown in different parts of the world or in different parts of the country, for that matter, did not contain consistent levels of nutrients—at least in part because the quality of the soils varied from place to place and farmer to farmer. How could a physician rely on a nutritional remedy if it could not be measured or controlled? As the use of pharmaceuticals became more successful and more widespread, and as plants (and the soils they grew in) became an increasingly complex issue, nutritional remedies were slowly overshadowed.

Today, the issue of nutrition and its connection to health is hotly debated in medical circles. Medical schools, researchers, physicians, and governing bodies engaged in modern mainstream medicine generally allow little room for nutritional remedies. Healthcare providers in complementary healthcare argue that natural remedies, including food supplements, have a more viable place in healthcare than drugs. Others see the issue in neither black nor white, but in varying shades of gray—where there is room for integrative treatments that combine both mainstream and complementary practices.

Exploring this lively and sometimes intense debate is beyond the scope of this book. The intention, here, is to draw from solid scientific research to teach you about your own biology, to let you decide whether food supplements may play a role in your overall nutritional status, and to help you make informed decisions about which food supplements to buy. First, though, let's examine a few reasons to consider supplements at all.

SOME FREAKY FACTS

When you experience a nutrient deficiency, your body will try to alert you. It may send a message via any combination of seemingly inconsequential symptoms: aches and pains, circulatory problems, cognitive impairment (such as brain fog, poor concentration, or memory loss), dandruff, depression, fatigue, infections, insomnia, irritability, or low energy levels. As Dr. Timothy Smith indicates, these situations tend to "drive doctors up a diagnostic tree" (1999). This frustration occurs because the underlying cause is difficult to pinpoint—especially for those who have not been trained in the science of nutrition and nutritional deficiencies.

In these situations, standard medical tests seldom show anything is abnormal, leaving both physician and patient at a loss. This is the point at which you or your physician or perhaps family, friends, or employers may misinterpret the symptoms as laziness, a bad temper, hypochondria, some kind of mental or character weakness, or simply as normal aging (an old standby that patients seem to accept all-too-readily). Your body's message has been sent and received, but grossly misunderstood.

So you force yourself to go to work, to pull up your socks, to get on with it. It's the modern-day equivalent of flogging a sailor in the early stages of scurvy. Like those sailors, you want to regain your health—but how? As Dr. Smith points out:

> If doctors do prescribe treatment, they usually bypass nutritional

supplements in favor of drugs such as anti-inflammatories, antidepressants, tranquilizers, and the like. These not only mask symptoms but also deplete nutrient stores even further. This accelerates the degenerative process, which is the forerunner of disease and aging (1999).

If a physician cannot diagnose or treat your symptoms or if you simply choose to ignore them, you may succumb to a more serious illness (an *event*, as it's known in medical terminology). It's important to realize, however, that ill health is seldom an event—it's a process. You become ill one mouthful at a time, one sedentary day at a time, one nutrient-deficient, inactive week at a time.

Despite the best that medical technology can offer, a heart attack or stroke can kill you or permanently debilitate you or, at the very least, leave you unable to play a game of baseball with your children. If you have a leg amputated due to diabetes (which is the leading cause of amputations), you may never again hike a favorite trail or dance a much-loved tango. In fact, once you become ill, you may end up in treatment for the rest of your life.

As these examples illustrate, disease can severely affect your life. Unfortunately, many people do not realize just how severe the changes may be, nor do they realize how great the risks of developing a serious illness may be—but the evidence is all around them:

First, according to the *American* and *Canadian Diabetes Associations,* 22.8 million North Americans (about 7% of the population) have diabetes; of these, nearly one-third do not know they have it. To make matters worse, a recent Canadian study by Lipscombe and Hux published in the prestigious medical journal *The Lancet* reported the prevalence of diabetes in Canada

A SUPPLEMENTS SECRET

When combined with proper diet and exercise, some food supplements (such as those containing chromium, magnesium, manganese and certain B vitamins) may help patients control blood glucose levels.

increased by 69% between 1995 and 2005. The greatest increase was found among younger people aged 20 to 49 years.

It's a frightening situation because diabetes greatly increases your risks of cardiovascular disease and stroke. Diabetes often brings with it other complications that occur with far greater frequency than many people think: erectile dysfunction, blindness, nerve damage often leading to amputation, and kidney disease (with its own set of complications). In the middle-aged and elderly, high blood sugar often results in poor memory, as well.

A diagnosis of diabetes is life-altering and potentially life-threatening. Necessary lifestyle changes and monitoring practices may be portrayed as "simple" in everything from medical literature to television advertising, but diabetes is not necessarily easy to manage.

Second, the *U.S. Department of Health and Human Services, Centers for Disease Control and Prevention* reports that, as of February 2007, more than 25.6 million American adults (12% of the population) have been diagnosed with heart disease. It's the leading cause of death in the United States. In the United Kingdom, the BBC reports that one British adult dies every three minutes from heart disease.

Third, in recent years, medical practitioners have seen the prevalence of inflammatory response disorders take off like a rocket. For example, the *National Center for Chronic Disease Prevention and Health Promotion* (CDC) reports that, in a classroom of 30 students, an average of three will have asthma. In fact, in 2002, 14.7 million school

A SUPPLEMENTS SECRET

Genetic testing now can reveal certain gene patterns that place certain individuals at risk for heart disease. Specialized supplements have been developed to address the nutrient needs of these people—especially as these needs relate to plant nutrients. Essential Fatty Acids and B vitamins also help support heart health, and recent clinical trials have confirmed something that thousands of years of traditional medicine have shown all along: Garlic helps maintain cardiovascular health.

days were missed because of it. In addition, Alzheimer's disease, allergies, and many other life-altering illnesses all have been linked to inflammation.

Heart disease, the leading killer of North Americans, also has been closely linked to the inflammatory process. An increased inflammatory response also has been implicated in certain aggressive forms of cancer. Cancer is the second-leading cause of death in the United States, and the CDC reports one million Americans are diagnosed with cancer every year.

The CDC also reports that 20% of American adults have arthritis and that the disease limits the activity of about 19 million people. It's important to understand that arthritis is not part of a natural aging process (as arthritis patients often are told). It's also important to understand that if you're dealing with arthritis, or any other inflammatory response disorder, the inflammatory response is your immune system's first response to injury. The redness, swelling, and pain typical of any inflammation constitute a warning that problems exist at the cellular level and that your body is attempting to repair itself. When inflammation becomes chronic, however, it can damage healthy tissues.

A SUPPLEMENTS SECRET

Evidence is mounting that a totally terrific multi-supplement combined with nutrients such as calcium, magnesium, essential fatty acids, and mixed fatty acid esters (celadrin) may help douse the fires of inflammation. Informed supplementation may help support the body so it can heal—without the potentially dangerous side effects of popular pharmaceutical remedies.

In medicine, the suffix "itis" at the end of a medical term indicates the condition is an inflammatory response. Arthritis, bursitis, colitis, gastro enteritis, gingivitis, and any other conditions ending with *itis* are all inflammatory responses. It's crucial to address the source of an inflammatory response and not to simply mask the symptoms with anti-inflammatory drugs. Masking symptoms without adequately addressing the underlying cause can create a chronic condition. Failure to find the cause of the inflammatory response is a little like switching off the fire alarm in a burning building: You turn off that annoying warning bell, but it does nothing to put out the fire.

Fourth, thirty years ago, ADD and ADHD were not a diagnostic category. Today, depending on which report you read, statistics show ADD/ADHD wreaks havoc in the lives of as many as 25% of North American school children (Whiting, 2006). Common treatment tends to focus on drugs or psychiatric counseling or both.

In the schools, curriculum development for students with ADD/ADHD seldom does little more than mention nutrition or supplementation, almost as an after-thought. Before exposing these children to drugs and their side effects (and all drugs have side effects), maybe it's worth saying "Okay, let's look at the nutritional status of these children. Let's see if something is missing from their diets or if some nutrient or combination of nutrients might help alleviate this condition, somewhat like citrus fruits alleviated scurvy." With any change like this, get the advice of your health practitioner.

A SUPPLEMENTS SECRET

Dr. Steven E. Whiting of the *Institute of Nutritional Science* in San Diego strongly advocates nutritional options for ADD/ADHD in his booklet "Trace Minerals and Learning Disabilities—A Third Opinion" (2006).

Fifth, fifty years ago, osteoporosis was considered a disease that afflicted elderly people, mainly women. Today, this killer disease costs the American healthcare system $14 billion per year and poses a major health threat for 44 million Americans. Of these, an estimated 10 million already have the disease and another 34 million have low bone mass. Most surprising, perhaps, is that those at risk now include young men (yes, men) and young women in their early thirties.

The *National Institutes of Health* define bone as "living, growing tissue. It's made mostly of collagen, a protein that provides a soft framework, and calcium phosphate, a mineral that adds strength and hardens the framework." As you already have read, inadequate intake of Vitamin C can lead to inadequate production of collagen, and fairly widespread Vitamin C deficiency is suspected in North America. Further, many published studies show that inadequate intake of calcium and its complementary nutrients throughout a person's lifetime (not just in the elder years) increases the risk of osteoporosis. Calcium deficiencies left unattended will lead to serious bone mass issues—especially in children and seniors.

Osteoporosis is caused by certain lifestyle factors and dietary choices. Lifestyle factors include smoking and sedentary habits; dietary choices include excessive protein intake, high phosphate intake (meat and soft drinks), high sugar intake (especially through processed foods), and low nutrient intake. When you add up all these factors, you may not be surprised to learn that the *National Institutes of Health* warn that one in two American women and one in four American men will suffer an osteoporosis-related fracture.

A SUPPLEMENTS SECRET

Many people know calcium is needed for strong bones, but they may not know that, if the body is to lay down bone properly, calcium also requires magnesium, Vitamin D, and Vitamin C with bioflavonoids.

It's important to realize these fractures can be deadly, especially when they occur in the hip or spine. It's important to realize, too, that this life-threatening disease is both preventable and treatable. If you're willing to modify your lifestyle and food choices, informed supplementation can go a long way to help prevent and treat osteoporosis.

Sixth, viruses such as SARS, Avian bird flu, and new strains of influenza (including the much-anticipated flu pandemic) threaten to overwhelm the healthcare system. These diseases have no cure. Influenza vaccines may improve immunity, but only for about two months and only for certain individuals.

According to the Canadian Association of Naturopathic Doctors, a flu vaccine is effective only about 75% of the time for healthy individuals under the age of 65. The success rate drops to less than 30% for those over the age of 65. Every year, medical science develops a new influenza vaccine—only to have the virus mutate into an even more powerful strain the following year. Each mutation demands another new vaccine.

Many people think there is a medication (a magic bullet) for whatever may ail them, but the cure for these diseases, and many others, still frequently eludes North America's over-burdened healthcare system and leaves patients with severely altered lives.

YOUR INTERNAL PHYSICIAN

The hunt for new medicines is not only frustrating and costly, it may cause you to lose sight of the incredible healing power of your own body and the need to maintain its natural, healthy state. As Drs. Lopez, Williams, and Miehlke have stated:

> A SUPPLEMENTS SECRET
>
> At the first tell-tale tickle of a cold or flu, many people find that taking a combination of Echinacea, Garlic, and Vitamin C with bioflavonoids, can help support the immune system so it can successfully fight a virus. The trick is to take three or four doses through the day as soon as the first symptoms appear.

> …it's not medicine which 'cures', not the drug. No doctor can heal a wound. He or she can contribute toward its healing, can relieve the strain on the body in many ways, support it, but healing and maintenance of health is the responsibility of the body's own defenses (Lopez, p. 145).

One of your body's main defenses is your immune system. It's your internal physician, on call 24 hours per day. Its job is to protect you against pathogenic organisms and some toxins. In the face of new viral and bacterial threats, medical professionals now are advising people to do all they can to enhance their immune function as a first line of defense.

Unfortunately, many people have weakened immune systems that may not be fully up to the task of defending against disease. Not all that long ago, a cold or sore throat was something the immune system could handle fairly readily. Today, it seems more and more people are suffering through multiple bouts of flu and colds each year, and it's not uncommon for children or adults to have a cough or sore throat for several weeks. If this is you, your body is not in its optimal state of well being and it's time to make some changes.

You may say, "But I don't need to change. I'm really pretty healthy." The question, however, is whether you are truly healthy or if you have learned to merely cope. If you have allergies or arthritis or asthma or brain fog or cholesterol problems or constipation or cravings or fatigue or frequent colds (more than one or two per year) or gingivitis or high blood pressure or infections or insomnia or irritable bowel or mood swings or chronic muscle pain or rashes or sinusitis or stomach pain or tonsillitis or weight problems or zits or any other symptom from a to z—whew! what a list—then you are not healthy: you are coping. These symptoms are signs of disease, not a healthy state of being. They have to be addressed, at least in part, by improving your nutritional status.

As you finish this chapter, you may feel as if you're operating in a huge void—a void in your understanding of nutritional matters, a void in your understanding of the role supplements may play in supporting your body's natural defenses, and void in your understanding of which supplements may be right for you.

Sadly, it's quite possible you're right. This book is designed to help you fill that void. It's also designed to help you scrutinize the various brands of supplements on store shelves so you can recognize the good, the bad, and the totally terrific.

BOTTOM LINE SECRETS

THE FOOD-HEALTH CONNECTION remains of secondary interest in most research that favors drugs to combat disease. This situation leaves a serious imbalance in the way North Americans approach health issues. It appears many people are fighting disease rather than preventing it, and prefer pharmaceutical drugs to natural remedies. It's a situation repeated throughout history.

INCREASES IN CHRONIC CONDITIONS and life-threatening diseases create a swelling burden on healthcare systems, in spite of impressive gains made in understanding and curing disease. Unfortunately, many people have forgotten the human body can be incredibly effective at healing itself—if it's given the proper support.

YOUR IMMUNE SYSTEM is one of your body's main defenses against disease. It's your internal physician, on call 24 hours per day. Unfortunately, however, many people have weakened immune systems which cannot adequately protect against disease. Informed supplementation may be able to help.

THE SECRET TO USING SUPPLEMENTS effectively is, first, to acknowledge they may play a proactive role in supporting the body's natural defenses. Second, you must learn to tell the difference among the good, the bad, and the totally terrific on the supplements shelves; that is, you must fill any void in your knowledge of nutrition and supplementation so you can make informed choices that are right for you.

A **ANECDOTE** My childhood memories center on farming life. I remember, each spring, my father having our soil checked for missing minerals and nutrients. He would say, "This year we need to plant flax here. Next year, we will rest that field, and the following year, we will plant oats." His intention was to ensure the soil remained rich in various minerals.

My father's concern for his soil extended beyond those minerals and nutrients he could measure to all the components of healthy soil he couldn't measure. Every year, he enriched the soil with organic matter; that is, manure. I still recall the odor of the well-rotted manure as my father spread it on our fields. When the west wind blew, the pungent smell wafted right through my bedroom window. Definitely not my favorite odor, but you gotta love the healthy soil it made!

It was a science based on centuries of caring for the earth the way we cared for our animals. In those days, no chemical fertilizers were used. Farmers at that time also followed an Old Testament rule: every seven years, a field must be left to summer fallow, allowing it to rest and restore. My dad, and most farmers of his day, didn't wait seven years: they summer-fallowed fields each year on a rotating basis.

Years later, I started researching food, food supplements, and soil in my quest to find answers to problems of disease. I interviewed several farmers who informed me things have dramatically changed: many fields are seldom left to summer fallow, because farmers cannot afford to let a field rest. Every field is planted with whatever the market dictates—not necessarily with crops that enhance the soil. Similarly, chemical fertilizers are now the norm and well-rotted manure is left for hobby gardeners or organic growers.

It's easy to spot nutrient-deficient foods. The commercially-grown strawberries in the grocery store may be larger than those my father grew, but they taste more like cardboard than the luscious fruit I recall from my childhood. The freckles on potatoes indicate they've been grown in mineral-deficient soil. And let's be clear: If the nutrients aren't in the soil they're not in you. So, when I subsequently started searching for a totally terrific supplement, I knew the first place to look would be the soil.

– Gloria

CHAPTER 2
THE NUTRITIONAL VOID

When science is mute or ambiguous about nutritional issues, when marketers promote foods that have more flavor than nutritional value, when consumers fail to educate themselves and their children about sound nutrition, when the politics of food overwhelm both science and common sense—and especially when all those situations exist simultaneously—a Nutritional Void opens up. It's an empty space that fails to provide sufficient nutrients that are indispensable to lifelong vibrant health.

JUNK FOOD & THE NUTRITIONAL VOID

You likely have heard it all before: Eat plenty of fruits and vegetables, choose whole grains, have fish three times a week, avoid empty calories. You try, but it's often hard to withstand the onslaught of what has become the mainstay of the North American diet—junk food, which always tastes better when washed down with junk beverages.

So what is junk food? Well, it's all the sweet and salty prepared food that provides some immediate satisfaction, but offers low levels of nutrients— and it's loaded with insidious ingredients:

- **Refined sugars and starches,** which can contribute to the development of diabetes and depress your immune system

- **Chemical additives**, many of which have been implicated in a host of food sensitivities, allergies, and other diseases

- **Damaged fats** (turned rancid), which can harm your body at the cellular level

All these ingredients fail to adequately nourish your cells. Consistently ingesting such low-nutrient foods forces your body to keep adapting to keep you functioning. Skip meals or eat oversize meals, and you compound the problem. Not only does junk food increase your risk of developing the diseases discussed in the previous chapter, eating it also places

A SUPPLEMENTS SECRET

Specialized supplements have been developed to support liver health and function and to help protect liver cells. Ask your healthcare provider or supplements retailer for details.

an enormous strain on your organs—especially your brain, which is highly sensitive to toxins, and your liver, which must work harder to filter harmful substances from your blood.

It's sometimes difficult to recognize junk food when you see it, because it isn't always commercially prepared. Sometimes, junk food is made at home. You may say, "I don't eat junk food. I cook at home myself." But if your home-cooked meals consistently include white flour, fried foods, or sugary baked goods, you are cookin' up junk food and you need to make some changes.

FACTORY FOOD & THE NUTRITIONAL VOID

Let's say you decide to try eating more healthfully—starting tomorrow at breakfast. At this first meal of a new day, you decide to eat cereal. Many brands are advertised as healthy. It's true that whole grains are an excellent source of valuable fiber, but many popular cereals and breads are so heavily processed that they contain too few nutrients and too little fiber.

Three-quarters of the nation suffers from constipation (which has a profound effect on the immune system), and this is often due to low intake of water and fiber. When vague symptoms emerge, many people look for answers by trying various cleanses (such as liver cleanses) without knowing much about them (or whether the liver actually needs treatment). Seldom, do they consider bowel hygiene—which is most often the best place to start.

Prepared cereals also tend to offer questionable nutritional value. Did you know, for example, that a serving of instant oatmeal will send your blood sugar soaring faster than some candy bars? Have you noticed that a serving of many cold cereals—including many promoted as "whole grain" and "heart healthy"—contain more salt than an equal-size serving of potato chips? Surprised? Next time you're in the grocery store, check the labels yourself.

This doesn't mean candy bars and potato chips are good breakfast foods, but it does show you need to know something about the Nutritional Void in which you live. Rather than instant oatmeal, a tasty and nutritious breakfast might include a half cup of slow-cooking oatmeal or other whole grain cereal served with a half cup of goat's milk or plain yogurt (not yogurt with sugary fruit syrup swirling in the bottom), some phytonutrient-rich blueberries, a sprinkle of cinnamon, and a handful of raw nuts. If you must use packaged cereal, choose the one with the least salt and other additives, the most nutrients, and the highest fiber content (3 – 7 gms). And make sure it's not sugar-coated.

A SUPPLEMENTS SECRET

When you buy milk or yogurt, don't get caught by the fat-free foolishness of the modern dairy industry. Small amounts of saturated fats are critical to optimum health. You need them to act as a solvent for Vitamins A, D, E, and K. In addition, dairy products contain lactose (milk sugar); you need some healthy fat to balance the sugar and to prevent your blood sugar levels from rising too fast.

Rather than cereal, let's say you choose an egg and toast for breakfast. Here, again, it helps to know what you're eating. According to data from the *U.S. Department of Agriculture* (USDA), eggs from free range hens contain as much as 30% more Vitamin E, 50% more folic acid, and 30% more Vitamin B-12 than commercially-produced eggs from hens raised in confinement (Long and Keiley).

Any cook familiar with free-range eggs will tell you their flavor is better, their shells are stronger, and their yolks are brighter yellow (indicating more beta-carotene) than their commercially-produced counterparts—

although some commercial growers feed their hens marigold flowers to enhance the pale color of the yolks. If you're not eating free range eggs, it would appear you're not getting optimum nutrition from your morning omelet.

And there's more. Choose white bread for your toast, and you've chosen to eat refined flour. Refined flour (which is often called *enriched flour* or *white flour*) is made from whole kernels of wheat that have been refined until virtually all the nutrients have been removed—among them, wheat germ and wheat bran, which are then repackaged and sold back to you. In an article entitled *Modern Bread, the Broken Staff of Life,* Dr. Elmer M. Cranton, M.D. describes the refining process and its results this way:

> When grain is made into refined white flour, more than 30 of the essential nutrients are largely removed. Only four of those nutrients are added back in a process called "enrichment." Using this same logic, if a person were robbed of 30 dollars and the thief then returned 4 dollars to his victim for cab fare home, then that person should be considered "enriched" by 4 dollars, not robbed of 26 dollars. How would you feel in that situation? You should feel the same about "enriched" white flour and bread. Only vitamins B1, B2, B3, and iron are added back. Nutrients which are removed and not returned include 44% of Vitamin E, 52% of the pantothenic acid, 65% of the folic acid, 76% of the biotin, 84% of the vitamin B6, and half or more of 20 minerals and trace elements, including magnesium, calcium, zinc, chromium, manganese, selenium, vanadium, and copper. If consumers would just educate themselves in the principles of good nutrition and show an educated preference at the checkout counter, the food industry would be forced to respond with more nutritious products.

Dr. Cranton's example is just one of many that demonstrate how the Nutritional Void is created by manufacturers interested in speed and profit, and how many consumers support the Nutritional Void by making uninformed choices in the grocery store. When it comes to nutrition, how many times have you been robbed?

Your best choices for breads and cereals (and pastas, too) are those brands using 100% whole grains, preferably stone-ground. Stone grinding helps retain nutrients. In contrast, high-speed, steel-roller mills suited for mass production operate at temperatures up to 400°F. This high temperature heats the flour to near burning and destroys vital nutrients.

And don't be fooled by advertising claiming a product is healthy. Advertising is advertising—not nutritional information—and it's largely

A SUPPLEMENTS SECRET

The Harvard School of Public Health and *The American Medical Association* now advise that everyone would benefit from taking a daily multivitamin. Supplementation was once an option, but in our nutrient-robbed world, it's now become a necessity.

unreliable. In a March 21, 2007 interview on CTV television, registered dietitian Leslie Beck warned that even advertising such as "100% whole wheat" printed right on the bag may be misleading. You ought to check the nutrition label on the back of the package, not the advertising on the front.

Look for the words "whole grain" at the beginning of the ingredients list—which should be short. For the most part, you only need whole grain flour, water, sea salt, and yeast to make delicious and nutritious bread with a high fiber content of 3 – 7 gms. Avoid brands with long lists of additives as well as multi-grain and 60% whole wheat bread. Both tend to be nothing more than white bread with a handful of grains or bran thrown in. Often, the grains end up in the bottom of the bag. Similarly, dark rye bread may be nothing more than white bread with molasses (sugar) added for color.

The lessons learned about bread can be applied across all your nutritional choices—including your choice of supplements. When you next shop for food and food supplements, don't make choices that are based merely on advertising claims and low prices. Choose those foods and food supplements that are closest to the natural, whole food Mother Nature intended, rather than a product that has been processed within an inch of its nutritional life.

ADDITIVES & THE NUTRITIONAL VOID

If you manage to make it through breakfast, you may be surprised to learn that other foods in your pantry may not be quite what you bargained for either. According to Dr. Janet Hull, Ph.D., M.ESc., over 14,000 chemicals are added to foods in the United States today.

The *Australian Academy of Science* warns that the long-term effects of food additives on the body are often unknown and difficult to research. So far, in hundreds of studies around the world, scientists have linked additives to conditions such as allergies, cancer, diabetes, headaches, hyperactivity, nausea, and obesity. Nevertheless, free flowing agents make salt flow; emulsifiers prevent oil and water from separating; thickeners ensure consistency; bleaching agents make flour white; and colors, acids, flavor-enhancers, and artificial sweeteners make packaged foods look and taste more appealing.

Even if you try to avoid them, additives may creep into your diet without your even realizing it. For example, once consumers started to avoid MSG, manufacturers changed its name on product labels. Terms such as *natural flavoring* and about 25 others have been adopted to make label-reading more difficult for consumers. Even restaurant owners who advertise their foods contain no MSG may not be able to recognize it on a label and may unwittingly serve it to their customers.

FRESH FOODS & THE NUTRITIONAL VOID

By now, you may be getting the idea that processed foods may not be your best nutritional bet. Good. For the most part, they're not a particularly nutritious choice. Unfortunately, problems can also exist with various fresh foods. *The Environmental Working Group (EWG)*, a research and advocacy organization based in Washington, D.C., analyzed the results of over 100,000 U.S. government pesticide tests.

Their well-publicized work named twelve fruits and vegetables (now known as *The Dirty Dozen)* as those that are most contaminated with pesticide residues, even after thorough washing:

apples	bell peppers	cherries
imported grapes	peaches	strawberries
nectarines	red raspberries	pears
potatoes	celery	spinach

For more information, see www.foodnews.org and www.ewg.org.

EWG recommends that consumers buy these fruits and vegetables from certified organic growers—unless, of course, you grow them yourself without chemicals. Buying from certified organic growers is perhaps the most effective way of letting commercial food suppliers know you don't want to be ingesting pesticides with your salad.

As a consumer, your concerns about food and toxins don't end with the grower. Botanists will tell you that fruits and vegetables continue to ripen after they are picked until, at some point, they begin to rot. You know this; you've seen foods spoil in your kitchen when they've been stored too long. Food producers and marketers know this, too. They also know the following statistic cited by the *Organic Consumers Association:* "the average supermarket apple travels 1,500 miles from farm to table" (Long and Keiley). It's a journey that promotes neither high nutrient content nor delicious flavor because plant chemicals that offer significant nutritional benefits and provide enticing colors, scents, and flavors are lost during storage and transport. To add insult to injury, commercial produce often is picked before its peak, sprayed to retard spoiling, and waxed to make it look glossy and appealing.

You may be tempted to buy these eye-catching baubles simply because you've been conditioned to find them appealing, but consider their smaller, less shiny, less symmetrical, certified organic counterparts for their superior flavor and nutritional value.

SOIL & THE NUTRITIONAL VOID

The nutritional benefits of plants are affected by more than conditions of growing, harvesting, transporting, and storing. If you do a little research, you'll soon discover there is considerable discussion and study among scientists, farmers, and consumers about the quality of the world's agricultural soils—the soils that produce the food you eat and the nutrients the food provides to your cells.

It's pretty obvious from many studies and reviews that land degradation is a global problem. This situation threatens all facets of life "because of its adverse impact on agronomic productivity, the environment, and its effect on food security and the quality of life" (Eswaran).

You might think soil problems are in the hands of the world's farmers, but most farmers are unavoidably focused on making a living in the face of overwhelming economic, social, and political pressures. These circumstances leave food producers in a situation where they cannot necessarily look after their soil in the way they might like, and it leaves consumers at a terrible loss when they attempt to fill the Nutritional Void.

The problem of poor soils is not a new one. André Voisin, a French farmer and scientist, raised this issue internationally decades ago in various papers and in his book *Soil, Grass and Cancer*. Dr. Gary Farr's 2002 review of Voisin's book summarizes his clear and helpful warning:

> Healthy soil, according to Voisin, is more than a collection of minerals. In fact, he demonstrated that people who ate the products of heavy clay soils suffered numerous health problems, such as thyroid disease and cancer, in spite of the fact that the soils were rich in minerals. He pointed out that organic matter served as the catalyst for mineral absorption. Minerals must first be consumed by earthworms and microscopic life and excreted as humus before they can be easily taken up by grazing animals.

If you think of yourself for a moment as one of those grazing animals

35

(an eater of plants), soil quality becomes an important issue for you. Simply put, plants grown in organically-rich soils have a much better chance of supplying essential nutrients.

Dr. Charles Northen, an American physician and an associate of Voisin, was prompted to devote most of his medical life to the issue of soils. He coined the phrase some 60 years ago that "we must make soil building the basis of food building in order to accomplish human building" (Beach).

But the task is daunting because a complex relationship exists among the organic matter, minerals, microbes, and earthworms that make up healthy soil. So far, scientists simply don't know enough about the critical balances in healthy soil to be able to produce it with a chemical fertilizer that comes from a bag.

A SUPPLEMENTS SECRET

When you buy plant-based supplements from certified organic sources, query the manufacturer on where the plants are grown. The plants for totally terrific supplements will have been grown in soils containing sufficient organic matter, earthworms, and microsopic life to ensure the minerals can be more readily taken up by your body.

Sustainable agriculture specialist Charles Benbrook, PhD. argues a nutrient decline in crops is due, at least in part, to dependence on chemical nitrogen fertilizers. Such fertilizers cause plants to grow fast and grow big. As a result, the plants absorb more water, and their nutrient density is compromised. Benbrook contends that, compared to organically produced foods, commercially raised foods contain lower concentrations of nutrients and provide consumers with an inferior nutritional bargain (Benbrooke in Long and Keiley).

Soil scientists such as C.J. Barrow from *Cambridge University* described the issues of food security, environmental balance, and land degradation as "the challenge of the 21st century" (Barrow). They argue there is a pressing need to develop an objective, quantifiable, and precise definition of healthy soil anchored in sound scientific principles. It appears they're right. Any search into the state of North American soils and the nutrient content of the crops grown in them (let alone around the world) results in an overwhelming complexity of data and conclusions that are difficult for even soil specialists to analyze.

The *Organic Consumers Association (OCA)* concurs. While their research clearly shows commercial eggs, meat, and dairy contain lower levels of nutrients than certified organic products, it's less obvious whether nutrients in vegetables and fruits may be declining. Statistics obtained from the *United States Department of Agriculture* reveal declining levels of nutrients in many fruits and vegetables, but not all. Several variables may contribute to this somewhat confusing situation: "Variety type, soil quality, fertilizers, crop rotations, maturity at harvest time and the distance from farm to table all play a role in determining the vitamins and minerals in our food" (Long and Keiley). The challenge for consumers is to know which crops have been adversely affected at any given time and in any given place.

While scientists generally concur that soil degradation constitutes a global threat, more research needs to be done on the relationship between depleted soils and the apparent decline in the nutrient content of crops. It's a situation that should concern all consumers because the effects of degradation often are irreversible, and technological advances tend to merely mask the severity of the underlying problem.

So far, governments have been slow to act, but consumers may be able to exert their influence by undertaking four relatively simple actions:

1. Purchase food as much as possible from local farmers and certified organic growers rather than huge factory farms where high yields and high profits take priority over sustaining the soil and the nutrient content of the plants.

2. Choose supplements made from certified organic plants— and make sure the plants have been grown and harvested using sustainable methods that replenish the soil, rather than depleting it. Again, query the manufacturer.

3. Look for individuals and organizations that treat the soil as a living organism. Find out if they are conducting annual soil tests, using cover crops to help prevent erosion, rotating crops to enhance the soil, and generally focusing on creating a healthy ecosystem.

4. Demand more research and better information from government officials.

The alternative—to ignore existing evidence and wait until governments act—is no alternative at all.

SUPPLEMENTS & THE NUTRITIONAL VOID

Junk foods. Factory foods. Food additives. Pesticides. Herbicides. Degraded soils. All of these contribute to a Nutritional Void where many North Americans simply are not getting sufficient levels of nutrients in their diets. Throw in a busy lifestyle that includes eating on the run, skipping meals, following certain fad diets, engaging in too much or too little exercise, smoking, drinking excessive amounts of alcohol, taking prescription drugs or over-the-counter remedies, and a person's nutrient stores can be depleted even further.

Despite all this, some healthcare professionals maintain that a person can get all his or her nutrients from a balanced diet. This could be true for a small percentage of people, but for most North Americans, a balanced diet is difficult to define let alone achieve.

Sure, your Uncle Pete may have lived to the age of 102 and smoked all his life, but the contaminants his body had to deal with and the contaminants your body has to deal with are far different. The toxic load in the 21st century combined with problems of soil degradation and nutrient depletion explain why even the most diligent consumer needs proper and informed supplementation.

Unfortunately, many people are confused by the array of supplements that is available and by reports that some supplements may be ineffective or even harmful. One of the most disturbing concerns often raised about supplements, especially by physicians, is that the supplements industry is poorly controlled. Is that correct? Let's have a look.

In Canada, vitamins and minerals, herbal remedies, homeopathic medicines, traditional medicines such as traditional Chinese medicines, probiotics, and other products such as amino acids and essential fatty acids are regulated under the *Natural Health Products* (NHP) regulations that came into effect in January 2004.

Under NHP regulations, companies must demonstrate they adhere to Good Manufacturing Practices (GMP) before they can get a license in Canada.

A SUPPLEMENTS SECRET

Exceptional manufacturers voluntarily strive to follow the GMPs for pharmaceuticals, which are much stricter than food GMPs. These standards, however, are not designed for supplements; they are designed for pharmaceuticals (see Chapter 12).

Appropriate standards and practices regarding testing, manufacturing, storing, handling, and distributing of natural health products must be met to ensure safety and quality. It's the responsibility of the manufacturer, packager, labeler, or importer to ensure that on-site Quality Assurance Persons possess appropriate training, experience, and technical knowledge so they are capable of executing all necessary quality testing.

There's the rub. It appears all manufacturers are not meeting these standards. According to a July 2007 news report on CBC television, supplements labels are not accurate. In addition, at a time when toxins are finding their way into everything from fresh produce to pet food, toxic ingredients have found their way into some brands of supplements. According to the report, increased government monitoring is being called for, but the Canadian government has yet to respond.

In the United States, supplements are regulated by the *Food and Drug Administration (FDA)*, but they are regulated as food, not drugs. *The National Center for Complementary and Alternative Medicine, National Institutes of Health* advises:

- The FDA does not analyze the content of dietary supplements.

- At this time, supplement manufacturers must meet the requirements of the FDA's *Good Manufacturing Practices (GMPs)* for foods. GMPs describe conditions under which products must be prepared, packed, and stored. Food GMPs do not always cover all issues of supplement quality.

- Some manufacturers use the term "standardized" to describe efforts to make their products consistent. However, U.S. law does not define standardization. Therefore, the use of this term (or similar terms such as "verified" or "certified") does not guarantee product quality or consistency.

In addition, information obtained from the FDA in May 2007 states that a company "does not have to provide FDA with the evidence it relies on to substantiate safety or effectiveness before or after it markets its products." In other words, American consumers are pretty much left to their own devices when it comes to the safety and efficacy of supplements.

Obviously, issues of safety, quality, and consistency should prompt you to do a little research into your supplements before you pop any into your mouth. Here's a case in point: In quality control tests spanning three years (2000 – 2003), the independent testing facility *ConsumerLab.com* tested 500 nutritional products sold under the labels of 157 brands.

Results showed problems in approximately 33% of multivitamin-mineral supplements. Other products (vitamins, minerals, herbals, protein drinks, energy drinks) failed their evaluations in ranges from 15% – 59%. Reasons for product failures include:

- Too little active ingredient, or too much, or the wrong ingredient altogether

- Contamination with toxins such as lead, mercury, and PCBs

- Rancidity, especially with fish oils

- Insufficient or misleading information, including unsupported health claims

- Dangerous or illegal ingredients, including those that may boost products

- Unsatisfactory disintegration times

In the face of these problems, how are healthcare professionals or consumers to know what a person really is ingesting—or whether a supplement actually may be harmful?

For example, one of the most disturbing of *ConsumerLab.com's* findings is that lead was found in several popular brands of calcium-magnesium supplements and in a popular multi-vitamin marketed to children. Lead is a heavy metal that accumulates in the body, and it's particularly dangerous for children. No parent or healthcare professional would ever knowingly supplement a child with lead, but the manufacturer did not seem to share this concern.

A SUPPLEMENTS SECRET

A totally terrific calcium-magnesium supplement or children's supplement will be assayed (analyzed) for heavy metals. Get it in writing from the manufacturer. In fact, look for a manufacturer that assays its entire product line for heavy metals, microbial pollutants, and toxins.

ConsumerLab.com's testing most often reveals that vitamins, minerals, and multivitamin-mineral supplements contain lower levels of certain ingredients than cited on labels. The reason for this is fourfold. First, some raw materials are particularly expensive (essential fatty acids or saw palmetto, for example). Second, some raw materials may simply degrade over time (such as Vitamin A). Third, manufacturing practices and machinery may not be up to the exacting task of measuring raw materials. Fourth, labeling may include the weight of inactive ingredients that bind the active materials (*ConsumerLab.com*, p. 10).

ConsumerLab.com's testing of ingredient levels listed on product labels revealed a range of problems. Here's a sampling:

- Despite claims that potency had been tested or verified, several brands of essential fatty acids contained less DHA or EPA than the label indicated.

- Healthcare practitioners know folic acid is essential for proper development of the brain and spinal chord of a fetus, yet some supplements contained less folic acid than the label indicated

- Some brands of Vitamin C, including a children's product, contained less of the vitamin than the label claimed, while other brands simply did not break down adequately, which would impede proper absorption into the body.

A SUPPLEMENTS SECRET

It's a good idea to find out just what the coatings on your supplements are and how quickly they dissolve. Thirty minutes is the maximum time allowed to ensure they are prepared with your food in the stomach and ready for uptake in the small bowel.

Skimping on raw materials may reduce the costs of supplements manufacturing, but it also may account for conflicting findings in clinical trials and unsatisfactory results at home. After all, if people take a supplement containing less than optimum amounts of ingredients, achieving the desired effect may not be possible.

Achieving the desired effect may not be possible for another reason: some supplements don't dissolve at the right time. Many people think absorption of nutrients occurs in the stomach, but most of it actually takes place in the duodenum, which is the first part of the small intestine beyond the stomach. Once ingested, a supplement must dissolve, mix with the food also in the stomach, then together be passed along to the duodenum. Therefore, the protective coating on the supplement must dissolve within about 30 minutes so its nutrients are available for absorption once they enter the intestinal tract.

When you're assessing supplements, it's important to understand that

ConsumerLab.com testing may provide a starting point, but it doesn't address two very important matters:

1.   The source of the raw materials in the supplement

2.   The manner in which they are extracted

Many supplements are made solely from synthetic sources, rather than primarily from natural plant sources, resulting in a lack of important plant nutrients known as *phytonutrients* (see Chapter 12). Science is just beginning to identify these plant nutrients. You probably have heard about some of them: beta-carotene, lutein, and lycopene, for example. But did you know there are about 25,000 others?

While research certainly is making progress in this area, scientists just don't know exactly how phytonutrients support human biology. Until they do, scientists simply cannot replicate the full spectrum of Mother Nature's nutrients in a lab.

So, what's the point? Well, here's an example. Most people know that Vitamin C is ascorbic acid, and scientists will tell you that ascorbic acid is ascorbic acid is ascorbic acid—it's a molecule, and it doesn't matter whether you get it from a laboratory or a certified organic orange. Technically, this is true, but it doesn't take the larger nutritional picture into account. In an orange, for example, Vitamin C does not exist in isolation. An orange also contains *phytonutrients* (plant nutrients) that help maximize absorption and retention of vitamins. If you take ascorbic acid on its own, you may not be absorbing the amount you expected to.

Even if you do take a plant-based supplement with the intention of ingesting all the phytonutrients provided by the source plant, you still have to ensure the materials in the plants are carefully extracted. Harsh refining practices can destroy the nutrients in plant-based supplements in much the same way that harsh refining practices can destroy the nutrients in bread.

Because *ConsumerLab.com*'s testing doesn't consider source materials and extraction processes, you can't rely solely on third-party evaluation of supplements. As we've said, their work provides a good starting point, but you need to do a little investigative work on your own. Ask your supplements provider about the source of the raw materials in your supplements and how they're grown and extracted. If you don't get a satisfactory answer, keep looking.

Another important factor that affects the efficacy of a supplement is the synergy (working together) among the nutrients it contains. For example, nutrition professionals know B vitamins work together, not in isolation. Nevertheless, many companies buy isolated vitamins and isolated minerals, stuff them into a tablet, and sell them at bargain prices. But this is no bargain. If you take isolated Vitamin B6, for example, without a B-complex supplement containing at least seven B vitamins, you're at risk of creating a deficiency in your other B vitamin levels. Similarly, Vitamin E works synergistically with selenium, calcium with Vitamin D and magnesium, and Vitamin A with zinc. You'll learn more about such interdependence as you read through the following chapters.

By now, you may feel like tossing your supplements in the trash. This act may be prudent if you don't know what they contain and how they're manufactured. Consider whether you're one of the many people who place their trust in media people covering highlights of the latest research, television actors strolling through laboratory settings, health store clerks promoting their most popular product, or even healthcare providers who haven't researched the products they recommend.

If so, it's time to learn the nutritional basics of supplements yourself. Put yourself in charge—that's how to move out of the Nutritional Void.

BOTTOM LINE SECRETS

JUNK FOODS AND PROCESSED FOODS contribute to the Nutritional Void.

FRESH PRODUCE provides a far better nutritional bargain. To get the highest levels of nutrients and the lowest levels of pesticides and herbicides, choose certified organic fruits and vegetables.

SOIL DEGRADATION is one of the major challenges of the 21st century; the effects of degradation often are irreversible, and technological advances tend to merely mask the severity of the underlying problem. According to American physician Dr. Charles Northen, "We must make soil building the basis of food building in order to accomplish human building" (Beach).

A BALANCED DIET is difficult to define, let alone achieve, in North America, so *The Harvard School of Public Health* and *The American Medical Association* now advise that everyone would benefit from taking a daily multivitamin. Food supplements were once thought to be optional, but they now have become essential.

THE NUTRITIONAL VOID unfortunately extends to supplements. As some physicians have warned, the multi-billion dollar supplements industry is poorly controlled. Testing has revealed a range of problems, including contamination, rancidity, misleading information, and dangerous ingredients. This means you *must* do some research into the food supplements you put in your mouth.

ONLY A FEW COMPANIES produce totally terrific supplements— the trick is finding them. Before you buy, be sure to ask some hard questions of the manufacturers. This book will help you do that.

ANECDOTE

I've taught all the grades—from Kindergarten through University—and I wish I could share all the discussions about nutrition I've had with hundreds, perhaps thousands, of young people. One memorable story involves a college class where I noticed an adult student sitting in the front row with a can of soda pop and a long, white slab of bread glazed with processed cheese. It was a noon hour class, and this assortment of brain-busting sugars, starches, damaged fats, and chemicals was the student's lunch. It was also his first meal of the day.

I hovered over him. From experience, he knew what was coming. In preceding weeks, I had spent a few minutes of every class teaching about the connection between food and health, ranting about the way junk food affects sensitive brain cells, and citing studies proving better nutrition equals better grades. Junk food was forbidden in my class. Of course, I felt the student's lunch display was my invitation to pontificate on his poor choices. How could I teach his mind if his body and brain were not prepared? It seemed so simple.

I hesitated, his eyes on me. Obviously, this bright student needed something concrete to bring all that nutrition theory home. So, I asked him to look at the palm of his hand and to place a dot right in the centre with his pen. Curiosity piqued, he dotted his hand and looked at it. The other students craned to see and listened. Some regarded the palms of their hands.

"Now," I said, "imagine that dot as a single cell. Imagine it as a single cell among all the cells that constitute your hand. And consider what that little cell, which houses and protects your DNA, will do with the rush of toxins you're sending its way. Do you think it will thrive from the blessing?"

He grinned as I waited for his answer. (I always wait.) Finally, he shook his head. Then, to my surprise, he asked to hear more about how cells respond to nutritional decisions. We agreed to meet after class. The story of our ensuing meetings is too long to narrate here, but the thought of that one, teeny cell seemed to move him. Over the next two months, I witnessed his skin clearing up, his energy increasing, and his focus improving. I never saw junk food on his desk top again, at least, not in my class.

In the spirit of that experience, we offer you a similar introduction to that one little cell in your hand—and to all the cells in your whole body.

- Jerre

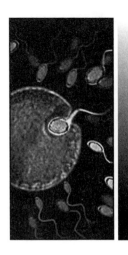

CHAPTER 3
THE HUMAN CELL

Consider placing a dot in the palm of your hand and referring to it from time to time as you read this chapter. That dot might help you imagine just one cell on your palm, and it might help keep you grounded as you read about something virtually invisible to the naked eye. Even if you aren't all that fond of biology lessons, don't avoid this chapter. Think of it more as a look into your own unique metabolism and your own personal heredity—and as the opportunity to have some say in both.

The previous chapters provided a detailed overview of the Nutritional Void and focused on the world "out there." This chapter will zoom in on the world "in here" where the consequences of your nutritional choices have their ultimate impact. This chapter will lay the foundation for all the chapters that follow because it will teach you about nutrition, starting at the cellular level.

Your cells look after everything to do with your metabolism and your heredity. In fact, cells are the base of all life on earth. All bodily functions happen through cells. When you say something is wrong with your metabolism, you're really saying your cells are not able to do their work for some reason. When you talk about your genes, you're really talking about a single little structure in your body's cells. So, if you can learn how to look after the metabolism of a single cell, including the cell dotted in the palm of your hand, and if you can learn how to ensure that cell receives the nutrients it needs to operate effectively, you'll go a tremendous distance in achieving optimal nutritional status. That may make learning a little biology well worth the trouble, yes?

This short book cannot discuss all the complexities of cells nor the myriad of interactions that occur among them. It can, however, help you understand a little about the way your own body works and how nutritional choices, including supplements choices, affect you at the cellular level.

You see, cells are the building blocks of life. Your body is comprised of about ten trillion of them, and they're organized into a complex array of about 200 types and functions. Scientists know that groups of cells perform specific tasks. Some combine to become human features such as noses and hair; others become part of systems, such as the lymphatic system or the immune system or the skeletal system.

Despite all this complexity, human cells tend to operate in the same general way, are susceptible to the same threats, and require the same kinds of nutrients. That's not surprising, really, because you came into this life because two human cells united to make a new one. Then, from that single cell, came trillions of others. One single cell eventually became you.

INSIDE YOUR CELL

Think of that one cell that became you or that one cell in the palm of your hand as a little, organic balloon comprised of a membrane on the outside that houses all sorts of mechanisms on the inside. You likely have heard of some of these mechanisms: DNA or mitochondria, for example.

Most of these mechanisms have one primary task—to organize things. They take raw materials, such as proteins and water, break them down, and organize the bits into new materials. That is called *metabolism*, and it involves countless numbers of operations.

Something has to orchestrate all those operations. In your modern car, that something is a small computer that ensures gas and oxygen are mixed precisely and that spark plugs fire in a timely way. In your body, that something is the *nucleus*. Almost every cell has a nucleus, and it's more complex than any computer.

As the illustration below shows, the nucleus is located way down deep in the center of every cell. The nucleus houses most of your DNA material.

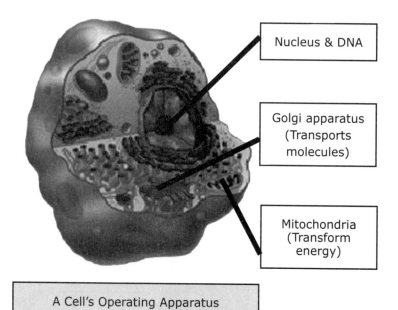

Nucleus & DNA

Golgi apparatus
(Transports
molecules)

Mitochondria
(Transform
energy)

A Cell's Operating Apparatus

DNA provides the master plan for all the operations of your entire body, and it's the strongest biological influence on who you are and who you'll come to be. Let's look a little closer.

DNA (Deoxyribonucleic Acid)

If you grabbed one end of the DNA inside the nucleus of a cell and pulled it out, the DNA would stretch about six feet. Have a look at the dot on the palm of your hand. Amazing—all that material packed into a single cell.

Structurally, a strand of DNA looks like a fine rope ladder that somebody twisted into a spiral. The ladder's two sides are connected by many linking bars—much like rungs on any ladder. These "rungs" are made up of chemicals called *bases*. Scientists have assigned letters to each of the individual bases. They're A, C, T, and G. That's all!—just four letters. If you look closely at the illustration, you'll see that each rung actually is made up of a pair of bases. These are called *base pairs*. You've about six billion base pairs in your body.

Okay, this is getting a little technical, here, but stay with it for just few paragraphs. There really is a nutritional point.

49

If you think of each individual base (on a single side of a DNA ladder) as a "letter", you can then think about how you might combine these letters with one another to form "words" in a marvelous new language. You might write AT, CG, TA, and so on. Now, imagine grouping those words to form long "sentences", sometimes a thousand words long or longer: "ATGCTAGCATAT" and so on. These sentences are your genes.

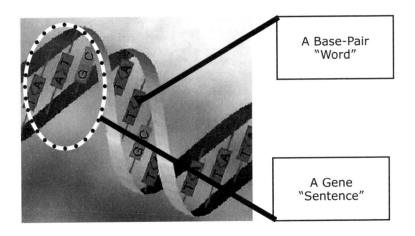

A Base-Pair "Word"

A Gene "Sentence"

When you talk about genetics, you're talking about the all those instruction sentences, the genes, passed along to you by your parents. You have about 30,000 genes in your body. They constitute very precise instructions detailing how every single cell in your body is to be built and how it's to operate. You emerge as a unique individual because of all this complex sentence building.

But what happens if a word or two, or even just a letter or two, gets altered? To illustrate, let's consider the simple instruction "Kiss your pet." Now what

A SUPPLEMENTS SECRET

When you're buying a multi-supplement, look for a brand containing sufficient varieties of plant nutrients (phytonutrients) shown by various studies to help repair DNA damage.

happens if you alter just one word or even just a couple of letters in the original sentence? The instruction might become "Kick your pet." Whoops! That's an alarmingly different instruction from the original. Similarly, each gene passed along to you by your parents can become altered by any of a myriad of influences—including the air you breathe, the water you drink, and the nutrients you ingest or don't ingest. See? We promised there was a nutritional point to all this.

The Human Genome Project

In the field of human genetics, scientists have identified about three million locations where single bases can differ in humans and cause disease. Understanding these single-base DNA differences promises to revolutionize the processes of finding genetic sequences associated with such common diseases as cardiovascular disease, diabetes, arthritis, and cancers.

The work began in the mid-1900s when scientists developed an international effort called the *Human Genome Project*. Their task was to identify each and every gene in human DNA. Their expectation was that if they knew which gene was responsible for each part and each function of your body, you could take preventative action against disease. Motivation and anticipation were high.

In 2003, after years of exceptionally complex work involving thousands of scientists around the world, a remarkable feat was accomplished. The researchers figured out the base sequence of the entire human blueprint, the *human genome*.

Since then, medical scientists' understanding of the human genome has become very helpful as they study how to solve the problems of any one individual's vulnerability to diseases. For example, medical statistics show that 50% of all North American heart attacks are atypical: the person is young, physically fit, of optimum weight, and has normal blood pressure and cholesterol. A similar percentage of all North Americans have a gene variance known as IL-1.

The IL-1 gene variance is directly linked to the predisposition for heart disease. This variance causes the DNA (via the RNA) to send a message that leads to over-production of the IL-1 protein. It's as if you tried to make a photocopy and the print button got stuck. This sets up an inflammatory response. If it becomes chronic, it predisposes you to heart disease (as well as a range of other inflammatory diseases).

51

The Supplements Secret You Need to Know

The science that helps you determine your genetic predisposition to disease and the response to nutrition is called *nutrigenomics*—a name reflecting the important link between nutrition and genetics. And here is one of the most exciting supplements secrets to come along in many years: A nutrigenomic supplement now has been developed to provide targeted nutritional support for people who test positive for IL-1. Yes, thanks to the Human Genome Project, it recently has become possible to take a

A SUPPLEMENTS SECRET

Many people are buying supplements without much direction, and many feel like walking supplements stores. Now, you can obtain a risk assessment with immediate information on specific supplements for your very own DNA, as well as any personalized lifestyle changes that may be needed.

sample of your genes with a simple cheek swab you can take yourself and then send the sample to a lab for analysis. Genetic analysis will tell you whether you test positive for IL-1 and whether you should consider targeted nutritional support for that gene variance to give you the best chance at prevention.

Other DNA tests target different issues:

1. How efficiently your body assimilates B vitamins. These tests are relevant because deficiency in folic acid, B6, and B12 significantly increase homocysteine levels, one of ten factors that indicate a risk for cardiovascular disease.

2. How efficiently your body handles oxidative stress and how that relates to your risk of contracting certain cancers (breast cancer and prostate cancer, for example). Healthcare professionals now recognize oxidative stress as a leading cause of chronic disease and premature aging.

This means you can have your personal DNA analyzed to determine whether you have a predisposition to specific health problems. DNA analysis promises to revolutionize the prevention of degenerative disease as we know it. While identifying a predisposition doesn't mean your problem can be fixed by repairing or replacing your genes, it does mean you can identify your risks and take specific nutritional action to lessen the chance of developing a gene-related disease. This cutting-edge science recognizes the relationship between genetics and nutrition, and it helps you deal even more effectively with the Nutritional Void right at the cellular level.

Organelles

Once you understand DNA, it's hard to imagine that cells are comprised of even more mechanisms, but they are—a lot more. Surrounding the cell's nucleus are all sorts of teeny organs called *organelles*. Organelles consist mainly of proteins (which may give you a little insight into why proteins are important in your diet).

In many cases, the work of organelles consists of various bio-chemical reactions enabled by one special type of protein: *enzymes*. The DNA tells the cell how to make proteins, including enzymes. You see, enzymes have to be designed in particular ways so each may play a unique and critical role in all chemical functions in your body. Those functions include digestion, energy transformation, and repair of tissues, organs, and cells—even repair of genes themselves.

No plant, animal, or human could exist without enzymes. They're the sparks of life of each and every cell. Without enzymes, your organelles couldn't function—which means you couldn't breathe, walk to the corner, hear the phone ring, read the pages of this book, or even lift a finger.

Poor nutritional choices can seriously inhibit the production and operation of enzymes, and that in turn can inhibit the activity of organelles. When this happens, your body manages to adapt so you can, in fact, continue breathing, walking, hearing, and reading. Yes, you usually can lift a finger, too. But if you consistently ingest toxins and make other poor nutritional choices, what are the consequences? Can you breathe easily? Is there a spring in your step? Do you remember what you read? You may be able to lift a finger, but can you lift your arms and legs with ease and without pain? If not, you may have an enzyme-related problem.

Entire books have been written on the importance of enzymes and on the various types of organelles. We won't go into that much detail here, but we will look briefly at two organelles: the *mitochondria* and the *Golgi apparatus*. Together, the mitochondria and Golgi apparatus use and process oxygen and proteins, enzymes, carbohydrates, and fats to transform energy that is used to manufacture other cellular products. To do all that work, these organelles also require vitamins, minerals, and other plant nutrients known collectively as *phytonutrients*. In short, the mitochondria and Golgi apparatus are major players that ensure your metabolism functions completely and effectively. They can do their work effectively only as long as you feed them with all the proper nutrients.

Mitochondria

Mitochondria are the energy transducers of the cells (they change the energy of various molecules into a form your body requires). In fact, throughout your whole body, mitochondria act as little, mobile furnaces. They're the powerhouses of the cell. Their primary job is to convert oxygen and various nutrients into a life-essential chemical called *Adenosine triphosphate*, or ATP. ATP is the principal form of chemical energy your body uses for all its metabolic

> **A SUPPLEMENTS SECRET**
>
> *Co-Enzyme Q10* is essential in the production of adenosine triphosphate (ATP). Young people make CoQ10 naturally, but production drops off as we age—which means your need for CoQ10 supplementation increases as you get older.

work. Without ATP and without active mitochondria, humans could not exist.

And here's another interesting secret for all you armchair detectives: The tails of male sperm cells contain mitochondria. The mitochondria provide energy as the sperm frantically wiggle their way to the female egg. Once they arrive at the female egg, sperm cells drop their tails and their exhausted mitochondria. That phenomenon is responsible for making the term mitochondria familiar to many people. Television shows such as *Law and Order* and *CSI* often include the term in their plots. Forensic scientists use the special DNA inside the little mitochondria to track down criminals or find family links.

There's yet another interesting fact about mitochondria that has more to do with good health than crime stories: The more you need them for metabolic activity, the more there are in each cell. That means the more active you are, both physically and metabolically, the more mitochondria you have working on your behalf.

The Golgi apparatus

The Golgi apparatus is less exciting to TV programmers, so it may be less familiar to you. Part of its job is to move molecules around inside your cells—much like a forklift hauls containers around inside a warehouse. The Golgi apparatus takes product to where it's needed: important, but hardly the stuff of crime stories.

The Golgi apparatus does more than transport. It also modifies proteins, carbohydrates, and certain fats inside the cell, and it prepares them for export to the outside of the cell. The Golgi apparatus even tags the molecules it builds so they get to where they're supposed to go. Without the Golgi apparatus, all the ATP energy production of the mitochondria (and the work of other cell mechanisms) would be for nothing.

Organelles and your nutritional status

Unless you write scripts for crime mysteries or design warehouses, you may wonder why organelles are covered here. Well, the answer really has to do with the Nutritional Void and with proper choices of food and food supplements.

Take another look at that cell dotted in the palm of your hand, and consider whether you've provided its metabolic apparatuses with enough high quality nutrients today so they can do their work. Do you think they're flourishing or failing? Have you ingested junk food or skipped meals or taken incomplete food supplements? If so, you've not provided that cell in the palm of your hand, or any other cell in your body, with the fuel it needs to keep you alive at optimal levels.

It's a strange thing, really, that people are willing to eat junk food or second-rate nutrients when they would never put junk fuel in their cars.

They readily comply with a car engine's needs for the best sources of energy. If they don't, the car engine lets them know when something is wrong. It hesitates or bucks or doesn't start at all. Mitochondria and the Golgi apparatus also have a way of telling you when you're abusing them with poor quality nutrition. Unfortunately, many people are more attuned to the smooth running of their automobiles than they're attuned to the smooth running of their cells. They know something is wrong when their car engine stalls, but they don't know something is wrong when their metabolic engine stalls.

When your mitochondria are low in number and inefficient in production, you're low in ATP. When you're out of ATP, you're dead! When your Golgi apparatuses are struggling to find work to do or when they're working inefficiently, molecules aren't getting built and re-built and sent to where they're needed. Your organelles may not buck like a misfiring car engine, but they will send you a message by way of pervasive low energy or daily rollercoaster cycles of high energy followed by exhaustion.

Such down-times constitute a strong warning that a problem exists at the cellular level. It's a warning that needs to be addressed, just as you would address a problem with the engine of your car. Unfortunately, people suffering low energy may not understand they're running on empty. Rather than changing their dietary habits and investing in totally terrific supplements, they continue to eat junk food and junk supplements and, when all else fails, they kick their adrenal glands into overdrive with coffee and cola. They just don't understand that their cells are crying out for help.

THE CELL'S MEMBRANE

As you can see, the interior of a human cell is a very busy place. The DNA provides the master plan, and organelles such as the mitochondria and Golgi apparatus execute the plan. All this activity must be monitored to ensure the cells function with integrity. Some of this monitoring is the job of the *membrane*.

Earlier in this chapter, we described cells as little, organic balloons. The membrane is a bit like the rubber skin of a balloon. It holds the cell together. The membrane also may perform several monitoring functions, such as protecting the cell and regulating the movement of raw products and wastes.

Like everything else in life, a cell is made up of various molecules, some of which are shown in the illustration below. These molecules are linked somewhat like Tinker Toys or Leggo blocks to form complex structures. In the case of the membrane, the main building block is a special fat. Scientists call fats *lipids*, and the special fats in cell membranes are called

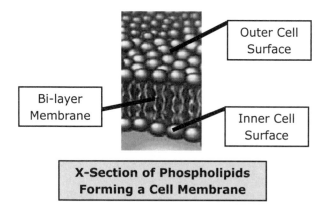

	Outer Cell Surface
Bi-layer Membrane	
	Inner Cell Surface

X-Section of Phospholipids Forming a Cell Membrane

phospholipids. The figure above shows phospholipids. Each phospholipid has a little round head and two wiggly legs. The heads love water; the legs hate it. Because the human body is comprised mainly of water, this situation poses a problem for the water-hating end of the molecule. So these water-loving, water-hating molecules arrange themselves with other phospholipids to create a structure that will enable their heads to dwell in water while protecting their wiggly legs from water. They accomplish this configuration by linking toe-to-toe, so to speak with one phospholipid on the upside and one on the downside. By linking up in this fashion, the phospholipids create a bi-layer membrane with a water-free interior.

Because the little round heads squish together and slip and slide around each other, the surface of a healthy human cell is flexible. It's fluid, not rigid like an egg's shell. That means (among other things) the membrane won't break. Even the cells that comprise bones have a certain, desirable degree of fluidity and flexibility. This built-in flexibility allows them to repair themselves easily, communicate with other cells (through membrane contact), and adapt to changing circumstances. Sort of sounds like a definition of life itself, doesn't it?

PUTTING IT ALL TOGETHER

Your cells are the means to the life you want to live. They're so marvellously designed, so utterly complex, it's tempting to keep describing their parts and functions.

It's like a Chinese puzzle, though: the deeper you get, the more you understand, the more you find there is to learn. So let's stop. For our purposes, we have revealed enough about your body's cells for you to appreciate how essential it is to meet their demands for the best nutrients.

In order for them to conduct their business of metabolizing proteins and enzymes, transforming energy, and communicating with other cells across the whole landscape of your body, they need to be topped up with only the best nutrients you can give them. No junk, no toxins.

The next chapter, *Powerful Proteins, Energyized Enzymes*, is the first of seven in which we focus your attention on the nutrients you need to understand if you want to achieve optimum health. So have a gander at the palm of your hand, imagine that single cell looking up at you, pleading for you to feed it well, and read with care.

BOTTOM LINE SECRETS

YOU WERE BORN TO LIVE on high-octane, energy-sustaining foods.

DNA IS THE TEMPLATE that tells the cell how to make its proteins and enzymes! That is all that DNA does.

ATTEMPTS TO DEVISE practical applications from the knowledge about the human genome will probably dominate biological research for many decades to come and may lead to exciting new ways to diagnose, treat, and prevent the many diseases that plague people of all ages.

NUTRIGENOMIC SUPPLEMENTS provide targeted nutritional support as part of a genetic screening program designed to reveal your predispositions to disease. These supplements and the screening program are available now as a result of the Human Genome Project.

THE SECRET TO ENSURING EVERYTHING is working properly in a cell, from the instructions-giving DNA to the hard-working organelles to the flexible membrane, is to ensure all the right nutrients are adequately supplied: It's no secret your cells abhor junk food.

A **ANECDOTE** I grew up on the eastern fringe of the rolling foothills that rise up to meet the Canadian Rocky Mountains. For me, it was a 1950s guy's world of lumbering and hunting. When my father wasn't operating his lumber business, he hunted deer, moose, elk, and mountain sheep. He fished prairie lakes and mountain streams for trout, whitefish, pike, and muskies. He hunkered down in the marshes waiting for ducks and geese to fly over his readied shotgun. He stalked the stubbled wheat fields, flushing pheasants and partridges from their hiding places. In a nutshell, he did the manly thing (for those days) of putting meat on our table. He was the protein provider, and he wanted me to follow in his footsteps. He was my hero.

My mother was the gardener and the cook. She garnished the protein with all sorts of tasty vegetables, mostly from her own garden. If it had been up to my father, we'd have eaten little more than meat and potatoes and corn, but my mother saved my life—or at least developed my palate. Thanks, Mom.

Despite my mother's skill with vegetables, in our household there was little doubt protein was King. Mom prepared it for hours, sometimes pounding the tougher moose steak into submission, and I helped her pluck all those darn birds. I didn't taste beef until I was nearly 20 years old.

Years later, I learned the wild meat, fish, and fowl my father brought home provided high-quality, lean protein with less saturated fat, more healthy Omega-3 fatty acids, and fewer toxins than the commercially-raised meat, fish, and poultry available in the average grocery store today. I also learned protein is essential for a host of cellular activities. The protein my father worked so hard to provide helped our cells function at optimal levels.

So, I cannot be too harsh on my father. He may have had the balance wrong, but his love of protein was not misplaced—especially given his remarkably active life. Although I didn't stictly follow in his footsteps, choosing to walk my mother's path as well as his, I have come full circle in my appreciation of the role of protein in our lives—but for some different reasons than those that served my father.

- Jerre

CHAPTER 4
POWERFUL PROTEINS,
ENERGIZED ENZYMES

The March 2007 *Journal of Oncology* warned that the number of cancer patients will increase by 55 percent by 2020. But that's not the worst of it.

Many North Americans are either sick or becoming sick with a range of degenerative diseases. Diabetes afflicts nearly 23 million, more than 25 million American adults have been diagnosed with heart disease, a high percentage of school children are afflicted with ADD/ADHD, and osteoporosis poses a major health threat for 44 million Americans— including young men and women.

Of particular note is that your body's response to chronic inflammation ("inflammatory response") has taken off like a rocket. Inflammatory response is your body's alarm bell warning that something is seriously wrong, and it's been linked to Alzheimer's disease, allergies, asthma, cancer, heart disease, and a range of other life-altering conditions. In the face of these alarming statistics, healthcare professionals are encouraging their patients to adopt healthier eating habits. Summing up current thinking, Dr. Anthony Cichoke argues in his book *Enzymes: The Sparks of Life* that degenerative diseases "are primarily caused by our modern diets and lifestyle, and for the most part, are preventable." He contends the solution lies in a "return to a healthful and balanced diet and lifestyle, of course" (Chichoke, p. 6).

MACRONUTRIENTS
Returning to a healthful and balanced diet begins with your choices of

the foods you eat every day: the *macronutrients*. Macronutrients are the proteins, carbohydrates, and fats that provide the largest proportion of metabolic energy and building material in the human diet. Hence, the prefix *macro*; it means "large."

In the human body, certain kinds of macronutrients are needed for particular cellular activities. **Proteins** are needed for an immense range of purposes. When digested, they serve as the basic building blocks of the body. They enable chemical reactions, defending your body against foreign microbes (microscopic living organisms), transporting materials, and regulating messages (including turning genes on and off). Primary sources of dietary protein include meats, fish, poultry, dairy products, eggs, and soy.

Carbohydrates provide the general energy base your whole body requires. They come from plants and from dairy products. **Fats** (especially *Essential Fatty Acids*) provide anti-oxidant protection, flexibility, lubrication, and structure. Fats come from both animal sources and some plants.

Understanding something about these macronutrients can help you make more appropriate choices when you spend your hard-earned money on foods and food supplements. Let's look, first, at proteins.

Powerful Proteins

Scientists estimate the human body consists of more than 100,000 proteins, and every one of them has a different purpose. Broadly speaking, all these proteins fall into two categories:

1. **Structural proteins** form most of the solid material in your body. Keratin and collagen, for example, are structural proteins. Keratin is the primary protein of skin, hair, and nails. Collagen is the primary protein of muscles, tendons, and connective tissues.

2. **Functional proteins** perform specific jobs. Hormones, antibodies, and various other components of the body are all functional proteins; that is, they *do* something. For example, the hormone insulin is a functional protein that regulates

blood sugar. Enzymes, which you'll read about later in this chapter, are a sub-class of functional proteins.

As you can see, proteins are hard-working macronutrients that are vital to the human body. It's important to understand, however, that your body requires a specific amount of protein for its many operations. Any excess is either excreted (small amounts) or stored as fat.

As well, eating too much protein (which is easy to do, especially at barbeques or at family feasts) can put a strain on your liver and kidneys and may set up an inflammatory response. Remember: Persistent inflammation is an initial warning that you may be experiencing damage at the cellular level.

Rather than skipping meals and then eating a huge 8-oz steak at dinnertime, it's a better idea to spread your protein intake throughout the day. Consider eating smaller portions at meals, all containing proteins, and having a protein snack mid-morning and mid-afternoon—especially if you feel hungry or tired during the day. Rather than that extra cup of java or a bagful of junk food, try a protein snack to help maintain energy, concentration, mood, and metabolism.

Sometimes, it can be a little awkward to work a protein snack into your day. After all, you can't very well pull out some roast beef in the middle of a meeting. Instead, you might find supplementing your diet with a protein shake or a protein bar more convenient. And we don't mean milk shakes or chocolate bars or fake protein snacks that contain more sugar than anything else. Once you identify a totally terrific supplier of supplements, check whether they also offer a totally terrific protein bar.

A SUPPLEMENTS SECRET

When students arrive home from school in the afternoon, they're often, in their words, "starving." Consider giving them a protein shake or protein bar. The protein can help balance blood sugar levels, which helps keep energy levels up and cranky behavior down.

Most people can benefit from mid-morning and mid-afternoon protein snacks, but some people absolutely should consider it. They're athletes and other people who are particularly active, pregnant and nursing mothers, growing children and teenagers (not infants), elderly people who may not otherwise get enough protein in their diets, people on weight-loss or low-fat diets, lacto-vegetarians, or anyone undergoing severe stress (whether mental, emotional, or physical).

Athletes may require 50 grams or more of protein in a protein shake plus a few grams of carbohydrate for energy. People who are not as active might find a shake containing 10 grams of protein per 45 calorie scoop is sufficient, and other people might find a few bites of a protein bar containing 20 – 22 grams of protein will be satisfactory. The Recommended Daily Allowance for the average person is between 50 – 65 grams per day depending upon weight and activity; those who exercise regularly might need twice that. An active 130 pound woman might need about 100 grams; an active 200 pound man might need around 150 grams (Tarnopolsky). In all cases, the amount of protein your body needs depends upon three things: your weight, your percentage of body fat, and your level of physical activity. For more specific information, seek advice from a qualified health care professional.

And here's a tip that will help your health (no matter who you are) and lend support to your budget at the same time: Break down those proteins in your mouth—that's really where metabolism starts. Most people would benefit from developing the simple art of chewing, the first step to healthy digestion. Many common digestive conditions can be reduced or eliminated through more conscious and diligent use of the pearly whites. Mahatma Ghandi condensed all wisdom about health into just one admonition: "Chew your drink, and drink your food." That is, chew your food until it turns to liquid in your mouth. Chewing effectively will also slow you up a bit, calm you down, make it seem less necessary to eat a lot of food, and it will get you the most out of the food you buy.

Amazing Amino Acids

You probably think of meats, eggs, dairy, legumes, and nuts when you think of proteins, but have you ever thought of jewellery? Well, here's a new way of looking at your morning egg or dinnertime cutlet.

Proteins are large molecules made up of smaller molecules. The smaller molecules are *amino acids*. A helpful way to think about proteins and amino acids is to imagine proteins as necklaces and amino acids as beads on the necklaces.

If you were to make a protein necklace, your selection of amino acid beads would be limited to only twenty different kinds. You could, however, use any kind of bead as often as you liked and in any order that you liked. As a result, you could string any number of amino acid beads together in any sequence, and you could make the protein necklace thousands of beads long if you wished.

A very long necklace laid out in a straight line might not be very interesting, so you might want to give it shape. Perhaps a simple loop or circle would do. You might decide to make something more complex. You would do that by folding the necklace over itself, twisting and looping it to create any number of interesting shapes.

Eventually, you'd want to create useful patterns and shapes, not just random ones. You might buy a book of necklace designs and use them as your patterns. In fact, that's what your body does. It uses a book of plans—your DNA—and builds amino acid necklaces of pre-determined sizes and shapes. Each size and shape has one single function to perform in your body—just one!

Here's an image of such an amino acid necklace, along with a magnification showing its amino acid beads:

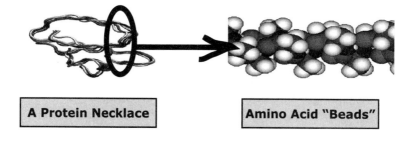

A Protein Necklace   **Amino Acid "Beads"**

The particular way an amino acid necklace is folded determines how and where your body will use it. The folding plan has been compared to the Japanese art of origami (paper folding). If you've ever seen origami, you know a flat piece of paper can be folded—carefully and according to a plan—to form a completely different thing. One manual on origami shows how to fold a dollar bill into a turtle or a flower. More complex designs involve folding a sheet of fine paper into a graceful swan or a colorful hot air balloon. You just need to know the technique, the master plan. In your body, that plan is your DNA.

Sources Of Amino Acids

You may wonder where your body gets amino acids for all that marvellous folding. Well, your body manufacturers eleven of them without your having to do anything but stay generally healthy. The remaining nine have to come from food. These nine are said to be *essential* because it is essential to get them from food. Your body uses the essential nine to build the others.

Some foods contain all nine of the essential amino acids. These foods are called *complete proteins*, and they include:

- Meat, fish, and poultry

- Eggs

- Dairy products

- Soy (depending on how it's processed)

Other foods contain some amino acids, but not all. They're called *incomplete proteins*, and they include:

- Legumes such as peas, lentils, and beans

- Nuts and seeds

- Rice and other grains

- Vegetables

Some incomplete protein foods contain certain amino acids; others contain other amino acids. Nuts and beans are high in them. Combining these foods incorporates all nine essential amino acids. Rice, other grains, and vegetables contain lesser amounts. Combining them will not provide all the amino acids you need.

A Protein Secret

Here's a secret about food sources of amino acids: By and large, your body doesn't really want them. Proteins generally are built to serve the organism in which they reside. What does your body want with a soy bean protein or a bovine protein or a moose protein? Do you want toes that look like beans? Do you want a cow's nose? A moose's ears? No—what your body is interested in is the building blocks of plant and animal protein. It wants the nine types of amino acids it cannot produce itself so it can fashion them into human-useable forms.

> **A SUPPLEMENTS SECRET**
>
> A totally terrific protein powder will contain all nine essential amino acids (see *Shake It Up*, later in the chapter).

When you eat a protein food, your digestive system breaks it apart, stripping off its various amino acids. Once stripped from the protein food, the amino acids travel to your liver. The liver cells absorb them, arrange, twist, and fold them into new protein necklaces according to your unique DNA plan. That way, you get your own toes, nose, and ears.

It's important to know that if even one essential amino acid is missing when a cell attempts to arrange, twist, and fold a string of amino acids into a new protein, the cell will stop manufacturing (synthesizing) the new protein; that is, the cell cannot create a complete protein necklace if it doesn't have a complete supply of amino acids. When this process is truncated, vital cell functions can be impaired. That can lead to poor health.

A missing amino acid is one condition in which a protein-making process can be truncated. Another involves the concept of *synergy*. Synergy is an important and common phenomenon that exists in Nature. It occurs when two or more agents are combined and react in a way that produces a greater response than if the agents acted independently. It's a classic case of the whole being greater than the sum of the parts.

In the case of protein synthesis, you're in some trouble if your body is lacking sufficient quantities of Vitamins B6, B9 (folic acid), and B12. According to the *American Journal of Clinical Nutrition*, when adequate amounts of these vitamins are present, your body is able to convert one amino acid form (methionine) into another amino acid form (cysteine). It normally does this on a regular basis. In the absence of the B vitamins, though, your body is unable to make cysteine. Instead, it produces a toxin called *homocysteine*. This chemical contributes to inflammation and plugs up your arteries, leading to possible heart attacks and strokes (Miller).

A SUPPLEMENTS SECRET

There are many people with a genetic predisposition to poor assimilation of B6, B12 and Folic Acid. This is very good reason to consider having a DNA test done by way of a simple cheek swab—a little nutritional CSI, as it were!

The production of homocysteine is an example of a biochemical process gone wrong. It points to the specific roles that macronutrients take on (in this case, proteins), and it points to the interdependence of nutrients (in this case, proteins and vitamins).

Shake It Up

Now that you know which combinations of foods can cover all nine amino acids, and now that you know a deficiency of even one can lead to illness, you can make more informed choices when you shop—including when you purchase protein powders, shakes, or bars. Here are some secrets to choosing a totally terrific brand:

- Some brands of protein drinks are little more than sugary shakes, and some brands of protein bars are little more than glorified candy bars. If refined sugar ranks high on the ingredients list, keep looking.

- Protein products made from soy beans or animal sources typically contain a more complete range of amino acids than those made from rice. Those made from soy and/or milk proteins will provide all nine essential amino acids.

- Milk protein concentrate (whey protein concentrate) contains 80% protein plus minerals, fat, and lactose (milk sugar). It's more biologically active and less expensive than whey protein isolates.

- Whey protein isolates and soy protein isolates are the most pure proteins available. They usually contain more than 90% protein and little fat and lactose. There is no difference in the ability of either protein concentrates or protein isolates to support muscle growth and recovery. Athletes, however, may tend to prefer the isolates because athletes are interested in maximum amounts of readily-absorbed protein and have other ways of taking in carbohydrates. The specific needs of athletes are beyond the scope of this book and should be discussed with a qualified nutritional expert.

A SUPPLEMENTS SECRET

In a totally terrific protein powder, the soy isolate will be "Identity Preserved" (IP). IP means the raw material comes from non-GMO seed (not genetically modified) and has been segregated from any other genetically modified material—from the seed to the finished product. The milk for the milk concentrate should come from pasture-fed cows who have not been subjected to hormone treatments. Check the brand you're thinking about with a nutrtioinist.

- Hydrolyzed protein is, essentially, a pre-digested protein. This makes it more digestible and absorbable in the intestines, and reduces the potential for allergenic reactions. It's bitter, however, and must be used in small quantities and with other ingredients.

Therefore, a totally terrific protein powder will provide protein from a combination of soy protein isolate and milk protein concentrate. Eight grams from soy and two grams from milk for a total of ten grams would be excellent.

A secret for students—and others

An impressive body of research now has confirmed something about students that many parents and teachers have known all along: eating breakfast containing protein improves academic performance, as well as behavior and overall psychological well-being. In fact, research conducted by J. Michael Murphy, *Harvard Medical School, Department of Psychiatry* showed math grades for students who regularly ate breakfast were 40% higher.

What's true for schoolchildren and adolescents is also true for adults: eating a protein-rich breakfast improves intellectual, physical, psychological, and social performance. Why? Well, while you may think your body "turns off" during sleep, your cells actually use that time to rebuild and repair; that is, a lot of activity goes on while you're sleeping.

Much of that activity depends upon proteins. In fact, proteins are required in over 90% of all body functions, so it's important to replenish that supply after a night of busy cellular repair. Otherwise, your cells may be forced to steal nutrients from muscles and other tissues to keep you going. Cereal and fruit with a little milk, or toast and coffee just don't cut it. You need more protein at breakfast—every day. Most people's breakfasts are high in carbs and fructose and very low in protein.

Some nutrition professionals recommend eating protein before 10:00 a.m. Others say it's crucial to eat protein within 30 minutes of getting up because it helps balance blood sugar levels throughout the day. For reasons that are not yet clear, the benefit's reduced if this narrow window of time is missed. Try eating protein soon after you rise and judge for yourself.

Balancing blood sugar levels by eating protein at breakfast helps maximize brain function, facilitate weight loss, and alleviate that mid-afternoon energy slump common for so many people. Of course, maintaining blood sugar levels is especially important for people with diabetes, insulin resistance, and other blood sugar concerns.

Once people understand why eating breakfast is important (and that eating protein at breakfast is even more important), many resolve to change their morning routine. Some, however, feel rushed in the morning. If you feel you don't have time for breakfast, shake up a protein smoothie—using a high-quality protein powder, of course. Lots of excellent smoothie recipes include plain yogurt, ground flax seed, protein powder, and fruit, for example.

Energetic Enzymes

As you've already read, proteins are combinations of amino acids. Some combine, according to plan, to form body structures (everything from hair to muscle). Other combinations of amino acids produce a sub-set of protein called *enzymes*. Their primary (but not only) role is as catalysts: They provide the energy for chemical reactions that take place at incredible speeds.

No plant, animal, or human could exist without enzymes. They're the sparks of life of each and every cell. Without enzymes, your organelles couldn't function—which means you couldn't breathe, hear the phone ring, read the pages of this book, walk to the corner, or even lift a finger.

How Enzymes Work

Enzymes play a critical role in all chemical functions in your body, including digestion, energy transformation, and repair of tissues, organs, cells, and even the very genes that make them.

One explanation of how enzymes work is called the lock-and-key model. Each enzyme adopts a particular shape that enables it to "grab" only that molecule with a mirror-image shape. Once the mirror-shape molecule fits into the enzyme, the enzyme does its high-speed chemical work. It's sort of like a lock-and-key arrangement between an enzyme (the key) and an organic molecule (the lock).

> **A SUPPLEMENTS SECRET**
>
> As you're likely starting to see, nutrients don't work in isolation. Enzymes are no exception. They combine with other nutrients, especially vitamins such as Vitamin C, to get all their work done.

The following diagram shows a maltose sugar molecule captured by an enzyme designed specifically for only that sugar molecule. Once the maltose is captured, the enzyme will split it in two parts, creating two molecules of the sugar *glucose*. The enzyme, in effect, will make the original molecule ready for use by your body. And it will do it thousands of times faster than the most highly trained, technologically equipped scientist could do it—their speed is their magic. Interestingly, nothing much will happen to the enzyme itself—it retains its shape, ready for the next maltose molecule.

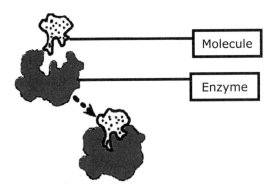

Enzymes are so specific in the work they do that the malfunction or absence of even a single type of enzyme in the human body can make life quite difficult. Unfortunately, and in the face of today's toxin-ridden environment, they can be vulnerable little spark plugs. Various toxins can block them from doing their jobs, and the absence of specific vitamins or minerals or phytonutrients can render them useless or ineffective. If genes in your DNA get damaged and unable to produce any more or in sufficient quantity, you can run low on specific types.

Enzymes also can be threatened by lack of variety in a person's diet. If you eat the same food every day for long periods of time, your pancreas may not be able to produce enough of the specific digestive enzyme needed to digest that specific food. When that happens, an inflammatory response will occur when you eat the food in question. Your white blood cells, the heart of your immune system, would actually start to become "irritated" by foods for which you no longer have the right enzyme. Your white blood cells identify such foods as foreign intruders and mount an offensive against them. It's a warning your body can't process the food you've just eaten. You've developed an allergy. To avoid this, simply vary your diet. Don't eat yogurt and fruit every morning, for example.

In the case of digestive enzymes, symptoms of impaired activity might include a chronic bowel or stomach condition such as bloating, gas, irritable bowel, Crohn's disease, and diverticulitis.

For people with these health issues, an appropriate dietary protocol would include a digestive enzyme complex containing enzymes that occur naturally in your body as well as enzymes that occur in many raw foods. These enzymes aid digestion by starting to break down food within about the first hour of eating. This activity occurs in the stomach where stomach acid and other metabolizing chemicals are produced. Once the food is prepared in the stomach, it moves into the small intestine where 90% of all nutrients are absorbed. Digestive enzymes are critical to this process.

> **A SUPPLEMENTS SECRET**
>
> A totally terrific digestive enzyme complex would provide peptidase and protease for proteins; lipase for fats; and invertase, lactase, cellulase, glucoamylase, and, amylase for starches and sugars; plus bromelain, a mixture of protein-digesting enzymes that aid cellular assimilation of essential materials.

An Enzyme Helper: Co-enzyme Q10

You've already read that cells depend upon mitochondria for energy production and that mitochondria—the energy factories in your cells—depend upon enzymes. The activity of enzymes largely depends upon organic molecules called *cofactors* or *coenzymes*. In the mitochondria, energy production ultimately requires a coenzyme called *Coenzyme Q10*, which is popularly called *CoQ10*. It's produced by your body, and you have the highest concentrations in your heart, kidneys, and liver.

As you might expect, food sources containing the most CoQ10 are organ meats. Since the liver and kidneys process toxins, some healthcare professionals warn against eating these meats. CoQ10 supplements provide an excellent alternative.

Research has linked low CoQ10 levels to heart disease, diabetes, and inflammation. There is, however, some good news. Placebo-controlled studies of CoQ10 have been conducted in several countries, and hundreds of physicians and scientists have presented hundreds of research papers at international symposia. Their research consistently shows CoQ10 treatment significantly improves heart muscle without adverse effects or drug interactions.

In addition, Dr. Richard A. Kunin, Founder and President of the *Society for Orthomolecular Health Medicine*, states that CoQ10 is an effective treatment for diseases affecting muscle tissue, including muscular dystrophy and heart failure. He also points to an impressive list of medical conditions that may respond well to CoQ10 treatment:

- **Heart conditions**, especially cardiomyopathy and congestive heart failure, as well as high blood pressure and mitral valve prolapse

- **Nerve tissue damage** (with applications to peripheral nerve disease and retinal diseases such as optic atrophy)

- **Blood sugar** in diabetes

- Some cases of **anemia**

- Some skin conditions, particularly **psoriasis**

- Inflammations, such as **gingivitis**

According to Dr. Kunin, CoQ10 also has been shown to strengthen immune function, improve resistance to infection, promote healing, augment muscle strength, and increase cardiac output. These properties can offer remarkable benefits to athletes, the elderly, people with compromised immune systems, or anyone wishing to enhance strength or vitality.

CoQ10 works in concert with certain vitamins (such as B2 and B3) and minerals (such as iron and copper). It also requires magnesium, which operates as a catalyst. In addition, Vitamin

> **A SUPPLEMENTS SECRET**
>
> Because CoQ10 works in concert with so many other nutrients, it's important to take a good, plant-based multivitamin-mineral supplement every day to provide the nutritional base the CoQ10 needs. In addition, a totally terrific CoQ10 supplement will contain Vitamin E in the form of natural d-alpha tocopherol and bioflavonoids (more about bioflavonoids later).

E helps prevent depletion of CoQ10. If these vitamin and mineral nutrients are missing from your diet, CoQ10 levels can drop and take your energy levels down with them. Additionally, if you tend to create excessive amounts of free radicals in your body by eating junk foods (especially fried foods and damaged fats) or by overeating, your body uses CoQ10 more quickly. Numerous toxins and some medications (such as cholesterol-reducing statin drugs) also interfere with CoQ10. It's important to note, too, that CoQ10 levels decline as we age.

It's easy to see that a complex inter-relationship exists among proteins, enzymes, coenzymes, vitamins, and minerals. If the Nutritional Void upsets this inter-relationship, the resulting damage can impair your cellular energy and, ultimately, put your quality of life or your longevity at risk. Eating moderate amounts of high-quality protein spread throughout the day, supplementing the diet with protein drinks or bars, and taking digestive enzymes or CoQ10 supplements if the need arises may prove helpful.

BOTTOM LINE SECRETS

EAT PROTEINS THROUGHOUT THE DAY, but avoid eating excessive amounts, because your body will convert excess to fat. For a good discussion of protein intake, visit www.hsph.harvard.edu/nutritionsource/protein.html, the *Harvard School of Public Health* website.

PROTEINS ARE NEEDED FOR AN IMMENSE range of purposes that include building, facilitating, defending, transporting, and regulating.

A PROPER BREAKFAST includes proteins and improves academic performance for students and intellectual, physical, psychological, and social performance for everyone.

THE B VITAMINS, especially B6, B9 (folic acid), and B12, are required for proper protein synthesis. Without them, your cells will produce a poison called *homocysteine*. High homocysteine levels put you at risk of arterial damage, strokes, and dementia or Alzheimer's disease.

PROTEIN POWDERS AND BARS from soy beans or animal sources can make it easy to choose the best between-meal snacks for kids and adults. Look for brands providing the quantity and type of protein that suits you best and avoid those that appear to be more like sweet drinks or candy bars.

ENZYMES are a sub-set of protein. They are the spark plugs of life. With help from other nutrients in your diet, including vitamins and coenzymes like CoQ10, enzymes play a critical role in all chemical functions in your body.

A TOTALLY TERRIFIC COQ10 SUPPLEMENT containing Vitamin E from d-alpha tocopherol and bioflavonoids may significantly improve heart muscle function, from congestive heart failure to high blood pressure. People who may particularly benefit from CoQ10 supplementation include those who wish to improve healing ability, immune function, muscle strength, and cardiac output.

YOUR PROTEINS AND ENZYMES require the support of coenzymes, vitamins, and minerals. Supplement wisely.

ANECDOTE

When I started my Nutritional Consulting business, medical science was just beginning to turn its attention to the issue of obesity—not only in adults, but in teens and young children. Physicians were noticing that a very high percentage of their patients needed medical treatment as a direct or indirect result of carrying too much weight. Conditions such as high blood pressure, strokes, Type 2 Diabetes, cholesterol issues, fatigue, and on and on, all related to obesity and high blood sugar levels. It was evident, too, that cancers were destroying people's lives with far greater frequency.

We healthcare providers knew this increase in a range of illnesses could be linked to the increase in the average North American's waistline. As I worked with moms and their children to address obesity and all its related issues, I couldn't help but become acutely aware of the huge amounts of sugars that were being consumed. They appeared in the form of candy and candy bars, soda pops, juices, baked goods, pastas, and a whole range of packaged foods. And then there were all those so-called "healthy" snacks containing more sugar than protein—popular cereal bars, protein bars, fruit smoothies, and syrupy-based yogurts (I like to call them "designer yogurt").

It seemed obvious that all this sugar was definitely affecting people's immune systems and impeding their bodies' natural ability to fight viruses and bacteria. Everything from frequent colds to allergies to other serious conditions alerted me that my clients' immune systems were crying out for help. In addition, many of my clients came to me complaining of constipation, IBS, and other digestive problems. Often, these problems could be corrected with simple measures, but they were being ignored until significant symptoms prompted a medical visit and, perhaps, medications.

As my business grew, I started public speaking engagements to teach parents about children's nutritional status—and their own. Knowledge is power, and it's my philosophy that each of us must take responsibility to learn about nutrition and health. We should not wait until symptoms arise and ultimately force us into an already over-worked healthcare system. I also believe people will do more when they know more. After you read this book, I hope you'll do more to look after your nutritional status because you know more.

- Gloria

CHAPTER 5
CRAVING CARBOHYDRATES

Of the three types of macronutrients (proteins, carbohydrates, and fats), carbohydrates probably have received the most media attention in recent years. Carbohydrates often are called "carbs," and it seems they've captured the spotlight about as often as Brad and Angelina. Is all the press coverage just more media hype, or is there some substance to all the nutritional celebrity? Let's see what the hoopla's about.

You've probably heard the arguments and advertising pitches as people debate the merits of low carb and high carb diets. This book isn't intended to assess weight loss programs, but a couple of comments are worth including here: First, your body needs carbs to provide the energy that fuels all kinds of biochemical reactions. Second, drastically cutting your carb intake can result in brain fog, weakness, and poor concentration because your main source of energy has dropped too low to support cellular activity.

Achieving sustained weight loss isn't a matter of eliminating carbs, but of incorporating appropriate types and quantities of carbs into a well-rounded program of balanced dietary choices, correct food supplementation, proper hydration with filtered water, and adequate exercise and rest.

These principles serve not only those people who may be trying to lose weight, but anyone interested in generating enough sustained cellular energy to create physical strength and mental balance—both of which are fundamental to your ability to enjoy life's many activities. In short, knowing how carbs supply energy could help improve everything from a child's grades at school to a golfer's handicap.

TWO GROUPS OF CARBS

Carbohydrates are molecules that provide your body with its principal source of energy. These molecules are made up of sugars, classified in two broad groups—*simple carbs* and *complex carbs*:

1. **Simple carbs** are made up of only one or two units of sugars. The most common simple carbs are glucose (which your body uses for energy), fructose (found in fruits), and sucrose (from sugar cane and sugar beets).

2. **Complex carbs** are made up of long chains of simple sugars that have bonded together. This more complicated structure gives these carbs their name: complex. They're found in plants—especially vegetables, grains, seeds, and legumes.

Notice that you do not get carbs from meat, poultry, fish, or eggs. You get some in dairy products, but you get most carbs from plants. Plants use the sun's energy to manufacture carbohydrates during photosynthesis. In fact, you could not survive without plants and the life-giving nutrients they contain.

THE GLYCEMIC INDEX

Simple carbs break down quickly during digestion and enter the bloodstream rapidly. This high-speed process can raise blood sugar levels too fast and too high. As a result, people have been warned away from simple carbs and advised to focus on complex carbs—which tend to digest more slowly, give up their energy more gradually, and generally treat the body more gently.

This advice was excellent as far as it went. After all, processed sugars have been linked to numerous diseases. Recent research, however, has revealed that some complex carbs actually break down and enter the bloodstream as fast as or faster than simple carbs.

The Glycemic Index (GI) was developed to measure the rate at which this happens. It ranks foods according to how high they cause blood sugar levels to rise. Glucose is ranked at 100 and provides the benchmark against which all other carbohydrates are measured:

- Rankings of 70 and above are High, indicating the food raises blood sugar rapidly

- Rankings of 56 – 69 are Moderate

- Rankings of 55 and below are Low, indicating the food raises blood sugar slowly.

Complete listings of foods and their GI ratings can be found on the internet or in books that focus on this subject.

As you might expect, high GI foods contain high concentrations of simple carbs. They include refined sugar, sugary foods, and certain fruits (bananas and mangos, for example). It may surprise you to learn, however, that certain vegetables and grains (categorized as complex carbs) also rank high. Root vegetables such as carrots and beets, for example, are high GI foods.

A SUPPLEMENTS SECRET

If you're faced with eating a meal of high GI foods, consider taking a supplement that can help block carbs. Carb blockers inhibit the activity of digestive enzymes that break down carbohydrates. Look for a brand that has been shown in clinical trials to block both sugars and starches while still permitting your body to absorb the vitamins, minerals, and plant nutrients in your food. Avoid those brands that make claims you cannot verify.

Studies at *Harvard Medical School*, as well as recommendations from the *World Health Organization,* link over-consumption of high GI foods to health conditions such as heart disease, diabetes, and obesity.

Nevertheless, considering only the GI of a food has an inherent drawback: GI looks only at the *quality* of the carb, but not the *quantity* consumed, nor at the way it's combined with other foods in a meal. As a result, you might be tempted to eliminate beneficial high GI foods from your diet. Carrots, for example, rank high, but they also are excellent sources of plant nutrients such as beta-carotene.

Rather than eliminating carrots or other healthy high GI foods from your diet, nutrition professionals recommend eating smaller portions of high GI foods combined with low GI foods, lean protein, and healthy fat. This will help slow down the rate at which carbs enter the bloodstream.

NEW WAYS OF LOOKING AT CARBS

New ways of looking at carbs are creating new ways of classifying them. While the simple and complex classifications still remain for various purposes, nutritional practitioners now also classify carbs into three other categories: *non-starchy* (fibrous), *starchy*, and *sugary*.

Non-starchy (Fibrous) Carbs

You might think of non-starchy carbs as the Arnold Schwarzeneggers of the carb world: They're bulked up. And you might think of them as the "governators" of blood sugar levels and colon hygiene.

Non-starchy carbs include a huge array of foods, especially vegetables, that are much too numerous to list here. If you eat leafy greens and cruciferous vegetables such as broccoli, cauliflower, and cabbage, you're eating non-starchy carbs. At meals, a general rule of thumb is to fill half your plate with these low GI foods; they make excellent snack foods, too.

Non-starchy carbs contain fiber. Fiber doesn't absorb into the bloodstream in the same way sugary or starchy carbs do, so it lowers a food's GI rating and provides the bulk that helps maintain proper colon hygiene.

The average person requires 25 – 30 grams of fiber per day. Fiber aids elimination of fecal matter, sweeps away excess estrogen that's linked to cancer, and creates a supportive environment for friendly bacteria that populate your digestive tract. Many people don't realize they need to have a bowel movement several times per week. Some healthcare providers argue you need to eliminate fecal matter every eight to twelve hours— that's two or three times a day. Others consider at least three per week to be normal. The most common pattern is one bowel movement per day, but everyone is different, so it's wise to discuss elimination with your healthcare provider to determine what's best for you. Of course, eating more fiber *and* drinking more water will tend to increase the frequency of bowel movements.

Whatever is optimum for you, it's important to ensure your body's sewer system doesn't back up. Constipation is as toxic and damaging as a sewer system backup in your house. You'd probably tell everyone if your household sewer system backed up, but you may be reluctant to tell even your healthcare provider if your internal sewer system backs up. If constipation goes unaddressed, however, your cells will be left to deal with the toxic effects.

There are two different types of fiber: *insoluble* and *soluble*. Insoluble fiber adds bulk to the stool, which helps food pass through your digestive tract more quickly. Soluble fiber will slow digestion and help your body absorb nutrients while still performing its important role in colon hygiene.

> **A SUPPLEMENTS SECRET**
>
> If your internal sewer system is clogged, consider soluble fiber supplements plus a broad spectrum probiotic. Totally terrific brands of soluble supplemental fiber contain *fructooligosaccharides*—which feed the friendly bacteria that naturally occur in your intestinal tract. Totally terrific probiotic supplements contain eight species of friendly bacteria to properly re-colonize the gut.

Soluble fiber helps regulate blood sugar for people with diabetes and other blood sugar problems. It also has been shown to help lower total cholesterol and LDL.(When you see the first L in LDL, think "Lousy"; LDL is the Lousy kind of cholesterol.) Lower total cholesterol and lower LDL may be linked to lower risk of heart disease.

Starchy Carbs

Starch is the most common complex carbohydrate. It's found in plants, especially grains, vegetables, legumes, and seeds. If you hold a starchy carb in your mouth, the digestive enzymes there will break down the starch until it actually melts. Next time you eat a baked potato, hold a little in your mouth and see what happens. If it's a high GI variety, you'll soon discover that it dissolves in much the same way as a teaspoon of sugar. What you won't see, though, is that the starch in the potato turns to glucose as it digests. As a result, it will enter your bloodstream almost immediately and create a rapid insulin response not unlike the insulin response induced by table sugar.

Starchy carbs such as this have high GI rankings. White bread ranks at 100, which is as high as glucose. Root vegetables such as beets, yams, and parsnips all rank above 70, and some varieties of potatoes rank over 100. The same is true of many grains (especially refined grains contained in rice cakes, cereal bars, breakfast cereals, crackers, and baked goods). Some grain products actually rank over 100, indicating they raise blood sugar even faster than glucose.

That's why eating cereal for breakfast can leave you dragging in the afternoon. If you don't have some protein to balance the starchy cereal, your blood sugar can rise too fast. Once that happens, you've purchased a ticket on a blood sugar rollercoaster with enough dizzying climbs and plunging drops to rival The Cyclone at Coney Island.

Sugary Carbs

Whew! Who knew getting the balance wrong with starchy carbs could give your cells such a ride? Unfortunately, whenever you overindulge in high GI carbs, your cells respond like the maintenance crew on an out-of-control rollercoaster. They're forced to work feverishly to avoid a crash, but it's a crash they often can't prevent.

If you thought the starch rollercoaster was a bit scary, wait until you see what's in store if you overindulge in the third category of carbs: sugary carbs. Ready? Fasten your seatbelt.

Foods that belong in the sugary category include health-giving fruits, as well as not-so-healthy manufactured sugars. Consuming these sugars in large quantities takes your body on a wild ride of soaring and crashing hormonal responses. Riding this biological roller coaster on a daily basis can drop you right into a not-so-fun-house of frightening degenerative diseases.

For the most part, processed foods containing sugary carbs are designed to entice, but not necessarily to nourish, and it's easy to overindulge. After all, these carbs taste sweet, and they're common ingredients in foods many adults, teens, and children consume several times every day. A partial list of foods laden with sugary carbs includes:

- Soft drinks, commercially-prepared fruit juices, and sweetened coffees

- Sugary breakfast cereals, even including brands boldly advertising whole grain ingredients

- Granola bars and other cereal bars and many energy bars

- "Designer" yogurts; that is, yogurts with syrupy fruit in the bottom; that fruit is essentially jam

- Baked goods, including everything from brownies to muffins to many multi-grain breads

- Condiments such as ketchup, relishes, and pickles

- Marinades

- Sauces

- Salad dressings and prepared dips for fruits and vegetables

- Frozen desserts, including those made from rice and soy

- Candy and candy bars, of course

In all likelihood, this list contains some foods you believe to be healthy or never really considered as sources of sugary carbs. The secret to discovering what's what is to read labels. Of course, manufacturers can make label-reading difficult.

If you're reading labels to determine whether a product contains sugars, look for the suffix "ose" in the ingredients list. Glucose, galactose, fructose, lactose (milk sugar), and maltose (malt sugar) are all sugars. Sugars also may be listed on labels as any of the following:

- Berry Sugar

- Brown Sugar

- Cane Juice

- Corn Sweetener

- Dextrin

- Honey

- Invert Sugar

- Maltodextrin

- Maltitol

- Molasses

- Natural Sugars

- Raw Sugar

- Refined Sugar

- Syrup

- Turbinado Sugar

Be sure to eat them in small quantities.

As you can see, sugary carbs can be fairly pervasive in the North American diet. Wherever sugary carbs show up, the use of two is particularly widespread in the food industry. They're *sucrose* and *fructose*.

Sucrose

Sucrose is common table sugar. It's often referred to as "refined" sugar. Because of its simple composition, sucrose passes quickly from stomach to intestines to bloodstream. When you eat it in large amounts, its rapid absorption into the bloodstream topples the precise balance of blood sugar and oxygen orchestrated by your adrenal glands. Large amounts literally drive your body into crisis. One of the most vivid descriptions of this sugar-induced emergency appears in William Dufty's book *Sugar Blues*:

> The brain registers it first. Hormones pour from the adrenal casings and marshal every chemical resource for dealing with sugar: insulin from the endocrine 'islets' of the pancreas works specifically to hold down the glucose level in the blood in complementary antagonism to the adrenal hormones concerned with keeping the glucose level up. All this proceeds at emergency pace, with predictable results. Going too fast, it goes too far. The bottom drops out of the blood glucose level and a second crisis comes out of the first. Pancreatic islets have to shut down; so do some departments of the adrenal casings. Other adrenal hormones must be produced to regulate the reversing of the chemical direction and bring blood glucose levels up again. (Dufty, p. 46-47)

Now that's a rollercoaster ride your cells don't want to be on.

Eating large amounts of sucrose affects your brain, adrenal glands, and pancreas as if they've been kicked—and kicked hard. The impact resonates throughout every system of your body. Bloating, gas, and Candida (yeast) overgrowth may occur in the digestive tract. You may feel foggy, moody, or anxious as your brain and nervous system succumb, and functioning of your immune system may be depressed. An inflammatory response may occur, resulting in arthritic symptoms in the musculoskeletal system or an asthma attack or infection in the respiratory system.

Repeatedly ingesting refined sugar throughout the day creates one biological event after another, producing a kind of whiplash effect that ultimately wears out the adrenal glands. For reasons that are not yet understood, this kind of unrelenting physical stress rapidly depletes the adrenal glands of their Vitamin C stores—with its attendant adverse effect on collagen production and immune system function.

Sadly, many people are addicted to refined sugar. After all, even cigarettes are cured with it, and soft drinks, of course, can be loaded with it. According to the *National Soft Drink Association,* the average American male age 12 to 29 consumes nearly two quarts of soft drinks per day. Two quarts? That's about sixty ounces. Since a ten-ounce soft drink (or can of fruit juice) can contain somewhere between eight and twelve teaspoons of sugar, the average American male may be consuming somewhere between 48 and 72 teaspoons of sugar every day. Wham! Now, there's a kick to the adrenal glands.

It's a habit that leaves boys and young men (or anyone consuming this much sugar) open to obesity, Type 2 diabetes, emotional and behavioral problems, heart disease, osteoporosis, and a range of other maladies. In her book *Natural Health Remedies*, respected health researcher Dr. Janet Maccaro argues "Excessive sugar consumption has been shown to suppress our body's immune response, which can lead to disease" (Maccaro, p. 26). This suppression leaves people vulnerable to viruses, bacteria, and other pathogens.

A SUPPLEMENTS SECRET

When you eat too much sugar, your body generates a powerful biochemical response that has more to do with biology than psychology. As a result, sugar cravings often are very difficult to resist because sheer will-power cannot override the physical need. These cravings can be reduced or even eliminated, however, over a period of weeks by including appropriate amounts of high-quality proteins in your diet at meals and whenever a craving strikes. Vitamin C supplements can help repair adrenal damage, and supplementing with chromium may help balance blood sugar levels. When you're choosing chromium supplements, look for a blend of chromium and niacin, which will be easier for your body to absorb and use.

Fructose

Fructose is the sweetest of all the natural sugars (about twice as sweet as sucrose) and one of the most important blood sugars, along with glucose and galactose. You know it best as the natural sweetener in fruits, beets, sweet potatoes, parsnips, and onions.

Like most foods, fructose can prove harmful when ingested to excess. Unfortunately, it's easy to ingest fructose in high concentrations. For example, the food industry uses it as part of their High Fructose Corn

Syrup (HFCS) formula for sweetening soft drinks, some fruit juices, and various other processed food products. Be wary, and do what you can to reduce the quantity of HFCS in your diet.

In very small amounts, however, fructose is either benign (no known health effect) or even metabolically helpful. As a minor ingredient in a supplement (perhaps designed for children) it's useful as a sweetener because such small amounts can be used to create a desirable effect.

PRO-BIOTICS: NATURAL IMMUNE SUPPORT

Chapter 1 referred to your immune system as your "internal physician" on call 24 hours per day. Poor dietary choices impair your immune system, but there are various ways to support it as well. They include everything that keeps a cell healthy: clean air, filtered water, nutritious food, and totally terrific supplements—all supported by adequate exercise and rest.

Another effective way to support your immune system is to look after the beneficial microbes (mostly bacteria) that naturally reside in your digestive tract. They're called *symbionts*. Symbionts are distinct organic entities that exist in a mutually beneficial relationship, and they aren't just exotic fictional creatures from *Star Trek*. They reside in the lower part of your small intestine and the colon and live in harmony with you. They need you and you need them.

Your digestive tract is the largest part of your immune system, and it contains three to four pounds of beneficial bacteria. In fact, the number of friendly bacteria in your gut exceeds the number of cells that comprise your entire body, which indicates just how important friendly bacteria are to your internal ecology.

Friendly bacteria are known as *probiotics*, bacteria that support life. According to D. Lindsey Berkson, consulting scholar for *Bioenvironmental Research* at Tulane and Xavier Universities, probiotics provide an impressive range of health benefits that include:

- Breaking down carbohydrates for energy and they help digest fats and lactose-based products such as milk and yogurt

- Producing some digestive enzymes that can help alleviate digestive disorders such as constipation, diarrhea, indigestion, gas, peptic ulcers, irritable bowel, colitis, and inflammatory bowel disease

- Possibly improving absorption of minerals, including calcium and magnesium and, perhaps, iron

- Protecting the immune system by producing natural antibacterial, antifungal, and antiviral substances (natural antibiotics)

- Enhancing liver function

- Maintaining optimal pH balance in the intestines; researchers now are linking reduced rates of disease to pH levels that tend toward alkaline rather than acid

- Making some B Vitamins such as biotin, niacin, folic acid, pantothenic acid, B6, and B12

- Making Vitamin K

- Producing by-products that protect against some cancers

- Deactivating many toxins, including chlorine and other chemicals in drinking water

- Preventing a parasitic infection from becoming more aggressive

- Protecting women from estrogen imbalance, which may be associated with a range of women's health problems, including PMS and some cancers

- Eliminating chronic yeast infections caused by an overgrowth of unfriendly bacteria known as *Candida albicans*

- Preventing blood poisoning after surgery, especially in elderly patients, by reducing or eliminating massive bacterial overgrowth.

In other words, the good bacteria in your gut actually help fight disease.

Unfortunately, however, these bacteria can be disrupted. Imbalances can be caused by excessive sugary foods, fatty foods, stress, constipation or diarrhea, chemotherapy or radiation treatments, or overuse of certain pharmaceuticals (such as antibiotics, birth control pills, cortisone or corticosteroids, prednisone, and ulcer medications).

Yeast infections are an all-too-common symptom of intestinal bacteria imbalance. Yeasts are fungi that live all around you and inside you. In a healthy individual, they're a harmless fact of everyday life. In a biologically weakened person, yeast can cause serious trouble.

Candida albicans is responsible for most yeast-induced illness. It makes itself at home in your mucous membranes. In women, vaginal burning and itching is a common sign of a yeast infection, but a yeast overgrowth can show up in both men and women as burning and itching of inflamed eyes, ears, throat, or rectum.

A SUPPLEMENTS SECRET

Probiotics can be especially useful following illness or surgery. Naturopaths and other practitioners of alternative health recommend diligent use of probiotics for a month after taking antibiotics, for several weeks after surgery, and for several days after food poisoning. Note, however, that people with severely suppressed immune function should not use probiotics in case the bacteria breach the intestinal lining. Check with your healthcare provider.

Mainstream medicine tends to downplay the serious nature of Candida overgrowth, but it can be connected to a host of conditions, such as allergies and chemical sensitivities, chronic infections, depression, fatigue, headaches, hyperactivity, irritability, jock itch, memory loss, menstrual disorders and PMS, mouth and throat infections (thrush), and skin conditions such as eczema and psoriasis.

Before reaching for a prescription to deal with these conditions, it may be worth consulting a naturopath to determine if a bacterial imbalance is the source of the symptoms. If Candida albicans overgrowth is identified, your naturopath may recommend a few things:

1. **Change your diet**. Reduce your intake of processed foods, use un-pasteurized apple cider vinegar in salad dressings to promote growth of friendly bacteria, and eat yogurt containing live cultures of friendly bacteria. Be aware, however, that probiotic yogurt may contain only one strain of bacteria, concentrations may be unclear or not stated at all, and sugary syrups in designer yogurts can reduce or even reverse the probiotics' effectiveness. After all, sugar promotes the growth of Candida.

2. **Kill the yeast**. You can do this medically or with herbals (only under the advice of your health care provider).

3. **Take probiotics supplements.** They will help re-colonize your gut with friendly bacteria. The probiotics will help maintain the delicate ecosystem that exists in your GI tract.

Dietary modification and daily supplementation with a totally terrific probiotic can help improve your overall immune health and digestive function.

If you're one of the many people who are confused by all the advertising claims, some guidance on how to buy probiotics probably is in order. Ready? Here's the scoop.

Probiotic supplements are available in a variety of forms. The secret to choosing something that's really effective is to avoid brands containing a narrow spectrum of bacteria. They may be cheaper, but they can't fully re-colonize the complex ecology of your gut. A totally terrific choice would be a product containing a broad spectrum of at least eight strains of friendly bacteria, starting with two you might be familiar with:

1. **Lactobacillus acidophilus** (also known as L. acidophilus) is becoming popular in the media, so you may have heard the term before. These friendly bacteria form a protective shield on your intestinal walls and help prevent overgrowth of Candida albicans. In addition, L acidophilus helps your

intestines absorb more nutrients. Preliminary research shows L. acidophilus also may help to balance immune activity.

2. **Bifidobacterium longum** (B. longum). You may have heard of B. longum, too. It's part of the largest bacteria group in the intestines of infants. In fact, B. longum bacteria colonize a newborn's intestines within days of birth, which may give you an idea of how important they are. These beneficial bacteria produce enzymes that break down food (including carbohydrates) and help to neutralize toxins. They also produce lactic acid, which discourages growth of unfriendly bacteria and promotes balance in the entire digestive tract, including in the large bowel where bowel movements start. Unfortunately, B. longum declines with age. Babies switched from breast milk to formula also experience a decline in the amount of B. longum, which can leave them susceptible to allergies and digestive problems.

While L. acidophilus and B. longum may be familiar terms, you may not have heard about others. Here are six more your probiotics supplement should contain:

1. **Lactobacillus casei** (L. casei) bacteria help L. acidophilus set up the protective shields in your gut referred to earlier

2. **Bifidobacterium bifidum** (B. bifidum) bacteria help break down carbohydrates; recall that carbohydrates provide energy

3. **Lactobacillus rhamnosus** can help relieve inflammation and hypersensitivity, especially in people with food allergies and eczema

4. **Lactobacillus salivarius** can help with bowel disorders

5. **Streptococcus thermophilus** breaks down milk products

6. **Bifidobacterium lactis** enhances the ability of natural killer cells (good guys) in the bowel; that is, it's immuno-stimulating.

All these friendly bacteria help to destroy harmful bacteria, maintain balance in the intestines, and promote healthy immunity.

When choosing a probiotic supplement, look for a brand that contains *fructooligosaccharides* (FOS). FOS provide food for friendly bacteria and encourage their growth; they're known as *pre-biotics*. Also make sure the supplement is enteric coated, so it bypasses the harsh acid in the stomach and is delivered to the intestine, where it belongs. Finally, look for a product that's stable at room temperature. If not, you'll have to refrigerate your probiotic supplements. Many people forget to take their probiotics if they're hidden away in the fridge.

BOTTOM LINE SECRETS

COMPLEX CARBS tend to digest more slowly than simple carbs, give up their energy more gradually, and generally treat the body more gently.

SIMPLE CARBS tend to be the main ingredients in processed foods. They're the ones you develop cravings for. They break down quickly during digestion and enter the bloodstream rapidly. This high-speed process can raise blood sugar levels too fast and too high. Repeatedly eating large amounts of simple carbs puts a huge strain on every system of your body.

THE GLYCEMIC INDEX (GI) measures the rate at which carbs break down and enter the bloodstream.

CARB BLOCKERS can help you avoid the consequences of excessive simple carbs when you're faced with eating the occasional carb-heavy meal (such as at weddings, birthday parties, and the like).

HIGH CONCENTRATIONS OF PROCESSED FRUCTOSE, especially as High Fructose Corn Syrup, can hinder the ability of the heart to use chromium, magnesium, and copper. Children, especially, are at risk from ingesting too much fructose on a regular basis in juices and sweet treats.

CRAVINGS can be eliminated by providing your cells with adequate nutritional support from nutrient-dense foods and supplements.

FIBER SUPPLEMENTS combined with adequate amounts of filtered water can help ensure proper bowel function. It's important to remember that your digestive tract is the largest part of your immune system. Proper bowel function is a strong indicator that your entire digestive tract is in good condition.

A DAILY PROBIOTICS SUPPLEMENT can help your intestinal tract re-colonize its natural bacteria.

A
ANECDOTE

I recall when television arrivied in my community, some time in the 1950s and just after Sputnik was announced. What a time in which to be a kid. I was terrified and excited at the same time.

The Roy Rogers Show, The Ed Sullivan Show, Tarzan, The Walt Disney Show, The Last of the Mohicans—ahh, those times were rich and influential, indeed. T.V. had such an impact, I recall to this day the test pattern that would start and end each television day.

My family would sit together especially to watch an evening of The Ed Sullivan Show and The Walt Disney Show, back to back. We'd watch everything, and no one but Mom got up during the commercials. We sat there with our new-fangled T.V. dinners that kept us rapt in the kaleidoscope of moving images, the stimulation of musical jingles, and the passion of talking heads promoting their products. Yeah, we even liked the commercials, such was the novelty of moving images coming through the air into our homes.

Among my strongest memories of television commercials is the television mom in an apron demonstrating the new, heart-healthy vegetable oils. Often enough, they were the cue for my Mom, suitably aproned herself, to deliver plates of food to our T.V. trays. How perfectly right everything seemed. It really did. No wonder we were so willing to buy whatever was being promoted.

I can no longer precisely hum the jingles that made everyone feel just right about the new vegetable oils, but I recall very clearly the image of a stock of corn affixed to a large bottle of oil and the T.V. mom so proudly presenting it to us. Her smile overwhelmed the music. The male voiceover accompanying the ad seemed entirely credible and persuasive. It was neat to realize that same bottle of corn oil was in our fridge.

We used television's new vegetable oils—and felt all the healthier for it. Little did we know back then that we should have been far more frightened of those oils than we were of Sputnik.

- Jerre

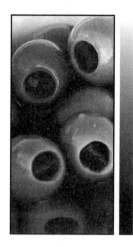

CHAPTER 6
BAFFLED BY FATS

Understanding fats is probably about as easy as deciding who's telling the truth in a court case. Fats have been accused of being unhealthy, the cause of heart attacks. At first, all the evidence looks valid. As the layers are stripped away, though, the reality becomes just downright baffling. Reviewing the history, the evidence, and the propaganda surrounding fats will help you determine if they're really guilty as charged.

THE CASE AGAINST FATS

Let's say you decide to first review some of the history surrounding fats. You'll uncover some truths, for sure, but you'll also uncover some big fat myths. You might start your review by scanning the first half of the 20th century. As you read, you'll find a steady increase in arguments against fats. Like any good detective, though, you'll soon find the evidence against fats isn't clear. In fact, you may find they've been wrongfully convicted.

As you begin your review, you might be surprised by the striking absence of fast-food outlets in the early part of the last century. You might be a little amused that most cooking and baking was done at home, but shocked that it was done with lard (pork fat), tallow (beef fat), butter (milk fat), and tropical oils (coconut and palm). Examining inventories of grocery store products, you'd notice there were few alternatives to these fats and little expressed need for any. The growing arguments against them went largely ignored throughout the first half of the century.

You might realize the vegetable oils of the day were not popular because refrigeration was difficult. These oils would have gone rancid quickly. As you continue your research, you might notice that many cookbook recipes called for solid fats—especially butter and lard.

As you continue your investigation, you'll find an interesting shift in the evidence around the time of World War II. The Japanese had invaded the Philippines, and trading with North America had stopped. The supplies of tropical fats (coconut oil and palm oil, for example) became limited. As a result, government bodies began supporting development of vegetable oils to replace the tropical oils.

Continuing on with your research, you'll come across some possibly unfamiliar terms:

- *Poly-unsaturated fats* linked with vegetable oils

- *Saturated fats* linked with animal fats and the increasingly-scarce tropical oils

You'll soon see the government was starting to identify saturated fats as a problem. In those years, people cooked, baked, and fried with saturated fats—probably because they provided convenience and taste, and no one was concerned they may not be good for their health.

Moving through the 1950s, 60s, and 70s, you'll find the soy and corn oil industries fully committed to altering their vegetable oils to make them look a lot like the saturated fats they were striving to replace. And a new term was coming into popular use: *partially-hydrogenated fats*, the new darling of the post-war era. These fats included margarine and shortening, and they were made from vegetable oils that had been heated to high temperatures, chemically altered, and served up on America's dinner plates as a healthier and less expensive alternative to butter and lard. Today, you might recognize partially-hydrogenated fats under their now common name, *trans-fats*. Partially-hydrogenated fats. Trans-fats. They're the same thing.

Your research will reveal the vegetable oil industry was quickly becoming a multi-million dollar operation entrenched in the American economy and a solid wall of defense had been constructed to protect the fledgling industry. In the middle of wars, embargos, industrial re-tooling, and the new economy, the advertising industry became closely linked with the vegetable oil industry. Your investigation will reveal that government health guidelines, various books, and media advertising adopted the term "heart-healthy" to describe the new vegetable oil products. You'll find, too, that "health-damaging" was the term used to describe the formerly popular saturated fats.

North American consumers, people just like you, were not baffled by all this—although they should have been. They fully accepted the new vegetable fats as good for them. Indeed, you'd find mothers serving up margarine and people flocking to all the fast-food outlets that had arisen. The new, cheap, stable, fats resulted in inexpensive, profitable, convenient foods: millions of hamburgers, billions of donuts, trillions of fries. All of this made possible by the inexpensive, so called heart-healthy vegetable oils. Fast foods, fast lifestyles, a burgeoning economy. People were eating up the new fats and rejecting the traditional ones. North Americans had taken government advice.

As you continue your research, you'll read the government proclamations of the late 1970s that everyone should reduce saturated fat intake to 10 – 20% of overall fat consumption. A figure now had been placed on just how unhealthy various authorities perceived saturated fat to be—without any consideration whatsoever for individual needs or genetic predisposition. Neither had there been much consideration of the link between fats and vitamins.

Then, if you look very carefully, you'll find some baffling information starting to emerge. Highly respected, independent lipid (fat) researchers, such as Mary Enig and Sally Fallon, had taken on the anti-fat campaigns of industrial giants and government policy-makers. Huge, longitudinal studies involving hundreds of thousands of people, such as the *Nurses' Health Study* and the *Framingham Heart Study*, began denouncing earlier studies that targeted saturated fats as the bad guys.

Their research introduced new evidence in the case against fats, and your eyes might widen with this discovery:

- During the 20th century, the amount of traditional animal fat (saturated fat) North Americans consumed fell from 83% to 62%

- Simultaneously, consumption of alternative fats (dietary vegetable oils such as margarine, shortening, and refined oils) increased by a whopping 400%

- Over that same period of time, heart disease increased to epidemic proportions—the opposite of what should have been expected if alternative fats were the better choice (Enig, 2001).

> **A SUPPLEMENTS SECRET**
>
> Vitamins A, D, E, and K are fat-soluble vitamins. If you've ever made the mistake of taking your multi-supplement with a glass of water, juice, or other fat-free beverage on an otherwise empty stomach, well—the fat-soluble vitamins simply passed right through you because there was no fat to act as a solvent.

This new evidence might make you question whether the charges against fats had been trumped up.

Looking for more expert testimony, you might come across the prestigious *American Journal of Clinical Nutrition* and read J. Bruce German and Cora Dillard's 2004 summary of research into dietary saturated fat:

> … reducing the proportion of energy from fat below 30% is not supported by experimental evidence and that advice to decrease total fat intake has failed to have any effect on the prevalence of obesity, diabetes, and cardiovascular disease.

Once you conclude your preliminary investigation of this case, you're likely to question what's fact and what's fiction. And you might feel a little baffled. If there were a jury in the case against fat, its members might feel a little baffled, too—there is a lot of baffle about fat.

If you were the judge in this case, you might instruct the jury this way: "You must determine which fats, if any, are healthy and which, if any, are not. Look only at the documented evidence before you, and be sure to look at all of it. Ignore preconceived notions, and make your own determination based on the evidence."

At this point, the jury might ask for more testimony from science experts before making a decision. All the facts have to be examined because the decision will affect every cell in a human being's body. Even though the science is going to get a little technical, it's needed to decide this case. So, the scientists are called in to present more expert testimony. Let's see what they have to say.

The Language Of Fats

The expert witnesses are going to use language that may not be familiar to you. Really, this language is based on three words: *saturated*, *mono-unsaturated*, and *poly-unsaturated*. These words refer to some common, everyday foods; for example, the butter you spread on a slice of bread, the olive oil you drizzle on a salad, or the safflower oil you use for a stir-fry. The experts also will refer to fats found in supplements: flaxseed oil and conjugated linoleic fatty acid (CLA), for example, are poly-unsaturated.

A SUPPLEMENTS SECRET

Research shows that, when combined with an appropriate exercise program, conjugated linoleic fatty acid (CLA) can help build lean muscle and reduce body fat. It's a favorite of body builders or anyone wanting to trim fat and build muscle.

Did you notice something here? People tend to refer to solid fats as "fats" and liquid fats as "oils". Think of butter or lard or the fat you trim from a steak. You likely refer to all of it as "fat", but when the fat in question is a liquid, you refer to it as "oil". This terminology offers a nice way to distinguish between the solid and the liquid forms of fats. After all, offering someone a salad drizzled with olive fat doesn't sound very appealing. So what's the point? Well—both terms refer to what the expert witnesses may lump together under the single term "fats."

In addition, when you hear from the expert witnesses, they'll likely use the terms *fat* and *fatty acids*. Often, the words are used interchangeably, but it's not technically correct to call a fatty acid a fat. To understand fat, however, you need to know something about fatty acids.

Fatty acids are those individual molecules that link up with other molecules to form the compound you know as *fat*. It's a little like fibers that link up to create a piece of fabric. You might refer to the fabric in everyday conversation, but it's really the fibers that make up the fabric. Similarly, fatty acids make up fat.

Mostly, the expert witnesses are going to talk about fatty acids, but from time to time, they'll interchange the terminology just as you often see in books, on television, on labels, and all over the internet. These expert witnesses may refer to fat when they really mean *fatty acids* simply because the term fat helps get to the real-life point. After all, most people (including the jury) are concerned in their daily lives about fat, not fatty acids.

Decoding Fats

Well—that was a mouthful of technical terms, wasn't it? Let's see if we can decode it all, now, and relate it to your food and food supplements. The terms saturated, mono-unsaturated, and poly-unsaturated refer to three main categories of fatty acids that people commonly refer to simply as fats. That's what we're going to do here: we're simply going to call them fats.

Saturated Fats

Saturated fats are solid at room temperature. Some come from animal sources: butter and other dairy products, tallow, lard, and the fats from meats, poultry, and fish. Others come from plant sources such as coconut and palm hearts—which are full of them.

Saturated fats also are manufactured by your body from excess carbohydrates. If you eat too many starchy or sugary carbs, the excess is stored as saturated fat. As a result, cutting saturated fat from your diet and then loading up on high GI carbs will do nothing to reduce the amount of stored fat in your body.

Here's an illustration of the saturated fatty acid molecule. It will combine with other molecules to form the saturated fat that ends up on your dinner plate.

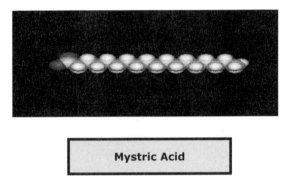

Mystric Acid

Notice the straight, rigid composition of this molecule. That's what makes saturated fats solid.

Mono-unsaturated Fats (MUFAs)

Here's an illustration of the mono-unsaturated fatty acid molecule:

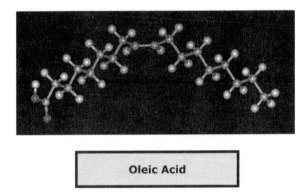

Oleic Acid

Notice the single bend in this molecule. That's where it gets its name "mono", which means "one". This molecule has one bend. That bend makes it a little less rigid than the saturated fatty acid molecule. Mono-unsaturated fats are liquid at room temperature, but they will turn solid when refrigerated. Let's avoid some of the tongue twisting, and call them *MUFAs* for short. Because MUFAs tend to be liquid, they commonly are called *oils*. Olive oil is the best known of them. If you refrigerate your olive oil, you'll see it turns solid. Return it to room temperature, though, and it turns liquid again.

Poly-unsaturated fats (PUFAs)

Poly-unsaturated fats are liquid at room temperature, and they remain liquid when refrigerated. Because of this, they're commonly called oils. Again, we can avoid some tongue twisting. Let's call them *PUFAs* for short. Here's an illustration of the poly-unsaturated fatty acid molecule:

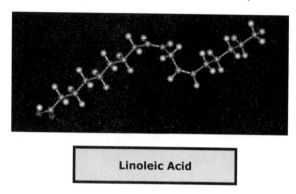

Linoleic Acid

Notice the two bends in this molecule; others have more. That's where these molecules get their name. "Poly" means "many". As you can see, PUFAs are well, "bendy". That makes these fats (okay, they're oils), fluid whether they're at room temperature or refrigerated.

PUFAs are easy to spot in your kitchen because they're the liquid oils that don't turn solid in the fridge. They come from corn, safflower, flaxseed, hemp, pumpkin seeds, sesame seeds, soybeans, and sunflowers. You probably recognize some of them as healthy oils, especially flaxseed oil and the increasingly-popular hempseed oil.

PUFAs and MUFAs and saturated fats. This decoding business gets a bit technical, doesn't it? But that's it for the technical terms the expert witnesses will be using. Now, you'll be able to understand what they're saying.

Okay, this probably is a good time for a break. Stretch your legs, take a little walk, do a few yoga poses. That's what we writers are going to do. Then come back, and we'll put this all together and see how the case against fats turns out.

The Testimony

Welcome back! Did you have a good break? If you did, it will serve you well as the case against fats unfolds. This case has introduced you to a lot of technical terms. Here's a summary you can use as a cheat sheet when the expert witnesses present their testimony:

- **Saturated Fats** are comprised of rigid fatty acid molecules that make the fat solid, even at room temperature. Think butter, lard, and other animal fat—including your own love handles. Think, too, of tropical oils such as coconut oil and palm oil.

- **Mono-unsaturated Fats** (MUFAs) are comprised of fatty acid molecules with one bend in them. "Mono" means "one". MUFA molecules are a bit flexible, so the fat is solid when refrigerated but liquid at room temperature. Think olive oil and canola oil. (Canola oil is about 60% mono-unsaturated fat.)

- **Poly-unsaturated Fats** (PUFAs) are comprised of fatty acid molecules with more than one bend in them. "Poly" means "many". PUFA molecules are really flexible, so these oils are liquid even in the fridge. Think of vegetable and seed oils such as corn oil, sunflower oil, safflower oil, and flaxseed oil.

Now that you have all this terminology sorted out, it's time to sort out the case against fats. We'll look at all these fats to determine which are the good guys and which are the bad guys. And if you don't have the terminology quite sorted out yet, don't worry; we'll get the expert witnesses to repeat things a little as the case proceeds. Ready? Let's hear what the experts have to say.

Saturated Fats

Industry and government campaigns have focused on saturated fats since at least the 1950s. In their collective language, these organizations have labeled saturated fats as the "bad guys." But are they?

You require saturated fats for energy, hormone production, vitamin absorption (Vitamins A, D, E, and K), cell membrane structure, and padding. Saturated fats also help individual cells facilitate signaling between their outer membranes and internal organelle structures. The familiar fight-or-flight reaction, for example, depends upon a complex signaling operation that requires specific saturated fatty acids. Different signaling and maintenance operations require the presence of different saturated fatty acids. It's all very complicated, and science hasn't yet figured it all out.

What science does know is that saturated fatty acids actually come in different sizes. We could write volumes about the different fatty acids, but let's look at two: *long chain* and *medium chain*.

Long chain saturated fatty acids are straight and rigid, and they have no openings for other atoms to get in. That's why they're called saturated. As a result, these molecules are relatively difficult to break apart, so saturated fat is not a good source of quick energy. It is, however, a good source of stored energy. In fact, it stores more than twice the energy of a carbohydrate or protein. That's why your body stores excess quantities of saturated fat—much of it just under the skin, which many of us know all about.

A long chain molecule has a difficult time getting through your body's cell membranes. That's a good thing because your cells don't necessarily want a lot of rigid, energy-difficult fats inside them. In fact, your cells will accept many long-chain fatty acids only when other kinds of fatty acids they prefer are not available.

Medium-chain saturated fatty acids are shorter and, for technical reasons, more readily absorbed through a cell's membrane and broken down into the individual components your cells require. Coconut oil is among the most popular and accessible of the medium-chain fats. Although it's referred to as "oil", coconut oil is solid at room temperature (like all saturated fats). But, it's just barely solid. If you scoop some of this white, aromatic substance onto your fingers, you'll find it literally melts. Coconut oil is excellent for cooking because it has a very high flash point, so it's less likely to burn and smoke (which is an indication of a damaged fat).

Further, you can store it outside the refrigerator at room temperature for several months without the fat turning rancid.

Sound, scientific research consistently demonstrates that coconut oil is indeed heart-healthy and that its benefits extend to the digestive, endocrine, and immune systems as well. Research suggests coconut oil can help protect against cancer, diabetes, heart disease, and many degenerative diseases. It also can help promote weight loss (Enig, 2001).

Mono-unsaturated Acids (MUFAs)

Recall that olive oil is a MUFA and that MUFA molecules have a single bend in them. That bend makes the molecules a little more flexible than saturated fat molecules, but it also makes them a little more delicate. While many cooks use olive oil for cooking, they may not be aware of one very important fact: When heated with sustained high heat, MUFAs such as olive oil oxidize.

You've seen oxidation take place when you've cut into an apple and watched it turn brown; a potato actually turns blackish. You likely don't find the discolored food appealing and tend to cut away the spoiled portion to get to the healthy (un-oxidized) flesh beneath. The discoloring has warned you the food is spoiling.

The reason oxidized foods are so bad is that they ultimately introduce an unwanted supply of oxidized molecules into your body. These oxidized molecules are known more commonly as *free radicals*, and they're the main culprits behind the aging process and a host of degenerative diseases. They can wreak havoc with your body's cells. It's kind of like rusting from the inside out.

This matter can be a little confusing because free radicals are not, in themselves, so very bad. Your body actually produces them as a result of its own chemical reactions. Free radicals are part of the aging process Nature designed, but you don't want to introduce them unnecessarily through poor dietary choices. Refrain from ingesting them in overwhelming numbers.

So here's a word of advice: If you heat any oil until it smokes, which is easy to do with a MUFA, you've oxidized it. Throw it out and start over.

And be careful what you buy in the first place. Today, cheaper oils are collected through a chemical extraction process, or they're refined with high-speed machines that produce tons of oil efficiently. This refining creates temperatures in the very high range. Sometimes, chemical extraction processes and high heat are used in combination, delivering a deadly one-two punch: oxidizing the oil and destroying many of the nutrients in the source plant.

A SUPPLEMENTS SECRET

Some brands of Saw Palmetto supplements contain the mono-unsaturated fat olive oil. It serves as a carrier of Saw Palmetto active ingredients and provides healthy fatty acids. Gentlemen: If it doesn't sound like Niagara Falls when you make that morning trip to the bathroom, you might consider Saw Palmetto supplementation. Native Americans traditionally have used Saw Palmetto berries to support the prostate gland. Research now has shown that Saw Palmetto (especially when combined with nettle root and pumpkin seed oil) supports the prostate gland and helps promote normal urinary frequency and flow.

As you can see, it's important to choose the right grade or quality of MUFA. Here's a guide for you:

- Always buy cold-pressed oil rather than refined.

- In the case of olive oil, look for cold pressed extra virgin olive oil. This oil comes only from the first, chemical-free pressing of a low-acid olive. It gives you the most nutritionally dense product.

- Virgin oil is also a first-press product and chemical free, but it's derived from an olive higher in acid than those chosen for extra-virgin oils.

- Pure oil sounds good, but don't buy it. Pure oils are, in fact, a combination of oils, including those that are chemically-extracted. They are typically sold as bulk, low-cost oils.

While you're shopping for cold-pressed oils, look for those that are certified organic in a dark, glass bottle.

When chosen wisely, handled well, and ingested in reasonable amounts, MUFAs contribute to healthy development of cells. These oils may protect against certain cancers, and they are thought to reduce the risk of heart disease (which has led to promotion of Mediterranean-style food as heart-healthy cuisine). In addition, MUFAs tend to be high in Vitamin E, which is often referred to as the most important free radical fighter.

Poly-unsaturated Fats (PUFAs)

Recall that PUFAs remain liquid, even when refrigerated. They're referred to as oils. In the human body, PUFAs such as flaxseed oil are needed for blood clotting and regulation of inflammation. They enable absorption of the fat-soluble vitamins A, D, E, and K (which will be covered in detail later in this book), and they're needed for maintenance of cell membranes. Obviously, PUFAs are an important part of a healthy diet.

A SUPPLEMENTS SECRET

Here's how to test if your flaxseed or fish oil supplement is rancid: break the capsule open or pierce it with a pin, and taste the oil. If it's bitter, it's rancid.

But, there's a problem. The molecular structure that makes PUFAs so fluid also makes them unstable—which means they can be easily damaged. Light and air damage these oils. Heat damages them, too. Expose them to light or air, fail to refrigerate them, or heat them, and the oil will oxidize. Oh! Oh! There's that word "oxidize" again. Oxidized oil is rancid oil, and that means it's toxic to your cells.

Many commercial establishments use these damaged oils over and over to prepare your food: donuts, French fries, fried eggs, deep-fried chicken, onion rings. At home, if you're not keeping your oils in the fridge and using them quickly, your home cookin' is toxic, too.

While you can't have much control over the way restaurants treat their oils, you can take charge at home. To avoid damaging PUFAs, be sure to refrigerate, and protect them from light and air. When properly handled, they're healthy oils suited for salad dressings and dips. Damage the oils with heat, light, or air, and they oxidize really very quickly, producing those ever-dangerous free radicals which, ultimately, can damage even your DNA.

When you're buying PUFAs, look for certified organic brands that are cold-pressed (not refined), and avoid those sold in clear containers. They may have started to oxidize before you even take them home from the grocery store. At home, keep these oils refrigerated after opening and use them quickly. In the case of flaxseed oils, buy only those that are refrigerated in the store, and keep them in the fridge when you get them home.

Concerns about oxidation extend beyond the oils you buy as food to those you buy as food supplements. Whenever you choose a flax oil or flax and fish oil supplement, for example, make sure it has not turned rancid due to harsh refining processes.

Trans-Fats

Trans-fats occur naturally in a few foods (milk is one of them). For the most part, though, trans-fats are man-made. Industries and communities in both the United States and Canada are just starting to remove this synthetic fat from products and restaurants after decades of pleas by informed groups and individuals (scientists and lay people alike). Remember your review of fat history: Synthetic fat was designed to replace natural, saturated fats and heralded as heart-healthy.

Synthetic fat is made from PUFAs. As you know, PUFAs are delicate— and that creates a problem for the food industry: Any PUFA that sits around at room temperature turns rancid really rather quickly. To address this problem and to increase the shelf-life of fats and products containing fats, manufacturers convert PUFAs to a solid form: they transform the molecules.

Through this process, the comparatively unstable liquid fats become stable. This means the transformed fats don't turn rancid quickly, and they end up looking and tasting much like the saturated fats (such as butter and lard) they are designed to replace. That change in state makes the synthetic fats very stable, indeed. Because trans-fats are so stable, the food industry can store them and use them much like saturated fats, but much more cheaply.

What's wrong with that? After all, if a PUFA is prone to turning rancid, why not transform it to a fat that won't spoil? And in our cost-conscious society, what's wrong with producing fats that are cheaper than their natural counterparts?

Well, here's the rub: The fats we're talking about here are made by heating nickel-infused oils to very high temperatures. The nickel acts as a catalyst to ensure a chemical reaction. Once the oil is heated, it's injected with hydrogen. The result is a "fake" solid fat in which a hydrogen atom has switched (or been transported) from one side of the fatty acid molecule to the other. This switch makes the oil solid at room temperature. The new molecule is called a *trans-molecule*, and the fat it produces is called a *trans-fat*. You'll find it listed on all kinds of food labels as either trans-fat or as *partially-hydrogenated fat*.

The problem is this: Your body doesn't recognize trans-fat as a nutrient. While trans-fat acts like a natural saturated fat outside your body, inside is another matter entirely. At the very least, it does nothing except replace natural fat with all its nutrients, leaving your body searching for the missing resources. This is the Nutritional Void. At the worst, and eventually, it interferes with cellular function.

Trans-fats are particularly harmful when ingested in large amounts, which North Americans tend to do because they eat so much processed food. In terms of present quantities ingested, trans-fats created by manufacturing processes remain a serious health problem linked to cancer, arteriosclerosis, and hosts of other degenerative diseases.

You may be aware that New York City is trying to get trans-fats off people's plates. The city has taken the lead in North America by banning trans-fats in restaurants and other eating places. Many other communities, small and large, are taking up New York's lead even as we write. It is good news that trans-fats appear to be on their way out. But don't celebrate quite yet.

Interesterified Fats (IE)

As we write, industry is introducing another fake fat known as the *interesterified fat* (IE for short). It likely will appear on food labels as *fully hydrogenated oil.* Start looking for it now.

The financial stakes are high for industries currently based on vegetable oils. If they can't render their fats solid, they can't compete with natural saturated fats. Do you think we should expect industry to sit back and take a big financial hit from the loss of trans-fats?

The research has only just begun on IE. So far, IE appears to afford no health improvements over trans-fats and certainly not over natural, saturated fatty acids. As fat researcher Dr. K .C. Hayes of *Brandeis University* in Waltham, MA has pointed out:

> From my perspective, natural fats are still nature's way of doing it. If nature's fat does something you don't like, try blending it with a natural fat that you do like, and that's the way to get to the best solution, as opposed to modifying it, as opposed to saying, we'll trick nature and make this partially hydrogenated or fully hydrogenated. (Wood, S. 2007)

His point of view appears to be well supported by sound, scientific research.

Summation

As the opening pages of this chapter described, North Americans have been encouraged by decades of government and industry persuasion to switch from saturated fats to PUFAs in the form of vegetable oils and trans-fats. Are saturated fats really bad guys and PUFAs good guys?

Certainly, PUFAs can provide huge nutritional benefits—especially in the form of flaxseed and flaxseed oil. Today, however, the North American diet is overwhelmed by PUFAs that have been oxidized—partly because cooks everywhere don't understand how gently these oils must be handled. As a result, many people are in serious need of significantly reducing their intake of oxidized oils, and they are in need of anti-oxidant supplements to help fight free radicals.

PUFAs are good oils, but they're not completely innocent. PUFAs turn into terrible bad guys if they're not handled properly. Choose only cold-pressed, certified organic brands sold in dark bottles. At home, keep them refrigerated and use them quickly. Avoid cooking with PUFAs such as corn oil, safflower oil, sunflower oil and the like because heat oxidizes them easily. They're best for salad dressings, drizzles, and dips.

Trans-fats are PUFAs that have been transformed by heat and chemicals, and they're guilty of promoting poor health. Trans-fats started out as good guys, but they've been turned bad the industrial way. It took decades to compile the evidence against trans-fats, but they're being moved out of the food supply.

Interesterified Fats (IE) are industry's new replacement for trans-fats. They're called fully hydrogenated oils, and you'll see them in store shelves now. Will they ambush unwary consumers? The jury is still out, but it appears likely IEs are no better than trans-fats.

As for saturated fats, they've been given a bad rap. They're not the bad guys they've been made out to be. Saturated fats are a good source of stored energy and, like all fats, they're needed for absorption of fat-soluble vitamins. Your body needs saturated fats for cellular communication inside and outside cells, hormone production, and padding.

Your cells especially prefer medium chain saturated fats—the tropical oils once described by industry and government as the cause of dreaded degenerative diseases. There was never any convincing research to demonstrate such claims, but good campaigning and faulty-but-convincing research convinced the public to avoid them. Industry marketed their synthetic vegetable oils to replace them.

Yes, your body will store excess saturated fat—and that can be harmful to your health—so eat saturated fat in moderate amounts. Nevertheless, one thing is certain: eliminating saturated fats by choosing fat-free meat and dairy products or by choosing foods containing hydrogenated oils rather than, say, butter or coconut oil is not a good idea. These foods not only have had the beneficial saturated fats removed, but they often have had sugars, salts, and flavorings added in an attempt to restore, however poorly, the flavor lost when the saturated fat was removed. It's a striking example of The Nutritional Void.

MUFAs are more stable than PUFAs. They're good guys, but they still need some careful handling so they don't turn into bad guys. While many cooks use olive oil and canola oil for cooking, they need to remember that MUFAs oxidize if they get too hot. If you heat your oil until it smokes, it's oxidized. Don't eat it. Oxidation contributes to disease because free radicals can cause damage at the cellular level.

The Verdict

Let's start with the worst verdict news and work our way up to the best— so you're left with a good taste in our mouths, so to speak.

GUILTY: Bad fats may be defined as those that interfere with your body's cellular activities. They can foster degenerative diseases, accelerate natural aging, and burden people with excessive weight. Fats that are guilty of damaging your health are:

- Trans-fats (partially hydrogenated fats)

- Refined PUFAs and MUFAs that have oxidized (turned rancid) during refining or through improper storage or handling

- Supplements containing oxidized PUFAs. Chapter 2 discussed the problem of rancid oils turning up in supplements. Query manufacturers about how they make their food supplements, and avoid those that damage their oils with excessive heat, air, and light during harsh refining.

The jury is still out on the matter of interesterified fats. It looks like these new synthetic fats eventually will be charged with harming your health.

INNOCENT: Good fats are those that enable natural cellular operations. Various energy-intensive chemical reactions in your body depend upon good fats. They help prevent degenerative diseases, slow and even reverse undue aging processes, meet structural needs such as padding of organs and joints against shock, and help people maintain proper body weight. The fats that are innocent of damaging your health and, instead, promote good health are:

- Coconut oil and moderate amounts of other saturated fats such as butter and lard

- Cold pressed MUFAs (such as olive oil) and PUFAs (such as flaxseed oil) that have been kept refrigerated and used quickly

- Properly-manufactured food supplements containing PUFAs. When it comes to supplements such as flaxseed oil, be sure to taste the oil. It should not be bitter.

Ironically, some of these good fats were replaced decades ago by synthetic fats. Your guiding rule as North America moves beyond the trans-fat era should reflect what you learned earlier in this chapter: Choose natural fat over synthesized fat so you can avoid lingering in The Nutritional Void.

BOTTOM LINE SECRETS

THE CASE AGAINST FATS is complicated. Some fats are good guys, and some are bad guys. Fats research shows that the traditional saturated fats may not have been as harmful as once thought, and that the refined vegetable oils and synthetic fats that replaced them can actually interfere with your cells and foster disease.

FATS CAN BE DAMAGED by heat, light, and air. When that happens, they become rancid. Rancid fats create huge problems for the body as they release damaging free radicals that wreak havoc at the cellular level.

LONG CHAIN SATURATED FATTY ACIDS, such as butter and lard (often touted as unhealthy fats), can be beneficial when eaten in moderate amounts.

MEDIUM CHAIN SATURATED FATTY ACIDS, such as those in coconut oil, are highly accessible to your cells. Solid research has shown medium chain fatty acids can benefit digestive, endocrine, and immune systems and may help protect against cancer, diabetes, heart disease, and many degenerative diseases.

CONJUGATED LINOLEIC ACID (CLA) is among the highly beneficial fatty acids that can help trim total body fat (especially abdominal fat) and build lean muscle: yes, fats to help reduce fats.

OLIVE OIL is a mono-unsaturated fat (MUFA). Like other MUFAs, olive oil contributes to healthy development of cells, and research now shows it may provide some protection against certain cancers and heart disease.

FLAXSEED OIL helps with blood clotting, regulation of inflammation, absorption of certain vitamins, and—very importantly, with maintenance of cell membranes.

A **ANECDOTE** Every Friday (winter, spring, summer, and fall) my Catholic family ate fish for breakfast, fish for lunch, and fish for dinner. I had a sense of the religious reasons for this regular departure from red meat, bird, and pork, so I never questioned it. But I had no idea it made nutritional sense, too. Regularly eating fish made certain we were ingesting reasonable quantities of Essential Fatty Acids. Often, ritual and science are found to be in sync.

When winter arrived in all its magical, snowy wonder, my mother made sure we were getting the benefits of fish every day. The thought was that when cold temperatures set in, so did flus and colds. Morning began with a hearty protein breakfast of eggs and bacon, slow-cooking oatmeal and creamy milk, or, on Fridays, kippers (and sometimes sardines) on toast covered with a delicious, buttery sauce. The kippers were a little hard for a kid's palate, but I nibbled away at them (and probably whined a lot), knowing something even worse was coming.

And it always came. Before I was allowed out of the house to walk to school, Mom met me at the door with a tablespoon heaped in yellow sugar—cod liver oil mixed with sugar, disguised as a "sweet." It didn't work, though. A spoonful of sugar did not make that medicine go down, I'll tell you. But Mom was Mom, so I grimaced and swallowed and, on my way to school, burped a lot. No wonder I had no girl friends during that part of my life. I didn't have a lot of colds or flus, either.

I survived the years of cod liver oil on a spoon, living long enough to witness the advent of gel caps. I don't recall whether they were filled with cod liver oil or some other fish oil, because I didn't care. My mornings were greatly improved by gel caps, and I think my Mom's life was improved, too. She ensured I got my fish oils, and I didn't make horrible faces at her.

I was lucky in a lot of ways back then. Mom strictly held to the common sense that fish oil supplements were good for her kids. What she didn't know, however, was that adults needed them as much as kids. Nor did she know she was not giving me the best fish oil supplements.

- Jerre

CHAPTER 7
INDISPENSABLE EFAS

In the case against fats, there's one group of PUFAs that's conspicuously absent in the previous chapter—maybe because they've never been charged as "bad guys." In fact, most researchers agree they're "good guys."

They're known as *Essential Fatty Acids* (EFAs). EFAs perform critical functions within the human body. Your body can't produce EFAs, so it's essential to get them from food—that's why they're called Essential Fatty Acids.

You can't survive without EFAs. Obviously, if you're reading this book, you're alive, so you must be getting EFAs from somewhere—so what's the big deal? Well, you may be surviving, but are you thriving? How's your performance at school or at work? How about on the football field? Can your relationships with people at work or at home stand some improvement? How about your sex life? More importantly, how's your ability to heal? What about that chronic illness or those persistent aches and pains that just won't go away? These are just some of the issues this chapter will address.

If you find the answers a bit technical or even a bit over your head, don't worry—and don't put the book down. It's true that parts of this chapter are a bit mind-boggling, but they're, well—essential, if you'll pardon the pun. Read through, and pick up what you can. Over time, it all will start to make sense.

And consider this: EFAs are important for optimum brain function. If you have trouble following this chapter, it's possible the information isn't too technical for you. Perhaps, instead, you simply need a better balance of EFAs in your diet. In all likelihood, you're pretty smart, but if you don't feel smart, if you can't concentrate, or if you experience brain fog, it could be your brain is starving for nutrients such as EFAs.

So, before you continue reading, go to your fridge and pull out some certified organic salad greens. Wash them in cool water with some organic liquid cleaner, pat dry, and place them in a bowl. Add some diced organic avocado, four or five ounces of raw or lightly cooked wild salmon, a teaspoonful of crushed organic flaxseed, and a small handful of chopped walnuts or Brazil nuts (raw—never roasted because, as you know, heat oxidizes the poly-unsaturated fats in the nuts).

Now, whisk together a salad dressing of equal parts organic flaxseed oil and un-pasteurized apple cider vinegar or fresh lemon juice. If you wish, add some seasonings such as coarse sea salt, fresh ground pepper, fresh garlic, or fresh herbs. Mix well. Drizzle the dressing over your salad. Toss and enjoy.

Once you have your salad prepared, nibble as you read. The avocado, wild salmon, flaxseed, flaxseed oil, and nuts all contain EFAs. By the time you finish, you'll have eaten all the molecules you're going to read about in this chapter.

And if this recipe made you exclaim, "Yuk!", then consider EFA supplements. You'll understand why by the end of this chapter.

HOW YOUR CELLS USE EFAS

Earlier in this book, we covered the molecules with little wiggly legs that make up the bi-layered membrane of a cell. Every one of the little wiggly legs is a fatty acid. There are many kinds of fatty acids, and EFAs are an indispensable member of this collection.

EFAs are needed for the manufacture of cell membranes, where they play a significant role in ensuring membrane fluidity and elasticity. The less fluid the membranes are, the more your cells have trouble communicating with other cells, and the more difficulty absorbing and releasing nutrients.

Further, cells lacking sufficient quantities of EFAs are more difficult for hormones to regulate. Diseases such as diabetes and heart disease can result.

The important role EFAs play in the life of a cell doesn't stop with the outer membrane. Recall that your DNA is housed in a nucleus. That nucleus has a membrane requiring the same degree of flexibility and elasticity as the main cell membrane. Without EFAs, therefore, your DNA cannot function properly.

Your cells also use EFAs for energy. Here's how it works: The cell receives the enzymes you provide in your diet, transports them to its inner mechanisms, breaks them down to access their amino acids, and converts their energy for other purposes. Without EFAs, your cells would be less able to metabolize nutrients, and the energy of every cell would be threatened. In the end, the very life of every cell would be threatened—and your life would be at risk, too. In fact, EFAs are entirely responsible for or play significant roles in:

> **A SUPPLEMENTS SECRET**
>
> EFAs support all your body's cells—which means they support all your body's systems: circulatory, digestive, endocrine, immune, lymphatic, muscular, nervous, reproductive, respiratory, skeletal, and urinary.

- Maturing of sensory systems in fetuses and children (especially brains and retinas), which points to the need for expectant and nursing mothers to have an adequate supply of EFAs.

- Lowering triglyceride levels (fat molecule levels) in your blood; regulating your blood pressure, blood clotting, and heart rate; and removing plaque from artery walls—all of which can reduce your risk of heart disease.

- Serving as important mechanisms by which your blood carries oxygen to the cells.

- Playing a role in the synthesis (making) of good cholesterol.

- Controlling inflammatory response, which can be a great benefit to people with inflammatory conditions. Recall that the suffix "itis" refers to inflammatory response. Arthritis, or any disease or condition ending with "itis," is a function of your body's response to chronic inflammation.

- Inhibiting the growth of viruses and bacteria (including yeast), which increases your resistance to disease.

- Supporting proper sleep-wake cycles.

When you appreciate the role of the cell in all bodily functions, it's not surprising to learn what the consequences of low EFAs might be, including decreased memory function, generally reduced mental abilities, inflammation of nerves (indicated in part by "tingling" sensations), vision problems (including the ability of the eye to re-focus readily), diminished immune response to disease (a couple of bouts of colds or flu per year), heartbeat irregularities, menopausal discomfort, and, significantly, learning disorders and growth retardation in infants and children.

Because EFAs are so important, Mother Nature has devised a way to compensate for dietary deficiencies, at least for a while. For example, when there is a shortage of EFAs, your cells will substitute saturated fatty acids as a source of energy. Saturated fatty acids serve only as a second-best energy resource—and a poor

A SUPPLEMENTS SECRET

Whether you're an athlete, an overworked executive, a busy parent, or all three, a shortage of EFAs can leave you feeling tired and sluggish and unable to perform. After all, if your cells can't function properly, neither can you. If you suffer from low energy, if you can't think, if you're moody, or if you're just plain tired, it's possible your cells are not getting the EFAs they need.

second choice, at that. Saturated fats take more than twice the energy to break down, which robs your cells of energy for other purposes.

So, let's think about this for a minute. Can you function at optimal levels if your cells are operating on a second-rate energy source or lacking flexibility or failing to communicate with one another? If you're a football player or a golfer, can you make that touchdown or sink that putt if your energy is low or if your body is stiff and lacking coordination?

NATIONAL FOOD GUIDES AND EFAS

When you consider the fact that you must get EFAs from food and combine it with the fact that EFAs are necessary for human survival, you'd think they would be featured in the national food guides of the United States and Canada. Surprisingly, they're not. In fact, the two guides are almost silent on EFAs. Here's what the 2005 American Food Pyramid says about EFAs:

> Most of the fats you eat should be poly-unsaturated (PUFA) or mono-unsaturated (MUFA) fats. Oils are the major source of MUFAs and PUFAs in the diet. PUFAs contain some fatty acids that are necessary for health—called "essential fatty acids."

This advice appears to ignore the inherent dangers of poly-unsaturated oils you read about in the last chapter, dismisses findings about medium-chain saturated fats, and only mentions EFAs in passing—hardly enough emphasis for such an important nutrient. Such outdated and empty advice simply perpetuates the Nutritional Void.

To be fair, on another page, the guide does refer to what it calls "limited evidence" that EFAs play a role in reducing the risk of heart disease. These comments hardly reflect what research says so clearly about the significance of EFAs—for a lot more than just heart disease.

We're focusing here on the American Pyramid because of the sheer number of people influenced by it. The Canadian Health Rainbow warrants consideration for its slightly different approach to nutrition and food policies, but concerns about the relative silence on EFAs hold true for the Canadian Health Rainbow as well.

By now, you've probably realized you must approach national food guides (and a great deal of other nutritional literature) with a critical eye because they tend to offer broad generalizations, and they're slow to respond to up-to-date research. By now, you've probably realized, too, there is a lot more to know about EFAs than you might find in a national food guide. Books such as this one can help.

Before you read any further, though, have another bite of your salad so you have the energy to read and the brainpower to remember what you've read. There's still a lot to learn.

TWO IMPORTANT EFAS

Recall that all fats are composed of fatty acids. There are many groups of fatty acids, and all these groups have sub-groups. This book will feature two groups of essential fatty acids that are particularly important to human nutritional status: *Omega-3* and *Omega-6*.

Omega-3 Fatty Acids

You likely have heard about Omega-3 essential fatty acids. This group of fatty acids has become very popular, but it's likely most people don't really know what Omega-3s are or what they do.

When we speak of Omega-3 fatty acids, we're referring to a group of fatty acids—all with a similar molecular structure. Omega-3, in other words, is a family of fatty acids your body requires. Two key members of the Omega-3 family are EPA and DHA:

1. **EPA** (Eicosapenaenoic Acid): EPA acts as a precursor for prostaglandin-3 (which inhibits blood platelet aggregation or coagulation—thickening of your blood, leading to increased blood pressure and related health problems).

2. **DHA** (Docosahexaenoic Acid): You already know that essential fatty acids, including Omega-3s, are important components of cells. DHA is particularly important to the structure of sperm cells, retina cells, and brain cells. As you might expect, then, deficiency is associated with impotence, vision problems, and mental disorders. DHA also may reduce serum levels of triglycerides (stored saturated fats). Lowering your triglyceride levels lowers your risk of heart disease.

Obviously, both EPA and DHA offer significant benefits. These Omega-3 fatty acids are found mainly in oily, cold water fish—which is why people are encouraged to eat fish or take fish oil supplements. When it comes to eating fish or taking fish oil supplements, there are, however, some pretty significant problems.

FIRST, many North Americans don't eat anywhere near enough fish.

SECOND, it turns out raw fish is the best source of EPA and DHA because cooking can damage or destroy these delicate Omega-3 fatty acids. Omega-3s are poly-unsaturated fats (PUFAs), so heat oxidizes them. Sushi lovers won't balk at eating raw fish, but many people do. Lightly cooked fish will provide Omega-3s, too, but raw fish is the best source.

THIRD, even if you enjoy raw fish, you can't just run off to the market and buy any old fish. Your best bet for Omega-3 fatty acids will be those fish caught in the upper regions of deep, cold ocean waters. They include wild salmon, mackerel, sardines, anchovies, and a few others. Albacore tuna was once a good bet, too, but toxicity due to heavy metals has become a headline-grabbing problem. It may be headline news, but savvy nutritionists have known about the problem with toxin-laden fish and seafood for years.

Oh! Oh! This situation brings us to the **FOURTH** problem that arises when you try to get enough EPA and DHA in your diet: heavy metals toxicity, and microbial pollutants. Fish caught or farmed in shallow waters such as lakes or streams or ocean shorelines, predatory fish such as tuna that eat smaller fish, and bottom-feeding fish and shellfish (such as shrimp, crab, and lobster), are not a good choice. They're too exposed to pollutants that settle in shallow waters and on the ocean floor. These pollutants collect in the flesh of the fish and shellfish and ultimately collect in the bodies of the people who eat them.

So, here's a secret that may especially please those of you who don't enjoy fish in any form: the very best source for EPA and DHA tends to be fish oil supplements (or for those with a fish allergy or for vegetarians, flaxseed oil capsules). Of course, in the case of fish oil, you must determine whether the manufacturers of the supplement have assayed for heavy metals. Unfortunately, much of the fresh fish for sale isn't assayed for toxins and neither are many fish oil supplements. You have to know what you're buying. Once again, it's important to ask the manufacturer and to get it writing.

Omega-6 Fatty Acids

Now that you know something about Omega-3s, it's time to turn your attention to another group of essential fatty acids: the Omega-6s. Okay, we're going to get a bit technical, again, so dip into your salad, then read on.

You may have read or heard that Omega-3s are the good guys (they are!) and Omega-6s are the bad guys (they aren't!). Here's why: Omega-6 fatty acids are a key component of cell membrane structure. They affect both membrane fluidity and the properties of a range of membrane-bound receptors, enzymes, and channels. In other words, they're important for basic cell operations, including communications. In particular, Omega-6 fatty acids are needed to maintain the barrier characteristics of membranes in the body—for instance, the ability of your skin to retain and absorb water. The permeability of your skin is increased (leading to more rapid drying out) if there is a shortfall of Omega-6s.

Through very complex operations, Omega-6 fatty acids support other molecules to help control inflammation, platelet aggregation (coagulation), and the ability of your veins and arteries to dilate and restrict. Omega-6 fatty acids also appear to help with the movement of cholesterol around the body, mainly by increasing its solubility.

Obviously, Omega-6 fatty acids are very good for you. As Peter Lapinskas, Ph.D., points out in his paper "Omega-6 fatty acids—What, Why, Where, How," a deficiency of Omega-6s can be more severe than a deficiency of Omega-3s. He emphasizes an Omega-6 deficiency can result in death.

Nevertheless, a deficiency of these fatty acids isn't the typical problem in North America. On the contrary, North Americans tend to get too much Omega-6 in their diets. Cooking oils such as corn oil, sunflower oil, safflower oil, soybean oil, and peanut oil all contain Omega-6s. So do various nuts and seeds as well domestically-raised meats. As a result, most people do not need to supplement with Omega-6 because they ingest enough (or too much) every day in the form of salad dressings, baked goods, fried foods, crackers, snacks, and meats.

In fact, the typical North American diet (and the Israeli diet, too) tends to contain 10 to 30 times more Omega-6 than Omega-3 fatty acids when it should contain no more than four times more. The problem is that these two EFAs actually compete for the attention of the enzymes that convert them into energy forms your body needs. Too much Omega-6 means Omega-3 will not get converted to the extent your body requires.

One major result of an imbalance is that too much Omega-6 can result in the loss of the production of prostaglandins, those substances that regulate everything from nerve impulses to inflammation to body temperature. This imbalance contributes to long-term diseases such as heart disease, cancer, asthma, arthritis, and depression.

Two Important Omega-6s

Like Omega-3, Omega-6 is a complex family of fatty acids. Two important members of the Omega-6 family are Linoleic Acid and Gamma Linolenic Acid.

1. **Linoleic Acid** (LA): LA comes mainly from poly-unsaturated cooking-oils (PUFAs). It's the starting point for the synthesis of other fatty acids in your body's cells, and it's a precursor to prostaglandins. Prostaglandins are potent tissue substances that help regulate important bodily functions, including inflammation, nerve impulses, muscle contractions, and body temperature. You read about conjugated linoleic fatty acid (CLA) in the last chapter and learned it can help build lean muscle and reduce body fat.

2. **Gamma-Linolenic Acid** (GLA): GLA helps regulate blood vessel, circulatory and immune systems. It's found in small amounts in organ meats as well as in Borage Oil (23%), Black Currant Oil (17%), and Evening Primrose Oil (10%).

GLA also comes from conversion of linoleic acid in your cells—unless you have some enzyme problems. In that case, you'll need to get GLA from dietary sources and, most importantly, from supplements.

In a paper delivered in the UK in 2000, Peter Lapinskas summarized Omega-6 fatty acids for a conference entitled *A Fitter Future for Fats.* Here's what he had to say:

> Omega-6 fatty acids play a key role in human metabolism but, because of various factors common in the Western societies, many people may be suffering from some degree of functional deficiency. There is therefore a case for some form of supplementation with oils containing GLA, which can alleviate this deficiency. Such supplements have been available and successful for many years.

His point is that some people have problems metabolizing Omega-6 and are therefore suffering from a lack of GLA. If you and your healthcare provider determine you have such a "functional deficiency," you may want to consider GLA supplementation. Most people are not in this situation.

The thing is, although GLA research is relatively new, increasingly convincing research indicates GLA supplementation is a no-side-effect remedy for a variety of serious diseases.

A SUPPLEMENTS SECRET

According to renowned fats researcher Mary Enig, supplementing with GLA has been shown to be effective in the treatment of diabetic neuropathy (Enig, 2004).

The *Journal of Nutrition*, 1998, elaborates:

> ...even though North Americans consume on average more than 10 times the amount of Omega-6 to meet minimal essential fatty acid requirements, the consumption of GLA may offer new strategies for treatment and prevention of certain chronic diseases. Potential Candidates, e.g., rheumatoid arthritis patients, will have to take GLA supplements in order to mimic clinical dosages, because GLA isn't readily found in common foods.

But it's worth repeating that you likely eat far too much Omega-6 relative to Omega-3. The question is whether you're converting the fatty acid LA into GLA—you might not be—so consult a knowledgeable healthcare professional who is up to speed on the latest research before pursuing GLA supplementation.

What About Omega-9?

You may hear that supplementing with Omega-9 will make up for deficiencies in Omega-3 and Omega-6. This isn't quite correct. In the first place, your body manufactures its own Omega-9 (it's not an essential fatty acid). You do not need to supplement it. In the second place, Omega-9 is an emergency alternative only for the -3s and -6s, and it's only marginally effective. For the most part, supplementing with Omega 3-6-9 concoctions is not warranted. Discuss this issue carefully with your healthcare provider if you are thinking of taking such supplements.

EFAS & INFLAMMATION

By now, you've read about all the EFAs in that salad you've been eating. Have you finished it yet? If so, Great! Your cells will thank you for it. If not, well, maybe the next few pages of information about EFAs and disease will give you the impetus to eat up—or at least to consider EFA supplements.

One of the greatest threats to human health is inflammatory response (your body's response to chronic

A SUPPLEMENTS SECRET

Research shows daily supplementation with adequate levels of Omega-3 fatty acids provides long-term benefits for patients suffering with Rheumatoid Arthritis. Omega-3s also may help people with inflammatory gastrointestinal problems such as irritable bowel, colitis, and Crohn's disease.

inflammation) and research has shown EFAs can be helpful here. You see, flexibility and elasticity are the responsibility mainly of Omega-3 fatty acids (and cholesterol). Without them as a central part of the structure of the cell, your cells would be less fluid, less able to metabolize nutrients and in a state of constant inflammatory response. Unchecked, the inflammatory response can lead to heart disease and cancer.

EFAS & HEART DISEASE

The *Nurse's Health Study* showed that EFAs can make the difference between life and death as a result of cardiac arrest. This study followed more than 123,000 nurses over 23 years, giving it considerable crediblity.

If your cells substitute saturated fat for poly-unsaturated Omega-3s, your cells become less elastic. That is particularly hard on your heart because it has to work much harder to relax after contraction. If your heart cells are less elastic than normal during cardiac arrest, recovery is less likely than if its cells had been sufficiently populated by EFAs.

EFAS & CANCER

EFAs have been shown in a variety of studies to enhance resistance against cancer, to slow its progress (in breast cancer), to relieve breast pain caused by tumor growth, and to benefit drug treatment in cancer patients suffering from bladder and breast tumors. One study indicated that Omega-3 may inhibit skin cancer (Davies, 1999).

EFAS & MENTAL DISORDERS

On March 6, 2006 the *University of Pittsburgh School of Medicine* posted the results of a study funded by the *National Heart, Lung and Blood Institute* of the *National Institutes of Health*. The study points to possible links between Omega-3 deficiencies and mental disorders:

> In a study of 106 healthy volunteers, researchers found that participants who had lower blood levels of Omega-3 poly-unsaturated fatty acids were more likely to report mild or moderate symptoms of depression, a more negative outlook and be more impulsive. Conversely, those with higher blood levels of Omega-3s were found to be more agreeable.

Somewhat more dramatically, Sarah Conklin, Ph.D. of the *Behavioral Medicine Program* at Pittsburgh points out that previous studies linked low levels of Omega-3 to bipolar disorder, schizophrenia, substance abuse, ADD/ADHD, and major depressive disorders. Dr. Michael Lyon, M.D. and Dr. Abram Hoffer, M.D., Ph.D., offer similar arguments backed by solid clinical evidence.

Further, the ability to circulate oxygen via your red blood cells to all parts of your body, especially your brain, would be critically hampered by a low intake of Omega-3s. If you experience brain fog or poor memory, you may be deficient in Omega-3s.

The point is this: DHA is decidedly concentrated in the brain. It's necessary for proper mental function, and

A SUPPLEMENTS SECRET

Here's a tip to help you remember DHA is good for the brain. Pronounce DHA as "Duh!" If you feel Duh!, you may need DHA.

it's also particularly important for proper communication between nerve cells.

EFAS & AGING

As you've read, DHA provides significant protection against mental deficiencies. This protection can be especially beneficial for the elderly Research shows that "…elderly people with cognition defects have low levels of DHA in red blood cell membranes" (Bryn).

The elderly must consistently replenish their supplies of DHA by eating fatty fish or, better yet, by taking a regular dose of fish oil supplements containing DHA. Deficiency in the elderly may manifest itself as Alzheimer's disease, dementia, depression, memory loss, and/or mood changes.

EFAS & PREGNANCY

If you think EFAs should be reserved for the older set or those with established diseases, well think again. A European study has found that pregnant women who took fish oil reduced the risk of pre-term delivery of their babies. You see, Omega 3 fatty acids increase placental blood flow—and that improves the growth rate of the fetus. Mothers who do not have enough EFAs in their diets are at higher risk of delivering low birth-weight babies. These babies tend to be deficient in DHA themselves, and are therefore more prone to problems with neurological development.

In addition, Omega 3 fatty acids are important in the development of visual acuity. Studies show that infants given DHA-enriched formula performed better on visual tests and mental tests.

EFAS & STANDARDS OF PRODUCTION

The *Council for Responsible Nutrition* (CRN) has set a standard for companies producing Omega-3 supplements. This standard is known as the *Omega-3 Monograph*. The *CRN Omega-3 Monograph* guarantees the highest quality of product. The Council's voluntary members (manufacturers) must adhere to a strong code of ethics, comply with dosage limits, and manufacture to high quality standards under *Good Manufacturing Practices* (GMP).

This combination of standards (CRN and GMP) is an important matter because of the degree of pollution found in our oceans today. Many manufacturers tend to cut corners during the catching, storage, processing, and distribution of fish products. Ask your supplements manufacturer if they adhere to the *CRN Omega-3 Monograph* standard (see Chapter 13's *Totally Terrific Questions* for help asking this question). If they do not, just keep looking for a company who does adhere to such a standard.

BOTTOM LINE SECRETS

EFAs are not made in the body and therefore they must be ingested as food and food supplements.

TOO MUCH OMEGA-6 (compared to Omega-3) is eaten by North Americans. In doing so, these people are threatening the healthy balance of EFAs in their cells. A typical diet takes in 10 – 30 times the Omega-6s compared to Omega-3s; a healthy diet should take in closer to 3 – 4 times the amount of Omega-6s compared to Omega-3s. People with such a diet need to cut back on Omega-6s and supplement with the Omega-3s (DHA and EPA).

GLA SUPPLEMENTATION may be required for some health conditions that result in the inability to convert Omega-6 into GLA. It's a good idea to consult a knowledgeable healthcare provider before supplementing with GLA, however. We encourage you to read a review article in the *Journal of Nutrition,* 1998 (Vol. 128 No 9, 1411-1414) for more detailed information than we can provide here.

FISH OIL SUPPLEMENTS are considered the best source of the two fatty acids EPA and DHA, although many people tend to use only flax seed oil for their source. Since flax seed oil requires conversion to EPA and DHA and fish oil doesn't, the latter is the preferred source, unless, of course, if you have an allergy to fish or are a vegan.

HEAVY METAL TESTING is also vitally important. In addition to testing for rancidity, be sure to find out if the manufacturer has assayed fish oils for heavy metals or microbial pollutants. This is one place you want to hold out for a proof of excellence. Get it in writing. If you can't, buy another brand.

A DIET RICH IN THE RIGHT BALANCE of Omega-3 and Omega-6 fatty acids can go far to give you the right amount of body fat, effective brain functioning, and (with reasonable exercise) a generally fit and ready body. In turn, these three benefits can combine to significantly reduce the threat of chronic disease throughout your life. A recent five-year study conducted at the *Bowman Gray School of Medicine* suggests adequate intake of Omega-3 fatty acids reduces death from heart disease 50%, Cardiovascular Disease 45%, and all causes by 27%" (Dolecek).

MANUFACTURERS VOLUNTARILY COMPLYING with GMP and the CRN (*Council for Responsible Nutrition*) standards are the only ones from whom you should consider buying EFA supplements. Expect premium results only when your EFA supplements are derived from sources that meet these standards.

A **ANECDOTE** Many more than a few years ago, I naively but eagerly entered a wonderful three year nursing program. As a young woman, I set out on my journey with dreams of walking in Florence Nightingale's shoes.

In class, I soon learned about Hippocrates, the ancient Greek physician known as the Founder of Medicine. Many people have heard his famous statement, "Let food be thy medicine and medicine be thy food." During my next three years, however, very little emphasis was placed on that theory. Granted, we did study Dietetics, but we didn't study Nutrition as it relates to a healthy cell or a healthy person.

Not much has changed. Today, in nursing and medical schools across North America, nutritional science is barely covered. As a result, most nurses' and physicians' understanding of nutrition and supplementation remains pretty rudimentary—unless they've taken on additional study.

Hippocrates also taught that the body must be treated as a whole, not just a series of parts. That philosophy, too, went largely ignored. I was taught that symptoms must be treated with conventional Western medicine approaches emphasizing specialization, surgery, and pharmaceuticals. Let me hasten to say that traditional medicine is wonderful and I thank God every day that these amazing experts are there; it's just that, in my view, we need to expand its scope with complementary healthcare practices—including treatments that address food and food supplements.

As you might imagine, my nursing curriculum largely ignored food supplements. In fact, the very concept of supplementation was explained this way: If you eat properly, there is no need to supplement. That philosophy (explained in no uncertain terms) provided the foundation for my thinking and my colleagues' thinking about supplementation for years.

But, over time, I started to see that nutrition and supplementation were part of treating the body as a whole, as Hippocrates had taught. One day, my good friend and colleague Dr. Carl Taylor offered this analogy, "When patients present themselves with symptoms, we typically pull down the spider webs, but we do not step on the spider." His words confirmed what I already had observed: conventional Western medicine tends to treat the symptoms rather than dealing with the root cause. If I truly was to follow my dream about learning all there is to know about health and healing, I simply had to learn more.

- Gloria

CHAPTER 8
VITAMINS FOR VITALITY

After reading the previous chapters, you likely have a good grasp on one broad classification of nutrients: the macronutrients. They make up the largest part of your diet. No matter whether you're talking about proteins, carbohydrates, or fats, the most important thing to remember about macronutrients is this: the more processed they are, the more damaged they are. Refined grains and over-heated oils provide two vivid examples of damaged macronutrients. In both cases, the heat of commercial refining creates changes that do not optimally support your cells and may even harm them.

MICRONUTRIENTS

Refining also depletes vital nutrients called *micronutrients*. The prefix "micro" means "small," and it's used to designate those nutrients human beings need every day in small quantities—perhaps in milligrams (one thousandth of a gram) or even micrograms (one millionth of a gram). You couldn't survive on a few milligrams of macronutrients, but when it comes to micronutrients, small amounts are all you need.

The micronutrients work together, and they include:

- vitamins

- minerals

- phytonutrients (plant nutrients)

Vitamins, minerals, and phytonutrients are necessary in the human diet because they enable the body to use proteins, carbohydrates, and fats. Without micronutrients in your diet, the macronutrients would do you little good.

Developing a deeper understanding of micronutrients' role in your nutritional status will help you determine which, if any, you may need to supplement your diet. This chapter will focus on vitamins, specifically Vitamins A, C, and E.

> **A SUPPLEMENTS SECRET**
>
> In 2006, the *Harvard School of Public Health* described daily multivitamin supplementation as a "nutritional safety net . . . [providing] about the least expensive insurance you can buy."

VITAMINS: A BRIEF HISTORY

Less than a hundred years ago, healthcare professionals knew nothing about vitamins. Today, however, most people know that certain vitamins prevent certain diseases: Vitamin C prevents scurvy, Vitamin B1 (thiamine) prevents beriberi, Vitamin B3 (niacin) prevents pellagra, and Vitamin D prevents rickets. These diseases are the full-blown consequence of The Nutritional Void, and they're referred to as *diseases of deficiency* because they arise when people are deficient in certain micronutrients.

It was the diseases of deficiency that first prompted research into and ultimately led to the discovery of vitamins. Although sailors and explorers had known for centuries that fresh whole foods offered a treatment for scurvy, it took until 1911 before the "cause was clearly recognized to be a dietary deficiency" (Pauling, p. 62). At that time, biochemist Casimir Funk published his theory that four substances exist in natural foods and that these substances can prevent scurvy, beriberi, pellagra, and rickets—all of which had caused untold suffering and death to millions of people.

In time, Vitamin C and all the vitamins we know today were discovered, and some scientists hypothesized that adequate intake of vitamins not only prevents the diseases of deficiency, but other diseases as well. For example, distinguished scientist and two-time Nobel Prize winner Linus Pauling argued that Vitamin C can help control the common cold. Professor George Beaton of the *University of Toronto* conducted controlled trials that supported Pauling's argument. Fifteen years after his first research was published, Pauling wrote that Vitamin C "exerts general anti-viral action and provides some protection not only against the common cold but also against other viral disease, including influenza, mononucleosis, hepatitis, and herpes" (Pauling, p. xi).

He also argued that sufficient intake of this vitamin (and others) can help control cancer, heart disease, and age-related diseases and that "there is much evidence that Vitamin C is essential to the efficient working of the immune system" (Pauling, p. 129). It was Pauling's view that if the practice of curing disease through nutritional therapy (orthomolecular medicine) were more widely accepted, it certainly would help to alleviate some of the enormous costs of healthcare (Pauling, p. 125).

Pauling's views, and those of others who favor using nutritional therapy, have met with sharp criticism, often reduced to ridicule, and sometimes resulting in unwarranted sanctions. It's a pattern that would be all-too-familiar to the physicians who first suggested lemons and limes could reverse scurvy. As a result, research in the area of orthomolecular medicine has remained largely ignored by mainstream North American society—including mainstream medicine and mainstream media. To make matters worse, American and Canadian physicians daring to treat illness with vitamins or other micronutrients risk having their licenses revoked because they're deemed to be using unproven methods.

Despite these obstacles, an impressive amount of clinical and anecdotal evidence concerning micronutrients has surfaced in recent years—much of it suggesting, and even confirming, that micronutrients play a central role in prevention and treatment of disease. Until recently, healthcare providers and supplements companies have been prohibited, by law, from claiming that any vitamin or other health product can prevent, treat, or cure a disease. New regulations now permit certain claims to be made—provided the benefits of a micronutrient have been scientifically proven. In addition, researchers are beginning to look more seriously at micronutrients as a method of treatment. For example, *CBC News*

World announced on March 30, 2006 that doctors in Montreal, Canada, are now conducting a Phase I study to research the theory that Vitamin C in high concentrations, given intravenously, may stabilize or even shrink cancer tumors. Further, the *Harvard School of Public Health* and the *American Medical Association* now advise that everyone would benefit from taking a daily multivitamin.

Before embarking on a vitamin regimen, however, it's important to understand a little more about the role vitamins may play in your overall nutritional status. Once you understand that, you can determine which, if any, are right for you. Because your body needs only microscopic amounts of micronutrients, it's also important to understand that supplements must be used sensibly. Many micronutrients work synergistically; that is, they depend on one another for proper functioning and results. Megadosing (taking very large quantities of vitamins) or taking certain vitamins in isolation from others can upset that balance. You may have heard some claims, for example, of very high doses of Vitamin A (retinol and retinyl esters) during pregnancy being associated with birth defects.

A SUPPLEMENTS SECRET

In 2006, the *Harvard School of Public Health* contained this statement: "Intake of several vitamins above the minimum daily requirement may prevent heart disease, cancer, osteoporosis, and other chromic diseases."

In addition, certain micronutrients can interfere with certain medications. For example, people taking thyroid hormone should be careful of supplementing with iron or calcium. Taking either mineral within four hours of taking your medication may interfere with your body's uptake of the medication and make it less effective. Similarly, iron and calcium also can reduce the effectiveness of tetracycline.

For all these reasons, it's important to tell your healthcare professional about your entire supplement regimen. Full disclosure is particularly important when medications are being prescribed.

FAT- AND WATER-SOLUBLE VITAMINS

Vitamins are called *essential micronutrients* because it's essential to get them from dietary sources; that is, your body cannot make them.

Vitamins enable chemical reactions in your body, but these reactions cannot occur if the vitamins are not eaten in the proper way. For example some vitamins need water to dissolve; they're called *water-soluble vitamins*. Others need fat to dissolve; they're called *fat-soluble vitamins*.

Because of their water-soluble and fat-soluble properties, vitamins are best taken with a meal so there is sufficient water and fat to act as the required solvent. Further, once you've eaten a meal, the blood flow to your stomach increases.

A SUPPLEMENTS SECRET

It's well worth repeating what we said in Chapter 6: Make certain you take your fat-soluble vitamins along with foods containing fat. If you don't, the vitamins will simply pass right through you, because they need fat as a solvent.

This increased blood flow facilitates improved absorption of the vitamins and other nutrients contained in your food and food supplements. Another very good reason to take vitamins with food is that release and absorption of vitamins (and other nutrients) typically is achieved in a more continuous and constant manner, which provides a better nutrient level in the blood.

The fat-soluble vitamins are A, D, E, and K. They're stored in your body's tissues and can build up to toxic levels if you take excessive amounts of them. Unfortunately, the risk of toxic build-up has received far more attention than the benefits afforded by fat-soluble vitamins. This situation has left them sorely neglected for several decades. Emerging research finally is starting to correct this situation. Scientists now concur that Vitamins A and E (along with water-soluble C) are powerful antioxidants, that Vitamin D (sometimes called the sunshine vitamin) is vital to the absorption and metabolism of calcium, and Vitamin K (mostly produced by bacteria in the intestines) is essential for blood clotting and, therefore, crucial for survival.

The water-soluble vitamins include all the B vitamins (there are eight of them) and Vitamin C. Because they dissolve in water, it's easy to pour water-soluble vitamins right down the drain if you boil your food and then discard the water.

It's important to understand that water-soluble vitamins are very sensitive. They're easily depleted or destroyed by the heat used for cooking (including steaming, baking, and microwaving), long periods of storage, and addition of synthetic chemicals. If you consider commercial processing generally involves all of these nutrient-destroying methods, you likely can see why processed foods help create The Nutritional Void. For example, as Dr. Cass Ingram points out, "milk stored in plastic jugs and glass containers loses the majority of its riboflavin [Vitamin B2] content by the time it's consumed" (Ingram, 2004).

Whole, unrefined grains are a rich source of Vitamins B1 (thiamine) and B3 (niacin), but refine the grains into breakfast cereals, cereal bars, crackers, and flour

A SUPPLEMENTS SECRET

Water-soluble vitamins are not stored in the body, even when taken in as a food source. So Vitamin C and B-complex should be taken every day.

(including even whole grain and additive-free brands) and you'll be hard-pressed to find B1 and B3 listed on the nutrition facts label. Fortification can help, but human beings are notorious for sullying Mother Nature's good work and then doing a poor job of repairing the damage. For all these reasons, it's important to purchase fresh, whole food that's free of chemicals and locally-grown or to seek out certified organic growers in your area. Then cook the produce gently, preferably in waterless cookware. Some orthomolecular physicians recommend eating about 75% of your fruits and vegetables raw to help preserve micronutrients that can be lost during cooking.

Similar concerns arise when choosing a multivitamin-mineral supplement. Totally terrific brands are made from fresh, whole plants grown without chemicals in nutrient-rich soil. For optimum potency, the plants must be harvested at the optimum nutrient stage, a minimum of time must elapse between harvesting and processing, and manufacturing must employ processes that are the least destructive to the plants' naturally-occurring micronutrients.

THE ANTIOXIDANTS

Vitamins perform so many inter-related functions that several categories other than fat-soluble and water-soluble have been developed to help everyone, from nutrition researchers to lay people, talk about these essential nutrients. Two of these categories are particularly well-used in nutritional discussions, and they're useful here: the *antioxidants* and the B vitamin group or *B-complex*. We'll look first at antioxidants.

The term antioxidant became a household word only about a decade ago. Antioxidants ("anti" meaning "opposing") help slow the decay process known as oxidation. In fact, advances in research show that over 100 various types of antioxidants protect your body against the damage caused by oxidation. This chapter looks at three antioxidants: Vitamins A, C, and E. Before you can understand the real value of antioxidants, however, it may be helpful to learn just a little more about the process of oxidation.

Dr. Michael Colgan describes oxidation as "the most pervasive process of decay on Earth." (Colgan, 1995). Rusting of metal is oxidation. The rust that appears on vegetables and fruits is oxidation. Apples turn brown after you cut them because of oxidation. What you witness in these situations is a process in which electrons are removed from atoms in a molecule. Once this removal occurs, the molecule becomes unstable and "creates a powerful electromagnetic attraction that sucks an electron out of the nearest whole molecule of any material it touches" (Colgan, p. 73). These unstable molecules are known as *free radicals*.

Healthcare providers frequently warn that your body can be damaged by free radicals. It's a mild statement, to say the least. Here's the translation: Free radicals, in essence, can damage virtually every part of your body— including the nucleus that houses your DNA, fats and proteins inside your cells, and all your body's tissues. Free radical damage, left unchecked by anti-oxidant activity, can create an endless chain reaction—like a cellular nuclear bomb.

Collagen is one of the many proteins damaged by free radical activity.

You've already read that collagen is a structural protein important for the formation of various organs and tissues—including skin. If you're beginning to put two and two together, you likely suspect that free radical damage shows up on your skin. Of course, you're right. Free radicals cause your skin to lose its elasticity—which is why some brands of skincare products include antioxidants in their formulations.

To see the power of antioxidants at work, cut an apple in two, apply a little antioxidant-rich lotion on one cut side, and leave the other cut side untreated. Let the apple sit uncovered for a few hours, and see what happens. If the lotion is effective, the treated portion of the apple will show few, if any, signs of decay while the untreated portion will start to turn brown and wither. It's a dramatic demonstration of oxidation and antioxidants in action.

Similar to an antioxidant lotion that helps protect your skin (or an apple) from free radical damage, antioxidant vitamins help protect every cell in your body. If you think back to your biology or health classes in school, you may

A SUPPLEMENTS SECRET

One way to help "ACE" your skin care is to include antioxidants such as Vitamins A, C, and E in your daily supplementation regimen. While quality topical lotions certainly can help reduce oxidative damage, glowing, healthy-looking skin really starts on the inside with the nutrients you ingest every day.

recall that skin is your largest organ. You can tell a lot about the oxidation occurring inside your body simply by reading the signs of oxidation that appear on the outside. As Dr. Nicholas Perricone points out in his book *The Wrinkle Cure*, if your skin has lost its elasticity, your other organs (and blood vessels and muscles and other tissues) likely are in similar condition.

In spite of the damage oxidation causes to your body, it's important to understand that it's a natural result of cellular activity. Even the simplest of everyday activities, such as breathing and moving about, cause oxidative damage. People eventually degenerate and die largely because of oxidative damage. Despite advertising claims you may see, completely reversing this aging process isn't possible, but slowing it by slowing oxidative damage may be. You see, it's not a matter of whether you're going to die, but a matter of how you're going to live until then. Will you age with grace and comfort, or will your golden years be fraught with sickness, pain, compromised mobility, and mental confusion?

The answer has a lot to do with those foods you put in your mouth. You see, free radicals are not just an inevitable result of biological activity—some come from the foods you choose to eat. Foods that introduce high amounts of free radicals to your body include:

- Damaged fats and foods containing damaged fats (including fats that have been oxidized due to overheating), trans-fats, and rancid fats such as butter and oils kept in the cupboard rather than in the refrigerator

- Saturated fats, but only if eaten in excess

- Charred or burned foods, including char-broiled and barbequed meats, burned toast, or any food that has been burned or charred

- Alcohol, perhaps with the exception of moderate amounts of antioxidant-rich red wine

A number of common stressors also promote free radical production:

- Physical stress such as illness, vigorous exercise, and eating a diet low in plants and plant nutrients

- Emotional stress such as fear, anxiety, anger, or depression

- Mental stress such as studying or working for excessively long hours

- Environmental stress such as pollution, smoking, and over-exposure to sunlight (including tanning beds)

Halting the production of free radicals isn't possible as long as you're living and breathing, but some modest dietary and lifestyle changes together with appropriate antioxidant supplementation with Vitamins A, C, and E can help curtail free radical assaults that otherwise can overwhelm your cells.

In addition, you may have a genetically predetermined inferior response to oxidative stress that makes certain food and lifestyle choices even more risky for you. This inferior response might explain why some people who have never smoked develop lung cancer: they may carry a particular gene variant that reduces their bodies' ability to handle oxidation.. Genetic tests can determine if you have such a gene variant.

While Vitamins A, C, and E certainly are powerful antioxidants, it's worth noting that these vitamins play other important roles in your body. Vitamin C already has been discussed fairly thoroughly in this book, starting from the first page, so let's look at the two that remain: Vitamin A and Vitamin E.

Vitamin A

Vitamin A actually is made in your body from a precursor known as *beta-carotene*. Beta-carotene is one of a colorful group of around 600 chemicals known as *carotenoids*. They "run the color range from yellow (peaches) to red (tomatoes) and occur in almost every plant"(Wentzler). If you eat plants, you most likely eat carotenoids. Your body converts one of them (beta-carotene) to Vitamin A as your body needs it.

From there, Vitamin A plays many important roles in your body. According to the *Harvard School of Public Health,* Vitamin A "stimulates the production and activity of white blood cells, takes part in remodeling bone, helps maintain the health of endothelial cells (those lining the body's interior surfaces), and regulates cell growth and division" (2006).

Obviously, Vitamin A plays a critical role in cellular production, activity, health, and growth. And there's more—lots more:

- Proper functioning of all cell membranes depends on Vitamin A. Too much makes the membrane lose some of its flexibility and too little makes it overly flexible; "…in both cases, the membrane malfunctions, allowing the bad molecules to sneak in and the good molecules to leak out" (Wentzler, p. 10).

- Small, hard bumps on skin of the triceps (back of the arms) may indicate a long-term Vitamin A deficiency. This "turkey skin" can indicate you're not getting enough beta-carotene or that you're having trouble absorbing, transporting, or converting it.

- Small structures in your eyes called *rods* help you see in the dark, and they depend on Vitamin A. Night blindness is one of the first signs of Vitamin A deficiency.

- Vitamin A aids in detoxification of the body's tissues and organs—a function that needs to be operating at peak efficiency in an increasingly toxic world.

A SUPPLEMENTS SECRET

Your body converts Beta-carotene to Vitamin A only in the amounts it absolutely needs. So choose Beta-carotene as your Vitamin A source.

- Vitamin A regulates the function of glands that produce hormones, and may help lower blood cholesterol by helping to raise the levels of certain hormones produced by the adrenal glands.

- Vitamin A is essential for the formation of tooth enamel and healthy bones in general.

And there's more, much of it the subject of considerable on-going research. While the results are not yet all in, you can see this multi-talented vitamin plays an important role in your nutritional status. For this reason, you may wish to supplement—especially if your eating habits tend to place you in the Nutritional Void. In addition, it's important to know that Vitamin A can be lost through the eyes as a result of exposure to overly-bright light, including computer monitors and certain fluorescent lights. It also can be lost during surgery.

If you're healthy, it's generally best to take Vitamin A supplements in the form of beta-carotene, and let your body do the work of converting it.

After all, a working body is a healthy body, so let it work. In addition, achieving the optimum amount of Vitamin A is more likely if your body controls the process. For this reason, pregnant women should use beta-carotene.

If you're ill or if your body can't store, convert, or transport beta-carotene, your healthcare provider may recommend pre-emulsified Vitamin A to make certain your body acquires the Vitamin A it needs. Those with hypothyroidism or severe liver malfunctioning or diabetes, for example, are better to take the pre-emulsified form. Be aware, however, that Vitamin A is fat soluble and thus stored. So follow Recommended Daily Intake (RDI) advice to avoid toxicity. Megadaoses of any supplement are never recommended without strict monitoring by a healthcare provider fully trained in nutritional science.

Vitamin E

Vitamin E is well known as a scavenger of free radicals. In fact, it often is called the most important of the anti-oxidants, but it has a range of other functions as well. Vitamin E is known to:

- Help stabilize cell membranes

- Help reduce the risk of cardiovascular disease by reducing platelet stickiness

- Improve immune function and reduce susceptibility to infection

- Protect against eye diseases such as macular degeneration and cataracts

- Work with Vitamin C to prevent oxidation of LDL cholesterol

It's an impressive list of benefits.

You should know, however, that the form of Vitamin E is important for these reasons: First, research shows that "natural vitamin E has from 34 to 50 percent greater bioavailability than synthetic vitamin E" (Pelton and Lavalle, p. 218); that is, it's more biologically active, more potent. Second, studies show that as little as one-third of synthetic Vitamin E actually is absorbed by the body (BLI 2005). It's a classic example of getting what you pay for—or not.

When buying Vitamin E supplements, be sure to spend the extra money to get the natural form. Natural forms of vitamin E are labeled "d"; synthetic forms are labeled "dl". Of the natural forms, there are two broad sub-classifications: 1) tocopherols (alpha, beta, gamma, and delta) and 2) tocotrienols (primarily, alpha-tocotrienols but also beta, gamma, and delta). The most potent and most biologically active form of vitamin E is d-alpha tocopherol. Be sure you're getting this form in your supplement, and make sure it's formulated with selenium because selenium works synergistically with Vitamin E.

BOTTOM LINE SECRETS

VITAMINS A, D, E, AND K are fat-soluble vitamins. They will be absorbed into your body only if you take them along with food containing fats. They do not dissolve in water.

VITAMIN C AND THE B-VITAMINS are water-soluble vitamins. They do not get stored in your body, so you have to take them every day.

VITAMINS work synergistically (together) as well as independently, so it's best to take a multivitamin-mineral supplement to build a solid nutritional foundation.

INDIVIDUAL VITAMINS AND MINERALS (or combinations of them) can be added to your multivitamin-mineral foundation, if you need them. If you require larger doses of an individual vitamin, consult with a healthcare professional who knows about nutrition and supplements.

VITAMINS A, C, AND E are known as powerful anti-oxidants. As a team, they are particularly effective as free-radical fighters. Excessive amounts of free radicals produced by nutritional and lifestyle choices can accelerate the aging process.

BETA-CAROTENE is, generally, the best way to get your Vitamin A. It's known as a Vitamin A precursor; that is, your body converts it to Vitamin A. Pre-emulsivied Vitamin A is best taken with zinc. They work synergistically.

VITAMIN E often is referred to as the most important of the antioxidants. It stabilizes cell membranes, helps reduce platelet stickiness, helps to improve immune function and reduce susceptibility to infection, and protects against eye diseases.

A **ANECDOTE** In Nursing School, I studied the human cell, but I somehow missed the fact that every single cell in your body is made from the nutrients you take in. Perhaps it just wasn't taught.

I subsequently went on to study nutrition and began to understand that the nutrients people ingest and the lifestyle choices they make can have a profound impact on their overall health and quality of life.

Through my extra study into nutrition, I realized that a healthy diet of high quality foods and high quality food supplements helps create healthy cells. I also realized that diseases such as ADD/ADHD and Alzheimer's disease were not even a diagnostic category when I took my training, but they're now at almost epidemic proportions.

It deeply saddens me that almost one million children line up every morning to take a drug before they go off to school when, perhaps, a diet and lifestyle change and appropriate supplementation may show they do not actually have ADD or ADHD. And it saddens me that many parents are unaware their children's lives can be turned around with proper nutrients that support those precious living cells in a child's brain.

It saddens me, too, that patients are being diagnosed with diseases such as Alzheimer's when they really are suffering a nutritional problem. Seniors who live alone on diets of "tea and toast" or other nutritionally limited meals can be especially at risk of conditions often incorrectly described as "a normal part of aging."

I notice the irony out there when our schools and hospitals sell candy, soft drinks, and other junk foods in the vending machines, while educational professionals and medical professionals try to handle the ravages of nutritional deficiencies on a daily basis. To me, Hippocrates was right: the body must be treated as a whole and not just a series of parts. When problems arise, I would like to see patients and their families explore nutritional deficiencies as well as pharmaceutical remedies as a standard part of disease investigation—and I would love to see governments support this type of investigation with significant revisions to current medical, insurance, and taxation legislation.

– Gloria

147

CHAPTER 9
MORE VITAMINS, MORE VITALITY

The previous chapter focused on Vitamins A, C, and E. Although these vitamins perform a myriad of functions in the human body, they tend to be known as antioxidants because of their prowess as free radical fighters. This chapter will focus on another group of vitamins—those known as the B-family or B-complex.

The B-family of vitamins is classified as water-soluble. There are eight of them currently published: B1, B2, B3, B5, B6, B12, folic acid, and biotin, nearly all of which are involved in the metabolism of carbohydrates and fats; that is, B vitamins are needed for energy. This fact may explain, at least in part, why many people feel an energy boost when they start supplementing with B vitamins.

The vital role of B vitamins doesn't stop with the metabolism of carbohydrates and fats, however. For example, folic acid is needed (either directly or indirectly) for pretty much every chemical reaction that occurs in your body. Folic acid is needed for synthesis of DNA and RNA. As Dr. Cass Ingram points out, this means "all cells depend on this vitamin for their growth and regeneration...there is no life without it" (Ingram).

Despite the central role that folic acid plays in the human body, the

Harvard School of Public Health warns that most North Americans don't get enough of it—at least in part because it's difficult to get adequate levels of folic acid from food, even though some foods are fortified. Part of the reason is that people don't eat enough dark green, leafy vegetables (foliage that contains folate), beans, or certified organic calves' liver.

Another reason people tend to be low on folic acid is that it can be depleted or entirely destroyed by light and cooking. Further complicating this situation is the fact that lifestyle choices can play a significant role. Alcohol, cigarettes, chewing tobacco, aspirin, antibiotics, marijuana, and hard drugs all can deplete or destroy folic acid. It's perhaps no surprise, then, that folic acid deficiency "is alarmingly common in the USA, with all age groups being adversely affected" (Ingram). Teenagers, particularly, are at very high risk. Studies show that as many as 90% consume less than the Recommended Daily Intake in their diets (Ingram).

What's even more alarming is that the RDI may not adequately support optimum nutritional status. Orthomolecular physicians have long argued that RDI levels are too low, and new research seems to support that view. As a result, RDI recommendations are "likely to change over the next few years as data from ongoing randomized trials are evaluated" *(Harvard Medical School)*. For now, however, the optimal level for B vitamin intake has not been established.

> ### A SUPPLEMENTS SECRET
>
> According to the September 29, 2004 edition of the *Health Sciences Institute* on-line newsletter, Vitamin B2 (riboflavin) can help to significantly reduce the frequency of migraine headaches.

Considering the current RDIs for B vitamins are likely too low and that only a small percentage of people get even those minor amounts, taking a broad-spectrum multivitamin-mineral supplement and a Vitamin B-complex appears to be much more important than healthcare providers once thought. Here's a summary of what researchers are learning.

B VITAMINS & HEART DISEASE

One important discovery receiving the attention of heart and stroke researchers is the relationship between higher intake of B vitamins and lower levels of homocysteine. Homocysteine is a by-product of protein that promotes plaque buildup on blood vessel walls. It was first implicated in heart disease following the fatal, massive strokes of two children in 1968. Since then, various studies (though not all) have linked higher intake of certain B vitamins with lower homocysteine levels and decreased risk of heart disease and stroke. So far, researchers know this:

> Homocysteine is a toxic amino acid produced in the metabolism of methionine (an essential fatty acid). Folic acid, Vitamin B6, and Vitamin B12 act as cofactors for the enzymes involved in methionine metabolism and thus the B vitamins affect homocysteine levels. Plasma homocysteine levels increase as B vitamin concentrates decrease. Several observational studies show that high levels of homocysteine are associated with increased risks of heart disease and stroke. Increasing intake of folic acid, Vitamin B6, and Vitamin B12 decreases homocysteine levels (Harvard 2006).

A SUPPLEMENTS SECRET

In addition to preventing the formation of homocysteine, folate (folic acid) plays a central role in building DNA.

At the moment, the exact role B vitamins may play in reducing heart disease remains the subject of ongoing research.

B VITAMINS & CANCER

While research continues into the link between B vitamins and heart health, research also has begun on another front: the role of B vitamins in cancer prevention. New research shows the risks of colon cancer and breast cancer appear to be lower in people "who get higher than average amounts of folic acid from their diets or supplements" (Harvard).

According to Harvard, researchers don't know if high intake of folic acid and the other B vitamins actually prevents cancer or whether there is merely a loose association between these vitamins and reduced risk.

The *Health Sciences Institute* (HSI) doesn't quite concur. They argue that a significant association exists "between dietary intake of folate (folic acid) and vitamin B6 and a reduced risk of colorectal cancer" (Thompson, February 9, 2006). HSI's comments are based on research conducted at Harvard and at its teaching affiliate *Brigham and Women's Hospital* where researchers followed nearly 38,000 female subjects for ten years.

Even more research is under way. Recent Canadian meta-research (the compiling of existing research on a subject) out of Toronto's famous *Hospital for Sick Children* reinforced widely-held thinking that taking supplements rich in folic acid guards against birth defects and are associated with reduction of three common types of cancer (reported online in *Clincial Pharmacology and Therapeutics*, February 2007):

- A 47% protective effect against neuroblastoma

- A 39% cut in rates of leukemia

- A 27% drop in rates of brain tumors

Whatever the relationship between folic acid and reduced cancer risk turns out to be, it appears that supplementing with a broad-spectrum multivitamin-mineral containing all the B vitamins, as well as a totally terrific B vitamin complex may offer inexpensive insurance against various types of cancer.

B VITAMINS & DIABETES

According to the *Linus Pauling Institute*, "it's been known for many years that overt biotin deficiency results in impaired utilization of glucose." The institute also reports two small studies involving a total of 50 subjects. One study showed that subjects with higher blood biotin levels had lower fasting blood glucose levels. The other showed that subjects' fasting blood glucose levels dropped, on average, by 45% after a month of supplementing with biotin. Obviously, it's difficult to draw firm conclusions from this research because the studies are so small, but the work underscores the need for more research.

In addition to biotin, Vitamin B3 (also known as *niacin* and *niacinamide*) may prove helpful for diabetics or for people at risk of developing diabetes. According to Dr. Abram Hoffer, diabetes may be caused by more than just excess sugar intake. He argues that:

> Evidence is accumulating that viral infections can destroy the Islets of Langerhans in the pancreas and this can be a main problem, even for people who do not eat much sugar. Genes have been found in some families which are possibly causal, but there is striking evidence that taking niacinamide will protect them from getting diabetes. In fact niacin and niacinamide (vitamin B-3) have valuable healing properties for every organ in the body, including the pancreas and kidneys (Hoffer).

It's critical, however, to undertake Vitamin B3 therapy only under the guidance of a qualified healthcare professional trained in nutritional therapies.

Even if you are under the care of a healthcare professional, you certainly should not relax your own vigilance when it comes to diabetes: The chances of your acquiring diabetes are on the increase.

The *World Health Organization* anticipated a whopping 39% increase in diabetes world wide between 1995 and 2005. That's high enough, but the prediction appears low.

According to a new Canadian study (published in *The Lancet,* 2007), diabetes in the Province of Ontario has increased a frightening 69%. Significantly, the greatest increase is in the age group 20 – 49. Should this trajectory continue, 10% of Ontario residents will have diabetes by the year 2010. If this study represents a North American trend, and it probably does, it isn't too far-fetched to think of the rise in diabetes as an epidemic.

A SUPPLEMENTS SECRET

According to the Linus Pauling Institute, "Long-term treatment with sulfa drugs or other antibiotics may decrease bacterial synthesis of biotin, potentially increasing the requirement for dietary biotin."

B VITAMINS & PSYCHIATRIC DISORDERS

It's a well-known fact that B vitamins affect energy and mood, and that they're critical for proper functioning of the nervous system. In fact, the entire nervous system is dependent on B vitamins. Early signs of B vitamin deficiency can include dry skin, itching, scaling, and even sores (especially in and around the mouth). More serious clues may come in the form of "…impatience, depression, or confusion, later developing into hallucinations, panic or complete withdrawal as neurosis becomes psychosis" (Wentzler).

Whole books have been written on the role B vitamins play in improving behavioural problems and treating psychiatric disorders. One of the more well-known figures in this arena is the late Dr. Abram Hoffer, MD, PhD, FRCP (C). Dr. Hoffer was Director of Psychiatric Research for the *Saskatchewan Department of Public Health*, Associate Professor at the *University of Saskatchewan, College of Medicine*, and one of the founders of the alternative health movement.

In hundreds of scientific articles and more than thirty books, he argued nutritional therapy is essential to the treatment of psychiatric disorders. It was his view that an enormous range of problems can be traced to vitamin deficiencies:

- **Perception dysfunctions** such as dyslexia, hallucinations, and schizophrenia

- **Thinking disorders** such as delusions, paranoia that isn't culturally induced, mental retardation, difficulty concentrating, and confusion—some of which may show up on standard IQ tests and some of which may manifest themselves as hyperactivity and ADD (or more adult forms of hyperactivity such as the inability to tolerate inactivity and, even, drug abuse and alcoholism)

- **Mood disorders** such as depression, manic depression, and suicidal tendencies

He argued that combinations of these problems culminate in behavioral problems that certainly can have a basis in a person's psychosocial experiences, but that such problems may be the result of nutritional deficiencies. He maintained psychotherapy and medications are helpful in controlling a psychiatric disorder, but these therapies "do not enable the patient to recover" (Hoffer, 2001).

Dr. Michael Lyon agrees that nutritional status and brain function are closely related. In his book *Is Your Child's Brain Starving?*, he states, "As a medical doctor and researcher I am firmly convinced that most non-optimum brain conditions can be significantly improved through nutritional change" (Lyon).

He also points to an alarming statistic: According to a recent Surgeon General's report, "one in ten North American children now suffers from a diagnosable psychiatric condition." Statistically speaking, this means three or four kids in a classroom of 35 are troubled by psychiatric problems that may range from a learning disability to violence. Certainly, some of this is due to societal factors, but some may be the result of vitamin deficiencies.

A SUPPLEMENTS SECRET

In research dating as far back as 1938, researchers have suspected sub-clinical pellagra (Vitamin B3 deficiency) may be responsible for multiple psychiatric complaints such as anxiety, forgetfulness, inability to concentrate, insomnia, mental fatigue, restlessness, and tension (Hoffer, 2001).

Educators have been on the front lines of this situation for a long time. In fact, researchers in the field of education have known for more than thirty years that the brain uses about 25% of the body's energy. This is why students get tired when they're studying. Their brains are using energy at a ferocious rate. It's also why students need diets that include appropriate amounts of healthy macronutrients (proteins, carbohydrates, and fats), plus sufficient levels of the B vitamins needed to metabolize them. Quite simply: low B vitamins = low energy for the brain.

One condition that affects many school children today is ADD/ADHD. Vitamin B6 is being studied as a possible treatment, but according to the *Harvard School of Public Health*, "there is little evidence that it works." As you likely know by now, it's not isolated B6 that may make a difference, but a whole range of B vitamins plus their complementary vitamins and minerals, toxin-free essential fatty-acids, and specific dietary changes that can make the difference.

A SUPPLEMENTS SECRET

Dr. Michael Lyon concurs. His view is that a range of nutrients including essential fatty acids, certain minerals, and "B vitamins, especially B1 (thiamine), B6 (pyridoxine), folic acid, and B12, are all brain critical nutrients." In designing studies, researchers need to be alert to the synergistic effects of a range of micronutrients.

The widespread B vitamin deficiency discussed earlier in this chapter has led some healthcare providers to speculate that a communication gap with teenagers is really a B vitamin gap.

B VITAMINS & AGE-RELATED DISEASES

While children's brains may be suffering from nutritional deficiencies, the brains of older adults appear to be suffering as well. Neurological problems in the elderly can include impatience, depression, and confusion. As you've read, all of these can be signs of B vitamin deficiency.

One of the more dreaded neurological diseases often associated with aging is Alzheimer's disease. It's important to understand that Alzheimer's absolutely isn't a normal part of aging. Nevertheless, the U.S. *National Institute on Aging* (NIA) reports that :

A SUPPLEMENTS SECRET

According to the *Harvard School of Public Health*, some people diagnosed with dementia or Alzheimer's disease actually are suffering from Vitamin B12 deficiency.

- Up to 4.5 million Americans suffer from this disease

- Alzheimer's typically begins after age 60

- Risk increases with age to the point where nearly half of people over the age of 85 may have it.

Fortunately, new research shows that "…individuals with early

Alzheimer's disease can benefit significantly by taking supplements that contain certain vitamins, minerals, and micronutrients" (Lyon).

The *Health Sciences Institute* reports that high homocysteine levels (covered earlier in this chapter) also are associated with Alzheimer's disease—as are memory loss, age-related macular degeneration, and fractures due to osteoporosis (Thompson, March 22, 2006).

Prevention and treatment of these apparent age-related diseases may include supplementing with folic acid, Vitamin B6, and Vitamin B12 because these vitamins appear to lower homocysteine levels. Of course, as we have said, these vitamins must be combined with the other B vitamins and their complementary micronutrients. In any case, consider such a regimen of vitamins only with the advice of your healthcare provider, as always.

B VITAMINS & BIRTH DEFECTS

While new research into B vitamins and various conditions isn't yet complete, the ability of one B vitamin to prevent birth defects has been proven. About twenty-five years ago, British researchers discovered folic acid is critical for prevention of neural tube defects such as spina bifida and anencephaly. These birth defects "occur when the early development of tissues that eventually become the spinal cord, the tissues that surround it, or the brain goes awry" (Harvard).

According to the *Harvard School of Public Health*, discovering the link between folic acid deficiency and neural tube defects changed the way medicine looks at vitamins—although many nutrition experts say the change is limited and slow. The ongoing debate aside, healthcare providers now understand that folic acid prevents neural tube defects.

Unfortunately, however, an adequate level of "folic acid, at least 400 micrograms a day [about the weight of 10 grains of salt] isn't always easy to get from food. That's why women of childbearing age are urged to take extra folic acid." (Harvard). In theory, this advice is absolutely right: women of childbearing age should be encouraged to take extra folic acid. In practice, however, this isn't happening. Many physicians never mention the need for folic acid to their female patients until several weeks after these women become pregnant—which may be a bit late since cells start to form immediately upon conception. When the *Harvard School of Public Health* says women of childbearing age should take extra folic acid, they mean *all* women of childbearing age who may become pregnant—not just those who are pregnant.

Taking extra folic acid is good advice for women of childbearing age, but new research indicates it may not go far enough. Remember: Every baby enters the world as a result of the union of two cells—one from the female and one from the male. The central role that folic acid plays in the life of a human cell provides a strong argument that men, and not just women, should take a good multivitamin-mineral supplement containing folic acid prior to conceiving a child.

Couples considering having children need to know, too, that estrogens rise significantly in pregnant women, and Vitamin B6 is needed for metabolism of these hormones. Raised estrogen levels resulting from pregnancy may result in Vitamin B6 deficiency.

Raised estrogen levels and possible Vitamin B6 deficiency also results from taking birth control pills. In fact, oral contraceptives deplete most B vitamins—

A SUPPLEMENTS SECRET

Recall from our discussion on Supplements and the Nutritional Void in Chapter 2, that some brands of supplements have been shown to contain lower levels of folic acid than cited on the label. As a result, it's critical to vigorously research the brand you choose before simply popping a supplement into your mouth.

including folic acid. And the list doesn't stop there. In their book *The Nutritional Cost of Prescription Drugs*, pharmacists Ross Pelton and James Vallee argue that, aspirin, corticosteroids, non-steroidal anti-inflammatory drugs, antacids containing aluminum or magnesium, and about thirty other drugs are known to deplete folic acid. Dozens more deplete the other B vitamins. All of this needs to be taken into account when you're considering whether to supplement with a B vitamin complex. We've already referred to the 2007 Canadian study at Toronto's famed *Hospital for Sick Children* that points to the advantages of pregnant women taking supplements, but part of that study warrants further attention here. While women have been advised to take folic acid *during* pregnancy to prevent birth defects such as spina bifida, the study advises that taking a multivitamin-mineral containing folic acid *before and during* may be even better. "This affordable approach," the study advises, "could contribute to a significant reduction in the number of childhood cancer cases diagnosed each year, which has huge implications for society at large."

Research such as this makes it obvious that supplementing with all the B vitamins in the form of a totally terrific multivitamin-mineral supplement and B-vitamin complex is a good idea for mothers and fathers-to-be. Right now, Canadian surveys show less than 50% of women take prenatal multivitamins-minerals before and during pregnancy. Healthcare providers say this percentage needs to improve significantly.

B VITAMINS & CARPAL TUNNEL SYNDROME

Despite their apparent benefits, deficiencies of certain B vitamins are alarmingly widespread in North America (Harvard, Ingram, Pauling). We've looked at a few, but the pervasive deficiency of B6 in North America has yet to be discussed here.

First, it's important to understand that Vitamin B6 is vitally important to protein synthesis and that, like folic acid, it's necessary for cellular reproduction. It also plays a significant role in immune function, synthesis of enzymes and fatty acids, and production of hormones.

According to several medical doctors and nutrition writers, B6 deficiency may result in clogged arteries, depression, fluid retention, hypoglycemia, insomnia, irritability, joint pain, and weight disorders (Ellis, Hoffer, Ingram, Spreen, Wentzler). It also may result in carpal tunnel syndrome, although there's quite a debate about that. In a quotation published in the *Health Sciences Institute*, Dr. Allan Spreen states:

> For carpal tunnel syndrome (which is involved with interstitial
> fluid taking up too much space within the carpal tunnel of the

wrist, resulting in pressure on the nerve and causing numbness, tingling, and pain), 90 days of B-6 treatment is often required for the symptoms to completely subside. Retained fluid in general, however, can start leaving the first night (and can be disconcerting to a person who's now urinating more than they know they've been drinking...the interstitial fluid is leaving) (Thompson, March 2, 2006).

The *Harvard School of Public Health* argues there is little evidence B6 can help alleviate carpal tunnel syndrome, but Dr. Cass Ingram disagrees. He concurs with Dr. Spreen and explains Vitamin B6 "is an invaluable aid in the treatment of a variety of conditions, including carpal tunnel syndrome, high blood pressure, diabetes, depression, anxiety, and insomnia" (Ingram).

> **A SUPPLEMENTS SECRET**
>
> It's ironic that birth control pills and hormone replacement therapy significantly reduce Vitamin B6—which is important for hormone production.

As these disparate views indicate, the vitamin debate still is underway, and more research needs to be done. It's a situation that can only leave patients wondering what to do. Some will choose conventional remedies; others will prefer to try supplements.

If you're one of those who chooses to try B6 for carpal tunnel syndrome or some of the other conditions cited here, take it only under the guidance of a qualified healthcare professional trained in nutrition and be sure to take it with a totally terrific multivitamin-mineral supplement and B-complex. Whatever you do, never take B6 without the support of the other B vitamins.

RULES TO THRIVE BY

It's important to understand that a totally terrific multivitamin-mineral supplement will contain all eight of the B vitamins—not just a few. This is important because B vitamins work together, and large doses of one may interfere with the efficacy of others. For example, as the *Linus Pauling Institute* points out, the B vitamins biotin and pantothenic acid (Vitamin B5) have similar structures. Because of this, large amounts of one may compete with the other for uptake in the intestines and cells. Also, excessive amounts of isolated B6 can cause nerve damage in the legs and arms, and supplementing with isolated B6 during pregnancy can lead to a dependency on B6 in the child.

For all these reasons, there are a couple of very important rules when it comes to supplementing with B vitamins:

1. Never take a B vitamin in isolation; always complement it with the other Bs—plus a few other complementary nutrients.

2. Proper balance is critical, and it's easy to get that balance wrong if you don't know what you're doing. For this reason, it's best to leave specific B vitamin doses to the specialists.

Rather than self-diagnosing and then mixing and matching isolated vitamins—which should be done only under the direction of a competent healthcare professional trained in nutritional science—choose B-complex and multivitamin-mineral formulations prepared by teams of nutrition scientists working for reputable companies who voluntarily adhere to Good Manufacturing Practices. Whether you buy supplements in a health food store, grocery store, or through the internet, it's important to check into the manufacturer's practices before you put anything in your mouth.

> **A SUPPLEMENTS SECRET**
>
> Grains containing a natural wealth of nutrition are robbed of most of their B vitamins when they become highly refined and processed.

BOTTOM LINE SECRETS

THE B VITAMINS ARE CRUCIAL throughout your life to all biochemical activities in your body.

VITAMIN B DEFICIENCIES in teens and young adults are being linked to mood problems, depression, energy, and even diabetes. These deficiencies also are associated with everything from cancer to dandruff in people across the ages.

ALZHEIMER'S DISEASE and dementia may be influenced by a deficiency in B-vitamins.

PEOPLE WITH GENETIC PREDISPOSITIONS to inefficient use of B vitamins may require specialized supplementation.

SUPPLEMENTING WITH B VITAMINS may be necessary for most people because these delicate vitamins tend to be easily depleted and even destroyed by a variety of factors—including heat, light, synthetic chemicals, alcohol, tobacco, and drugs of all types.

NEVER TAKE A B VITAMIN IN ISOLATION. Look for a totally terrific multivitamin-mineral supplement that contains ample doses of all eight B vitamins and a B-complex containing all but perhaps *biotin* (which may not be included in some stress formulations because it does not appear to contribute to stress relief).

A

ANECDOTE

Is Vitamin D toxic? I hear this question a lot. During my years of teaching nutrition in different medical clinics (which was not many years ago), we were warned that Vitamin D is, indeed, toxic. In fact, at one point, science even warned that it was the one vitamin to fear because once you had too much, the overload couldn't be reversed.

But since 1999, research has attempted to dispel unwarranted fears and hysteria surrounding Vitamin D toxicity. (Of course, you can get too much of anything, even water, but I'm not speaking of megadoses here.) Over the past few years, research has discovered the wonderful benefits of Vitamin D and how shockingly deficient many people actually are.

You may know your body generates Vitamin D, but it needs sunshine to do this work. And you likely know there are forces at work preventing many people from getting adequate sun exposure. Work, school, and play activities centered indoors, for example, can prevent you from getting adequate sun exposure and, therefore, adequate production of Vitamin D. Of course, people frequently are told not only to avoid the sun, but to slather on the sunscreen. Even applying sunscreen with an SPF factor of 8 reduces production of Vitamin D by 95%.

Avoiding the sun so completely can have a devastating effect on your health—unless you're supplementing with Vitamin D. Today, I recommend getting 15 to 20 minutes of sun directly on a large surface area of your skin every day (more, if your skin is dark). For those who cannot do that, I recommend supplements, but not just any supplement. It has to be a totally terrific one to be effective.

Since starting my nutritional consulting business, I've also encouraged all my clients to request a blood test to identify their Vitamin D levels. It's not routine, so you'll have to ask for it, but the test is 25(OH)D, also called "25-hydroxyvitamin D concentration." Optimal levels are around 50 ng/mL (125 nM/L).

I'm truly amazed at the number of people coming back to me and saying, "My doctor was very surprised to find I have such low levels of vitamin D that I actually have a Vitamin D deficiency!"

- Gloria

162

CHAPTER 10
DO-IT-YOURSELF
VITAMINS

Within the whole range of nutrients called vitamins, there are two that actually have been misnamed: Vitamin D and Vitamin K. Your body makes them, which disqualifies them from the strict definition of a vitamin; that is, they're not vitamins at all. Vitamin D actually works more like a hormone, and it's a precursor to steroid hormones naturally produced in your body. Vitamin K is a coenzyme. If you recall the discussion of enzymes in Chapter 4, you likely remember that the important activity of enzymes largely depends upon coenzymes.

Although researchers now understand Vitamins D and K more fully, the term "vitamin" has stuck, and it's unlikely to change. Whatever they're correctly called, these micronutrients perform vital functions in your body that you should know about, because deficiencies have been linked to common health problems.

VITAMIN D: THE SUNSHINE VITAMIN

Until reading this book, you may have considered scurvy to be a disease of a by-gone era, and you may think of rickets in the same way; that is, you may think rickets no longer poses a health threat to modern society. But think again. Rickets actually is on the rise in North America. The disease can occur in adults, but it most commonly affects children, and incidents are increasing, particularly, among African-American children.

Rickets is the softening and weakening of bones (and even teeth) caused by prolonged deficiency of Vitamin D (*Mayo Clinic*, November 7). Symptoms include skeletal deformities such as bowed legs and pelvic malformation, leg and skeletal fractures, impaired growth that can be severe, and dental problems, including slow development of teeth, holes in the enamel, and increased cavities. Sufferers also experience bone pain, muscle loss, and muscle spasms. Unless treated promptly and properly, pain can become chronic and deformities can become permanent.

So, why is rickets appearing again? Well, it appears many North Americans are suffering from a prolonged deficiency of Vitamin D. When your Vitamin D levels are low, your body's ability to absorb and retain calcium and phosphorus is reduced. Calcium and phosphorus are crucial for bone-building. Three important factors make this situation particularly tricky:

1. Your body needs sunshine to generate Vitamin D—which is why Vitamin D often is called "The Sunshine Vitamin." Unfortunately, though, many people don't get enough sunshine directly on their skin to make this process possible. In fact, many tend to avoid the sun altogether, or they slather on sunscreen because of warnings about skin cancer. Avoiding the sun so completely prevents the body from synthesizing Vitamin D. In addition, work and lifestyle choices keep people indoors, or in many cases, people live in regions where it's too cold to get enough daily sunshine.

2. Food sources of Vitamin D are really quite rare. Only liver, egg yolks from chickens fed Vitamin D, shrimp, and fish naturally contain it. Dairy products are fortified with it. As you can see, this is a short list of foods, and it's not necessarily a list that appeals to most kids. As any parent knows, getting a three-year-old to eat fish or eggs or liver can be an uphill battle.

3. Many brands of savory snacks (potato chips, crackers, cheese puffs, and tortilla chips) are made with olestra. Olestra depletes the body of Vitamins D and K, as well as Vitamins A and E (that is, the fat-soluble vitamins) because it binds

fat-soluble molecules and blocks their absorption. As a result, the FDA requires manufacturers to fortify olestra-containing products with Vitamins A, D, E, and K. The Health Sciences Institute, however, raises this pertinent question: What do you suppose the chances are that cheese puff manufacturers are making a special effort to use appropriate amounts of fresh, high-quality vitamins?

It's easy to see, then, why increased numbers of North American children are presenting in doctors' offices and hospitals with rickets. These kids simply aren't getting enough sunshine, and they aren't eating much fish or liver, either. To make matters worse, they're eating too many nutrient-robbing snack foods. It's a bone-crushing combination.

As a result, most children may need a daily supplement that includes Vitamin D. Despite the enormous benefits of breastfeeding,

A SUPPLEMENTS SECRET

According to the *Harvard School of Public Health*, 57% of patients admitted to a Boston hospital were shown to be deficient in Vitamin D (2006).

it's important for nursing moms to understand that breast milk doesn't contain Vitamin D. For this reason, breastfed infants may well require Vitamin D supplementation from an age as young as two months— unless they're exposed to the sun. Of course, you should discuss such supplementation with your healthcare provider.

So far, we've focused on Vitamin D supplementation for children, but it's important for adults, too, because bone health is important from infancy through to the senior years. According to the *Harvard School of Public Health*, Vitamin D supplementation may help prevent bone fractures that often lead to disability and death in older people. In fact, some healthcare providers now believe that Vitamin D is as important as, or even more important than, calcium in preventing osteoporosis. They recommend that postmenopausal women, particularly, get blood tests for Vitamin D and either get more sunlight or take supplements if their levels are low. (Mirkin, 2006).

Older people have a reduced capacity to synthesize Vitamin D and an increased risk of developing osteoporosis. So supplementing with Vitamin D is particularly important for seniors.

In addition to bone factures, preliminary studies point to a correlation between lower levels of Vitamin D and higher risk of certain cancers—specifically prostate, breast, and colon cancers. The explanation for this may lie in test-tube and in-vivo studies (those conducted on living organisms). These studies show that Vitamin D kills cancer cells and can help cells differentiate between normal cells and cancer cells.

> **A SUPPLEMENTS SECRET**
>
> According to the *Harvard School of Public Health*, Vitamin D prevents cancer cells from growing or dividing.

In France, a recent study of 800 subjects actually linked five nutrients with lesser risk of colorectal polyps. The nutrients were: Vitamins D and C, and three B vitamins (folate, beta-carotene, and B6). Other studies have linked Vitamin D deficiency with breast cancer. In 2001, the following statement appeared in the *British Journal of Cancer:*

> Women with breast cancer are twice as likely to have a fault in the gene required to make use of Vitamin D. Experts already believe Vitamin D protects against breast cancer and in some forms may even be used to shrink existing tumors. Now research in London suggests that women with genetic variations (polymorphisms) of the Vitamin D receptor gene may be less able to benefit from this protective effect (Bretherton-Watt, D., 2001).

It's a statement that reveals just how important Vitamin D supplementation may be and just how important genetic screening likely will become in the future. Until the science of nutrigenomics is further advanced, however, it may be wise to take the advice of the *Harvard School of Public Health,* who publishes this clear recommendation on their website:

> If you live north of the line connecting San Francisco to Philadelphia, odds are you don't get enough Vitamin D. The

same holds true if you don't, or can't, get outside for at least a 15-minute daily walk in the sun. African-Americans and others with dark skin tend to have much lower levels of vitamin D due to less formation of the vitamin from the action of sunlight on skin.

The website recommends starting with a daily multivitamin, but it warns that most multivitamins contain Vitamin D levels that are too low, so additional supplementation may be required to achieve optimal levels—which they say are considerably higher than the current RDI.

When your skin is exposed to direct sunlight, the cholesterol found in

A SUPPLEMENTS SECRET

Vitamin D may reduce your susceptibility to gingivitis, which is inflammation and bleeding of the gums that has been linked to heart disease. (*American Journal of Clinical Nutrition,* September 2005)

the cells of your skin is converted to cholecalciferol (called Vitamin D3) and then to calcitriol (the active form of D3). If you choose to supplement with Vitamin D, your best choice is Vitamin D3 from cholecalciferol because it's the form your body produces naturally. Vitamin D3 from cholecalciferol isn't cheap, but it's the best form. You may see Vitamin D2 (ergocalciferol) sold as a vegetarian Vitamin D. It's an inferior form.

When you're shopping for Vitamin D3, especially if you're a post-menopausal woman, look for a brand containing Ipriflavone. Ipriflavone is a semi-synthetic form of isoflavone. Isoflavones are water-soluble chemicals found in plants; ipriflavone is derived from soy. It helps the body absorb and metabolize calcium.

Ipriflavone has been researched in dozens of studies involving nearly 4300 patients for over twenty-five years. In virtually all the studies, ipriflavone combined with calcium has been shown to slow, halt, or perhaps somewhat reverse bone loss. In addition, researchers have found it may reduce the pain of osteoporosis-related fractures and may even reduce fractures of the vertebrae.

If you're interested in Vitamin D supplementation with ipriflavone, discuss your needs with a healthcare provider who is knowledgeable in the area of nutrition and supplementation. People with active ulcers should not use it, and your physician may monitor your white blood cell count and lymphocyte count if you take ipriflavone on a long-term basis.

VITAMIN K: KRITICAL FOR KLOTTING

Vitamin K is essential for your survival because it's involved in making six of the thirteen proteins needed for blood clotting. Without Vitamin K, you would bleed to death—either from even the smallest cut or from internal bleeding. Its name, Vitamin K, derives from the Danish word *koagulate*, which is *coagulate* in English. As writer Rich Wenztler humorously points out, "Without vitamin K, the blood kan't klot."

Fortunately, this kritikal vitamin—okay, enough is enough—this critical vitamin is plentiful in a range of foods, especially green, leafy vegetables such as spinach and salad greens, broccoli (especially broccoli leaves), horseradish (the best source), and vegetable oils such as olive oil.

The form of Vitamin K in these plant foods is known as K1; it's converted to K2 in the small intestine. You also get some Vitamin K in the form of K2 from liver, egg yolks, and fermented products such as yogurt and cheese.

Finally, and perhaps most importantly, the friendly bacteria in your gut make Vitamin K—lots of it—providing yet another good reason to take probiotics, as discussed earlier in this book.

To perform its blood clotting work, Vitamin K "shuttles back and forth between two enzymes to get its job done" (Wentzler, p. 144). Anticoagulant drugs interfere with this action by partially preventing Vitamin K from reaching the second enzyme, which in turn impedes the liver's ability to make clotting factors. Alcoholism, lead poisoning, and most medications (including seemingly innocuous over-the-counter medications such as aspirin) have a similar effect.

As if its critical role in blood clotting weren't enough for one little vitamin, Vitamin K also plays an important role in bone-building: "A report from the *Nurses' Health Study* suggests that women who get at least 110 micrograms of vitamin K a day are 30% less likely to break a hip as women who get less than that" (Harvard, 2006). In addition, abnormalities in bone and cartilage that occur as a result of Vitamin K deficiency can increase the severity of osteoarthritis (Thompson, 2006).

A SUPPLEMENTS SECRET

Long-term use of antibiotics destroys normal intestinal bacteria, in turn reducing synthesis of Vitamin of K. It's important, then, to take a totally terrific probiotics supplement between antibiotic doses.

And that's not all. You've probably heard that eating certain vegetables (especially horseradish, broccoli, and leafy green vegetables) may help prevent coronary heart disease and calcification of the arteries. A study conducted by a team from the *Harvard School of Public Health, Tufts University* in the United States, and the *University of Kuopio* in Finland researched 40,000 men over 15 years. The study found that those who consumed the highest levels of Vitamin K reduced their risk of fatal heart disease by 20%. Of course, those inclined to eat their greens also may be inclined to lead a healthier lifestyle—a fact that was not lost on the researchers who reported that Vitamin K intake and lifestyle choices both contributed to fewer coronary events.

At one time, Vitamin K deficiencies were considered to be rare, but the *Harvard School for Public Health* reports that a 1996 survey showed most Americans (especially children and young adults) are not getting enough Vitamin K. The culprits likely can be traced back to two factors: North Americans aren't eating their veggies, and many people have depleted the friendly bacteria in their intestines with poor dietary choices or antibiotics.

For all these reasons, it's probably good to use a multivitamin-mineral supplement that includes low concentration Vitamin K. Currently, however, Vitamin K is listed in the American Food and Drug Regulations and in the Canadian Natural Health Products Regulations as suitable only for use with a prescription. In Canada, these regulations are changing. Once completed, these changes will allow products containing less than 120 micrograms to be sold without a prescription.

BOTTOM LINE SECRETS

VITAMIN D is made by your body from sunshine.

VITAMIN K is made by the friendly bacteria in your gut.

15 MINUTES A DAY OF SUNLIGHT directly on your skin may be enough to replenish Vitamin D stores. If you cannot guarantee yourself that much sun time, consider Vitamin D supplementation.

HIGHER DOSES OF VITAMIN D, in combination with calcium supplementation, may help prevent falls (by strengthening muscles) and fractures (by helping increase bone density) among the elderly. Higher dose Vitamin D prevents first osteoporotic fracture (*JAMA* 2005).

RICKETS, a bone disease caused by a deficiency of Vitamin D, is on the rise in North America. Fifty seven percent of patients admitted to a Boston hospital were deemed deficient in Vitamin D.

THE BEST FORM IS VITAMIN D3 from cholecalciferol, which is the form of D your body produces naturally. Look for a Vitamin D3 supplement containing ipriflavone, which helps the body absorb and metabolize calcium.

VITAMIN D, according to the *American Journal of Clinical Nutrtion,* may reduce your susceptibility to gingivitis—which has been linked to heart disease.

THE HARVARD SCHOOL FOR PUBLIC HEALTH advises that Vitamin D prevents cancer cells from growing or dividing.

VITAMIN K IS ACTUALLY A CO-ENZYME that is essential for proper blood clotting.

THE HARVARD SCHOOL FOR PUBLIC HEALTH reports that most North Americans are deficient in Vitamin K. This has occurred because people aren't eating their veggies and because many have depleted the friendly bacteria in their intestines with poor dietary choices and/or antibiotics.

SUPPLEMENTING WITH PROBIOTICS, as well as a plant-based

multivitamin-mineral product containing low concentrations of Vitamin K may be a good idea for most people.

THE CANADIAN CANCER SOCIETY announced recently (June 8, 2007) that it recommends Vitamin D as a potent defense against cancer. It based its recommendation on a four-year study at Creighton University, Nebraska. Check with your healthcare provider about how or whether to proceed on a Vitamin D regimen.

A **ANECDOTE** Although I've never personally "taken the waters'" in a European resort, I've read about the many who do and all the claims about improved health from absorption of minerals. It is an old and respected practice. I'm not sure what science thinks about it.

When I lived in Hawaii, I talked with many people who made various claims about how much better they felt when they swam in the ocean regularly. One woman, in particular, impressed me with her tale of moving to Hawaii with a debilitating asthmatic condition. For some time, she did not go to the beach, perhaps because the hot, moist air triggered her asthma and the spectre of an even hotter public beach frightened her. Nevertheless, when she finally did start venturing to the water, she was surprised and pleased to notice, over a few months, a significant improvement in her ability to breathe—her asthma seemed to come under control. Was it the water? Certainly, the ocean is replete with minerals.

But my attention was really caught when my son, Jeremy, a victim of Crohn's Disease and the debilitating drugs that were given him to fight it, came to visit me in Hawaii from Canada. His Crohn's was so bad, he was frightened of the long plane trip. Once he arrived, though, he had no hesitation about going down to the ocean, swimming, surfing, and snorkeling for hours at a time. For most of the month he was with me, his Crohn's symptoms, horrible and disabling as they were, virtually disappeared. He began thinking of how he might move there permanently, so dramatic was his relief. Was it the ocean?

Once I started reading about minerals in our soil, in our plants, and in our cells, my thoughts about the ocean's minerals and the health they seemed to offer my son and others became more focused. I had no idea how utterly complex and wondrous dietary minerals are and once again wondered why I had not learned all this through decades of public education. I had taken minerals for granted.

And, of course, I wondered (and wonder) whether my son had to go through the terrible ordeals of side-effect-ridden drugs with no professional attention to nutrition in general, and to mineral intake and absorption in particular.

- Jerre

CHAPTER 11
MIGHTY MINERALS

Most people are relatively comfortable with their understanding of dietary minerals, although perhaps they shouldn't be. After all, many tend to get their information from news clips, magazine articles, and advertising. These media formats are necessarily simplistic, but they speak with such a tone of authority, people seldom question them.

As a result, it's not uncommon to think of minerals as isolated nutrients, little silver bullets of nutrition. A news clip reveals that signs of iron deficiency include fatigue and weakness, so people supplement with iron. A television ad proclaims calcium is needed for strong bones, so people take calcium. A magazine article says bananas contain potassium, which sounds vaguely nutritious, so people eat bananas.

The fact is, however, minerals are much more inter-related than that. They depend on other nutrients, especially vitamins, in order to be effective. For example, calcium must be balanced with magnesium, other minerals, and vitamins. Without these complementary nutrients, the body cannot use calcium effectively.

We're not suggesting here that you should avoid taking minerals. After all, there would be no life for humans if there were no minerals because they play a central role in a wide variety of metabolic processes. What we're saying is that you have to learn a little about minerals before you passively accept media-driven recommendations and start supplementing willy-nilly with the cheapest or most heavily promoted product.

Although many people tend to focus on vitamins, and the admonition to take your vitamins is pretty common, you really need to be taking a vitamin-mineral supplement. In fact, the most important thing you need to know about minerals is this: Minerals are primary to your good health; vitamins are secondary.

This statement is not intended to downplay the role of vitamins. Rather, it's intended to point out that, without minerals, vitamins have little effect on human health.

THE MACRO-MINERALS

So what are these minerals? How many of them are there? What does each of them do? For now, know that some minerals are called *macro-minerals*, and the rest are called *micro-minerals* or *trace minerals*. The macro-minerals are calcium, magnesium, sodium, potassium, and phosphorus. They are the subject of the next few pages.

Calcium and Magnesium

Of all the minerals, calcium is probably the best known—if only because, since childhood, North Americans have been told it is needed for strong bones and teeth. What most people don't know, however, is that calcium is needed for hundreds of interactions in the human body. In fact, calcium is the most abundant mineral in the human body. Most of it (about 99%) is found in the bones, but calcium also is found in muscle tissue, in the blood, and in the fluid between cells.

Not only is calcium the most important nutritional factor in bone density, but it also is essential for proper muscle contraction and relaxation (including the heart), blood clotting, immune function, transmission of nerve impulses, secretion of hormones, and enzyme activation. For these reasons, signs of possible deficiency include muscle cramps; hormone-related problems such as insomnia, irritability, and hot flashes; frequent nosebleeds in children; and bone-related symptoms such as softening of the bones, stress fractures (especially in the feet and legs), and of course, osteoporosis and its less severe form, *osteopenia*.

Dairy products are a popular form of calcium, but something obviously is wrong here, because milk has been promoted for forty years as a good source of calcium while osteoporosis has reached epidemic proportions. It's important to understand that cow's milk is not easily digested.

Poor digestion leads to poor absorption of the calcium. In addition, milk consumption recently has been linked to allergies, asthma, cancer, diabetes, and ear infections. This situation has led some researchers and practitioners to seriously question whether dairy products from cows are the best source of calcium.

For many people, green, leafy vegetables (such as spinach), eggs, tofu, and legumes offer a better alternative. It's important to understand that certain compounds derived from some foods can make calcium less available for absorption into the body. For example, phytates are a kind of "anti-nutrient" found in the husks of whole grains that can block absorption of calcium, iron, and zinc. Another example is oxalic acid, which is found in a wide range of plants, especially leafy plants in the spinach family and in seeds. Oxalic acid binds with minerals such as calcium, magnesium, sodium, and potassium to form salt compounds, which cannot be absorbed. For these reasons, it's important to find a totally terrific supplement that dissolves quickly in your stomach and that can be absorbed quickly.

> **A SUPPLEMENTS SECRET**
>
> Female athletes, menopausal women, people doing heavy exercise, as well as those on high protein and fat or sugar diets need greater amounts of calcium and would benefit from supplementation.

When attempting to increase your calcium intake, don't be fooled by products (including food supplements and, even, antacids) containing only calcium. Calcium is a team player. Without certain complementary vitamins and minerals on the team, your body cannot properly absorb calcium or lay down bone.

Obviously, you need to know what other minerals and vitamins combine with calcium to make it effective.

> **A SUPPLEMENTS SECRET**
>
> Brands blending three different sources of calcium (such as calcium carbonate, calcium citrate, and calcium amino-acid chelate) help to maximize absorption— especially if taken with meals.

Chief among these is magnesium.

Magnesium is the fourth most prevalent mineral in the human body, and it's involved in more than 300 biochemical reactions. Magnesium is a salt that's critical for proper absorption of calcium, proliferation of cells, production of energy, function of muscles (including the heart muscle), and working of the nervous, immune, and endocrine systems.

A SUPPLEMENTS SECRET

Taking a calcium-magnesium supplement about 30 minutes before bed can have a very relaxing effect, especially with a cup of chamomile tea.

Over twenty conditions may be sparked by or directly related to magnesium deficiency. They include:

- Bone and joint problems (including osteoporosis) or pain that requires frequent chiropractic treatment

- Muscle problems such as aching, cramps, stiffness, tics, twitches, and weakness

- Cardiovascular problems such as angina, arrhythmia (irregular heartbeat) high blood pressure, heart attack, and stroke

- Nervous system problems such as ADD, aggression, anxiety, confusion, depression, hyperactivity, and seizures

- Endocrine problems such as diabetes (including pre-diabetic conditions such as Syndrome X and Metabolic Syndrome), hypoglycemia, and insomnia

- Gynecological problems such as infertility, menstrual cramps, premature contractions, and PMS. Magnesium also is thought to reduce the risk of cerebral palsy and Sudden Infant Death Syndrome (SIDS).

- Elimination problems such as constipation and kidney stones

Any of these symptoms, especially in combination with others, may indicate you need to supplement with magnesium (Dean, 2007).

Because magnesium helps your body absorb calcium, your calcium supplement must contain magnesium; that is, you're not looking for a calcium supplement, but a calcium-magnesium supplement (cal-mag for short). It's not just calcium and magnesium that make up the team, however. In addition to magnesium and three sources of calcium, a totally terrific calcium-magnesium supplement also will contain Vitamins C and D3, zinc, copper, and manganese.

A SUPPLEMENTS SECRET

According to the *Health Sciences Institute*, magnesium has been shown to reduce the frequency and severity of migraine headaches (Thompson, 2006).

As we have said, calcium and magnesium are team players. A coach who wants to win The World Series fields a full team of the best players. If you want to win at The World Series of nutrition, make sure you have enough star nutrients on your nutritional team—and make sure you don't have any non-performers on that team. For example, some brands of cal-mag contain lead, which is a heavy metal that can build up in the body and impair mental function. Obviously, it's not something you want to be ingesting with your supplements.

A SUPPLEMENTS SECRET

If you experience occasional heartburn that prompts you to reach for an antacid, try chewing a totally terrific calcium-magnesium supplement instead. It may taste a bit like a mouthful of grass, but it's effective—and you don't run the risk of ingesting isolated calcium or lead.

Toxic build-up of lead is harmful to everyone, but children are especially vulnerable. For all these reasons, it's vital to choose a supplements manufacturer that assays its entire line of supplements for heavy metals. Also, lead can be transferred to a developing fetus, so pregnant women must be especially careful of the calcium-magnesium brand they choose.

Phosphorus

While we're talking about star nutrients, including those that combine with calcium, let's spend a moment discussing phosphorus. Phosphorus is a component of DNA and RNA, and it's essential for the survival of all living cells. When combined with calcium, phosphorus contributes to strong bones; when combined with lipids (fats), it forms the phospholipids of cell membranes.

If, in this short description, you noticed that phosphorus always seems to combine with something, then you have made an astute observation. In nature, this highly reactive element never exists as a free element. It's truly a team player.

In the human body, phosphorus exists as *phosphate*. While you may be familiar with the role of phosphate in commercial compounds for detergents, explosives, matches, fireworks, and pesticides, you may not be familiar with it as an energy source within your own body. Here's a quick summary:

- Red blood cells need phospate, in the form of an enzyme, to carry oxygen.

- Phosphate is a component of Adenosine Triphosphate (ATP), which is needed for the transfer of energy within cells.

- Muscles use Creatine Phosphate to store energy—which is vital because, when called upon to complete a task, muscles can quickly use more energy than your body can metabolize.

For most people, however, supplementation is unnecessary because phosphate is found in pretty much every food. Deficiency is unlikely because, as author Rich Wentzler points out, "phosphates are like clothes hangers; there are always plenty of them around." (Wentzler).

Sodium and Potassium

When people talk about *sodium* in the diet, they really are referring to *sodium chloride*. Pure sodium is a chemical element that rapidly oxidizes when exposed to air. Edible salt is predominantly sodium chloride, but let's just call it *salt*.

All living creatures depend on salt for survival. Yes, you do need salt in your diet; you just don't need lots of it. The amount of salt an adult needs is less than a teaspoon per day, but many people get far more of it, leading to warnings about high blood pressure, blood clots, heart attack, and stroke.

Excess salt is ingested in many kinds of prepared foods—which tend to be loaded with it. After all, if you can make chicken broth, for example, taste better by using a tablespoon of salt rather than real chicken bones, why not? Right? Wrong. Salt is used to enhance flavor, but it's also used to preserve food because salt inhibits enzyme action. Now that you've read about enzymes, you likely understand why you don't want to be eating excessive amounts of salt that may impede or even destroy enzyme activity. No enzymes, no life. Remember?

Nevertheless, as we have said, a little salt is essential. Too little salt can cause headaches, muscle weakness, and fatigue. Too little salt can even increase blood pressure, blood sugar, and cholesterol levels. That's why healthcare professionals recommend low salt—not no salt.

For some people, nutrition practitioners recommend salt substitutes that combine sodium and potassium. Others may be advised to use natural sea salt because it contains minerals such as calcium, magnesium, potassium, copper, and zinc. Some brands contain iodine; others do not. It depends on the iodine content in the region where the salt is harvested or whether iodine is added after harvesting. Iodine, as you will read, is important for proper functioning of the thyroid gland—which regulates your metabolism.

Just as calcium and magnesium work together in a harmonious balance, so do sodium and potassium. Once again, the concept of balance (homeostasis) plays a part in human nutrition—but we humans can do a great job of skewing that balance. In a baked potato, for example, the ratio of sodium to potassium is about 2:450 (that is, 2 mg of sodium to 450 mg of potassium). Turn that potato into a potato chip, however, and the ratio becomes about 220: 0. Similarly, Mother Nature's ratios of sodium to potassium are skewed when apples are processed into apple turnovers, tomatoes are turned into tomato soup, or fruits and vegetables are processed into pre-packaged foods.

Potassium is an electrolyte; so is sodium. This means that, when broken down in solution, sodium and potassium are capable of conducting electricity. Potassium is the major positively-charged ion in the fluid *inside* a cell; sodium is the major positively-charged ion in the fluid *outside* a cell. This imbalance across cell membranes is critical for nutrient transport as well as muscle contraction (including the heart muscle) and transmission of nerve impulses.

You probably know that bananas contain potassium and that potassium is somehow good for you. But that's about it. You might not realize your very survival depends on tight control of potassium and sodium ions inside and outside the cell.

A SUPPLEMENTS SECRET

Unless your healthcare provider recommends supplementing with isolated potassium, it's always best to take potassium in a multivitamin-mineral supplement. Otherwise, you may exceed your body's need for it, skew the delicate balance of potassium and sodium, and exceed the kidneys' ability to eliminate it. Acute excesses may lead to cardiac arrest. Doses of isolated potassium exceeding 100 mg per day should be supervised by a healthcare professional who can closely monitor your serum potassium levels.

As well, you might not realize how excess intake of salt can upset the delicate sodium-potassium concentrations in the human body, especially if coupled with low intake of potassium.

You may not know that fruits, in general, as well as the skins of potatoes, are the best sources of potassium. Nor might you realize that half an avocado, a serving of prunes, or five dried figs all contain more potassium than a banana.

You may understand that a diet high in salt may lead to high blood pressure, but you may not know that low potassium levels also have been linked to high blood pressure as well as stroke, osteoporosis, and kidney stones. In addition, the activity of certain enzymes is adversely affected if potassium levels fall too low.

For all these reasons, it's important to eat two servings of fresh fruit each day because fruits contain potassium; vegetables also contain potassium, but generally in lesser amounts. If you don't eat fruits and vegetables grown in a mineral-rich soil, be sure to supplement with a plant-based vitamin-mineral supplement that contains this important mineral.

THE MICRO-MINERALS

While the list of macro-minerals is fairly short, the list of micro-minerals (also called trace minerals) grows every year. In this book, we'll look at eight micro-minerals that are vital to human nutrition: chromium, copper, iodine, iron, manganese, molybdenum, selenium, and zinc. Your vitamin-mineral supplement should contain all of them—except, perhaps, iron. First, let's look at chromium.

Chromium

A SUPPLEMENTS SECRET

According to the 2005 *American Heart Journal,* supplementing with 200 – 1000 mcg per day of chromium picolinate can help decrease elevated cholesterol levels.

Chromium is essential to digestion of carbohydrates and fats. It's also been shown to help regulate blood sugar—which can help decrease insulin resistance, prevent weight gain, and reduce a person's risk of developing diabetes or suffering a heart attack. In addition, several clinical studies have shown that chromium is effective in lowering LDL cholesterol (the lousy kind) and raising HDL cholesterol (the good kind).

Whole grains are good sources of chromium, but processing tends to deplete it by as much as 90% (Colgan, p. 96). Also, diets high in sugary foods can increase the amount of chromium excreted in the urine. Physical stresses on the body (such as infection, pregnancy, lactation, physical injury, and extreme exercise) also can increase loss of chromium.

As a result, chromium deficiency is common in North America. Symptoms include uncontrollable urges to eat sugary and starchy foods and/or fatigue after eating these carbohydrates. Metabolic syndrome (a pre-diabetic condition that includes high blood sugar, high blood pressure, high triglycerides, and obesity) has been linked to chromium deficiency.

People interested in supplementing with chromium are best advised to take it, first, by way of their multivitamin-mineral supplement. The multivitamin-mineral also should contain Vitamin C and the B vitamins because they enhance chromium absorption. Additional chromium can be added in the form of chromium picolinate or chromium polynicotinate supplements. While the combination of low absorption and high excretion rates make chromium toxicity uncommon, people with blood sugar problems should chat with their healthcare provider.

Copper

When most of us think of copper, we think of pennies or other coins, household items such as copper plumbing or cookware, or electronics items such as copper wire or circuit boards. Less frequently, we think of copper as an important micro-mineral needed by all higher-level animals and plants.

A SUPPLEMENTS SECRET

Copper might be less available in today's commercially farmed vegetables and whole grains than it was in the mid-1900s because of depleted soil conditions. It is all the more important, therefore, that you supplement with a certified organic whole-plant multivitamin-mineral supplement.

In the human body, copper acts as a co-factor for enzymes; that is, it acts as a catalyst that makes the enzymes work. Now that you know copper is a co-factor for enzymes, you may have guessed that it's needed for cellular energy production. If you did, you'd be correct.

Copper also is involved in other biochemical functions: formation of connective tissue, metabolism of iron, proper function of the brain and nervous system, antioxidant function, and formation of melanin (the pigment responsible for hair, skin, and eye color).

Some possible signs of deficiency include low energy or even frequent fatigue, joint or bone problems, easy bruising, or frequent infections. Anemia that does not respond to iron treatment also may indicate a copper deficiency.

Iodine

While micro-minerals tend to multi-task, iodine is needed for one, single task: proper functioning of the thyroid gland. It's a critically important job because thyroid hormones regulate all metabolic processes in the human body. In fact, thyroid hormones "stimulate every tissue in the body to produce proteins and increase the amount of oxygen used by cells" (*U of Maryland Medical Center*). Without iodine, your body would have no energy for even the most basic functions.

You may have known someone with low thyroid function. The condition leads to fatique, impaired mental function, slow response times, protruding eyes (exophthalmos), depression, and/or weight gain. People with this problem frequently feel cold and, if undiagnosed, they may experience serious fatigue that leaves them unable to function. In women, the problem is particularly problematic because the thyroid hormone *thyroxin* is needed to break down estrogens. Too little thyroxin can lead to too much estrogen. Too much estrogen can result in menstrual problems, water retention, and a dangerous tendency toward blood clots.

To understand the wide-ranging role that iodine and the thyroid gland play, it's important to understand that the thyroid gland is part of the endocrine system. The glands in the endocrine system include the thyroid as well as the hypothalamus, pituitary, parathyroids, adrenals, pineal, pancreas, and reproductive glands (ovaries in women, testes in men). These glands release 20 main hormones into the bloodstream and, when one gland is out, they're all out. As a result, low thyroid function may impact the entire endocrine system and, subsequently, the entire body. As you can see, the micro-mineral iodine is critically important to human life because it's critically important to the thyroid gland. Iodine is found in the ocean and in fish and seaweed that grow there, and it also can be found in soils. Once again, however, degradation poses a problem, and the iodine content of soils often is not sufficient to provide adequate iodine to the body.

In the developing world, low thyroid function remains a common problem resulting in visible swelling of the thyroid gland known as goiter. In the United States, Canada, and other Westernized countries, iodine has been added to salt to reduce incidents of iodine deficiency resulting in low thyroid function.

Nevertheless, the prevalence of low thyroid function (hypothyroidism) appears to be on the rise. Recent research conducted in the United Kingdom concludes that the prevalence of hypothyroidism in young people appears to be double that of previous estimates (Hunter).

A SUPPLEMENTS SECRET

While treatment of the thyroid is far more complex than supplementation with a single mineral, iodine can help support this delicate gland. Kelp is a rich source of iodine as are plants grown in iodine-rich soil. It is therefore important to choose a broad-spectrum, multivitamin-mineral supplement containing kelp and other mineral-rich plants.

In addition, autoimmune thyroid conditions such as fibromyalgia and Hashimoto's Thyroiditis are increasing at an alarming rate. Bacteria, environmental toxins, fluoride, parasites, radiation, and genetic predisposition all are the subjects of current research because any combination of them can impact the immune system. So far, however, medical science is nearly powerless to deal with the immune system when it revs into overdrive and turns on the thyroid gland.

To make matters worse, blood tests commonly used to check for low thyroid function or an autoimmune condition do not always reveal there is a problem. If you suspect you have a thyroid problem, but standard thyroid tests show no measurable problems, see Mary J. Shomon's books listed in the bibliography for information on additional tests needed, and see a naturopath who specializes in thyroid and endocrine function.

Iron

Iron is used by all living organisms. In humans, it's needed for formation of the red pigment in your blood known as *hemoglobin*. Hemoglobin carries oxygen, which is vitally important for energy, mental clarity, and the ability to focus. Even a mild iron deficiency can be particularly difficult. A shortage of iron deprives your cells of oxygen, and that can lead to fatigue.

While iron supplementation is not necessary for everyone, some people may need it: children, women in their childbearing years, pregnant women, women who experience heavy menstrual bleeding, and some men.

Chronic iron deficiency can lead to an array of symptoms: brittle fingernails, fatigue, weakness, headache, and mental confusion. Severe deficiency leads to anemia. Anemia results in fatigue that may prevent any kind of physical exertion, including even the simplest of tasks. Anemia also been linked to miscarriages.

> **A SUPPLEMENTS SECRET**
>
> In the event you need an iron supplement, choose a brand containing Vitamin C, which can improve iron absorption. Pregnant women or women who may become pregnant will benefit from brands containing folic acid.

The best way to determine if you require iron supplementation is to get a blood test. Iron deficiency can be detected with a simple blood test that measures serum ferritin (the storage form of iron). Yet, this test is seldom performed. If you feel tired for no reason, ask your doctor about a serum ferritin test.

Manganese

Manganese is needed for many enzyme actions in the body—especially those involved in metabolism of carbohydrates as well as proteins and cholesterol. It's especially important for the action of a particular enzyme called *superoxide dismutase-2*. Isn't that a mouthful? Just call it SOD2 and remember this: SOD2 destroys free radicals in your mitochondria. You may recall that free radicals seriously damage your cells. Obviously, a trace mineral that can activate an enzyme to destroy them is a totally terrific thing. It's important to understand, however, that manganese doesn't work alone. It needs the help of zinc and copper to activate SOD2. As is so often the case in nature, synergy is critical.

In addition to its role with SOD2, manganese also supports bone growth, and it's needed to activate Vitamin B1 and biotin enzymes; that is, you need manganese so your body can use B vitamins. In addition, manganese is especially abundant in the pancreas. A deficiency can lead to high blood sugar (which is a dangerous step toward diabetes).

Molybdenum

While it's not as abundant as some trace minerals, molybdenum is needed by virtually all life forms. In humans, it's known to be an important co-factor for three enzymes. One enzyme (sulfite oxidase) is critical for human health because it's needed for metabolism of certain amino acids. Another (xanthine oxidase) plays a role the blood's antioxidant capability as well as metabolism of toxins and drugs. A third enzyme (aldehyde oxidase) also contributes to metabolism of toxins and drugs. Without the catalytic effect of molybdenum, the action of these enzymes would be interrupted.

A SUPPLEMENTS SECRET

Variations on the SOD2 enzyme gene can be detected by genetic analysis. Wise food choices and a multivitamin-mineral supplement containing a range of vitamins, minerals (including manganese), and other plant nutrients can provide a solid foundation to improve your nutritional status—which is especially important for people who test positive for the SOD2 variant. These people also should seriously consider supplementing with antioxidants beta-carotene or Vitamin A plus zinc, Vitamin C with bioflavonoids, and Vitamin E with selenium to help fight free radical damage.

Legumes and whole grains can be good sources of this micro-mineral, but it depends on the content in the soil in which the plants are grown. Many crops have a poor diet. As a result, plants may be unable to fend off disease if the soil they're grown in doesn't contain enough micronutrients. Although not much micronutrient is needed to activate a plant's resistance to disease, it is critical. It's critical in humans, too.

Selenium

Like manganese, selenium is needed by enzymes that destroy free radicals. But, like so many micro-minerals, selenium is a team player. It works with Vitamin E to deliver a solid one-two punch in the fight against free radicals. This is why a total terrific multivitamin-mineral or Vitamin E supplement will contain a balance of Vitamin E (in its natural form d-alpha tocopheryl) and selenium. Since selenium can be a bit expensive, it's often not found in adequate quantities, if at all, in cheap products.

In addition to its critical role in enzyme activity and free radical fighting, selenium plays an important role in detoxifying heavy metals from cells. And, there's more: selenium also is needed for healthy immune function because it stimulates natural killer cells (white blood cells) known to kill cancer. For all these reasons, it's not surprising that research has associated low selenium intake with a high risk of cancer.

> **A SUPPLEMENTS SECRET**
>
> Frequent colds (more than one or two per year) may indicate a selenium deficiency.

Selenium deficiency in soils has been chronicled for years, and its consequences for plants and humans have been discussed at length (Vanderhaege, 1999). Deficiency in soils has led to deficiency in crops and in the animals and people who eat the crops. This situation prompted certain livestock and poultry growers to use selenium-fortified feed for their animals. Fortification would improve the selenium content of human foods such as meat and poultry, but it would do little for plant sources such as whole grains. Of course, as you already have read, refining of grains destroys selenium. When it comes to the selenium content of grains, depleted soils and damaging refining processes pose a double threat to adequate consumption of this important trace mineral. You can minimize this threat through informed supplementation.

Zinc

While iodine (which was discussed earlier in this chapter) has only one function in the human body, zinc has a wide range of functions. In fact, the micro-mineral zinc plays so many important roles, your very life depends on it.

Zinc is actually an enzyme. As you likely know by now, enzymes are proteins that act as catalysts—which means zinc either speeds up or slows down chemical reactions. In addition, this particular enzyme serves as a structural protein in thousands of places in the human body. As you might expect, then, zinc is needed for proper functioning of cells, including metabolism of carbohydrates, proteins, and lipids (fats) and in RNA and DNA production. It's therefore critical to the development of a fetus and in the growth and development of children.

Whether you are talking about an infant, a child, or an adult, proper functioning

A SUPPLEMENTS SECRET

Zinc has been shown to significantly reduce the risk of developing macular degeneration when taken in combination with copper and antioxidants. Make sure your multivitamin-mineral contains all of these micronutrients.

of the immune system depends on zinc, and it works with copper and manganese to produce SOD2 (which destroys free radicals).

You might think this list of roles is enough for one little trace mineral, but there's more: Zinc also is needed for transport of carbon dioxide in the blood of all human beings. It's also important for the healing of wounds. In addition, the senses of hearing, sight, and smell depend on zinc.

Zinc is absolutely indispensable for proper use of Vitamin A in the body, and since every single cell in the body needs Vitamin A, every single cell needs zinc. Once you know this, you may be tempted to supplement with extra zinc. Don't do it—at least not in isolation. As Dr. Michael Colgan points out "Excess zinc disrupts copper metabolism, which disrupts iron metabolism, which disrupts. . . . You get the picture. Excesses of single minerals are bad news" (Colgan).

As you've probably gathered by now, minerals are vitally important to human nutritional status, and deficiencies have been linked to a variety of conditions and diseases. Here are a few.

MINERALS & MUSCLES

If you've ever soaked in an Epsom salts bath to relieve stiff, sore muscles, you'll understand some of the benefits magnesium offers to muscle tissue. You see, Epsom salts are magnesium salts. When absorbed through the skin in the bath, the magnesium helps to relax cramped muscles. Because of their muscle-relaxing properties, calcium-magnesium supplements can help relieve cramps in the legs and feet as well as menstrual cramps.

In addition to its important role in muscle relaxation, calcium also is important for muscle contraction. Other minerals needed for muscle health include potassium, which also is important for muscle contraction, and phosphorus (in the form of creatine phosphate) to help muscles store energy. And while too much sodium is not a good idea, too little sodium actually can cause muscle weakness and fatigue.

MINERALS & CARDIOVASCULAR DISEASE

If magnesium can help relieve cramped muscles in the legs and feet, imagine what it may be able to do for your heart. In fact, magnesium is known to promote a steady heart rhythm. Sodium also has been shown to help keep blood pressure normal, but it has to be properly balanced: either too much or too little can raise blood pressure. And don't forget sodium's partner potassium. Low potassium levels have been linked to high blood pressure and stroke.

MINERALS & THE IMMUNE SYSTEM

In the Hawaiian Islands, many people turn to the clear blue ocean to help relieve respiratory ailments such as asthma. These people know the minerals contained in the ocean, such as magnesium and iodine, help to balance the immune system, which can have a beneficial effect on asthma patients. In addition, because magnesium helps relax smooth muscle tissue, it also can help calm asthmatic constriction.

When it comes to looking after your immune system, you also want to consider selenium. This micro-mineral is needed for healthy immune function because it stimulates natural killer cells (white blood cells) known to kill cancer. In fact, research has associated low selenium intake with a high risk of cancer.

Take selenium in a supplement formulation that also includes the natural form of Vitamin E. Vitamin E is known to fight free radicals and, therefore, can help protect against cancer. Don't forget, too, that low manganese can put you at risk of free radical damage.

While you're considering magnesium, selenium, Vitamin E, and manganese, don't forget iodine and zinc. Both play a role in maintaining a strong immune system. Of course, zinc works best when combined with copper and manganese. A totally terrific multivitamin-mineral supplement will contain all of these minerals—as well as Vitamins A, C, and E, which all are powerful free radical fighters.

MINERALS & BLOOD SUGAR

Magnesium and chromium help to regulate blood sugar. Low levels of both of these minerals have been linked to diabetes as well as metabolic syndrome (a dangerous pre-diabetic condition that includes high blood sugar, high blood pressure, high triglycerides, and obesity). In addition, manganese is especially prevalent in the pancreas, and deficiency has been linked to high blood sugar levels. Other possible symptoms of manganese deficiency include loss of hair color and impaired hearing and vision.

MINERALS & MENTAL HEALTH

The human brain is a highly sensitive organ that can be profoundly affected by nutritional deficiencies, including mineral deficiencies. For example, iron is needed for proper mental clarity and focus, at least in part, because of its role in the formation of hemoglobin. As you have read, hemoglobin carries oxygen in the blood. If your brain cells are deprived of oxygen, your brain function is depleted. Recall, too, that phosphate also is needed to carry oxygen to the cells.

Reduced cognitive function, as well as depression, also has been linked to magnesium deficiency. Magnesium also can be helpful for mild cases of anxiety.

Sometimes, poor brain function can be linked to poor function of the endocrine system. For example, low iodine can lead to poor thyroid function, and poor thyroid function can cause a whole range of mental health symptoms related to the endocrine system: memory problems, tendency toward depression or moodiness, inability to cope, and insomnia.

If you suffer with insomnia, and endocrine problems have been ruled out, you may be low on calcium and magnesium. Type I insomnia (the inability to fall asleep) may indicate a calcium deficiency. Type II insomnia (waking up in the middle of the night for no apparent reason) may indicate a magnesium deficiency. To avoid confusing the two, here's a handy tip: the words "middle" and "magnesium" both start with the letter "M." Waking in the Middle of the night may suggest low Magnesium. Before reaching for sleep medication, you might try a calcium-magnesium supplement at bedtime along with a cup of hot chamomile tea. If that doesn't send you off to dreamland, you might try valerian root supplements as well.

MINERALS & ENDOCRINE HEALTH

When you consider that low thyroid function can have a profound effect on all the glands in your endocrine system, you will understand that the list of endocrine-related symptoms can be long indeed: declining cognitive function, extremely low blood pressure, blood sugar problems, low energy, fatigue, heart palpitations, and muscle weakness are just a few.

The thyroid gland needs iodine to produce hormones—including the hormone *calcitonin* which, together with *parathyroid hormone*, regulates the body's calcium balance. Calcium and magnesium contribute to hormonal balance, which is why PMS and prostate problems also may indicate low magnesium.

BOTTOM LINE SECRETS

HUMAN ENERGY depends on all the macro-minerals and micro-minerals available from plants and whole plant-based supplements. Low energy may well reflect a problem with mineral imbalance or mineral depletion in your diet.

MINERALS work synergistically with other nutrients, so it's always best to take minerals in a well-balanced combination of micro-nutrients rather than as isolated minerals.

IN NATURE, CALCIUM PARTNERS WITH MAGNESIUM, and your calcium supplement should always contain magnesium. As well, it should contain Vitamins C and D3, zinc, copper, and manganese.

SELENIUM should be combined with Vitamin E.

IRON should be combined with Vitamin C.

DEGRADATION OF SOILS is a global problem that directly affects availability of minerals to plants and, then, to people who eat the plants. That's why you need to buy certified organic food and food supplements to ensure you're getting the minerals you need (refer to Chapter 2 concerning humus).

A **ANECDOTE** I have observed for years how foraging deer and rabbits would pick and choose their way up from the lush river valley to feed in my yard—on my garden, no less! If I was fortunate and alert, I could even spot the odd hummingbird hovering at one of my flowering plants, always the bright red ones.

I noticed all these animals are very particular. They would eat only certain types of my very expensive bedding out plants—those with the high colored blossoms!—and they turned up their discerning little noses at the plants with pale colors. As I watched all this, I could only deduce these animals either have a funny sense of humor or they know something I could learn—that there is some nutritional magic in those little plants with so much color.

Of course, the pale colors were not entirely ignored. When I looked more carefully, I noticed insects of all sorts seemed to enjoy my garden. Some insects went for the pale pinks; others went for the light blues or butter yellows. Ants seemed to have particular favorites, aphids had theirs, and bees and wasps were pretty fussy, too.

All these animals, birds, and insects seemed to know something I did not—that the color and distinct scent of each plant attracted them to the particular nutrients they needed. The greater the diversity in my garden, the greater the diversity of living things that visited it.

It turns out, my garden visitors were not after just the vitamins, minerals, and fiber that plants offer, but thousands of different plant chemicals called phytonutrients. It turns out too, that not every plant has the same store-house of phytonutrients. While plants certainly share many of the same plant chemicals, the red ones have some the yellow ones or blue ones do not, and vice-versa.

The deer and rabbits and hummingbirds, the aphids and bees and wasps have all this figured out instinctively. And now, we humans are starting to understand and appreciate the miracle of **phytonutrients**.

- Gloria

CHAPTER 12
PHENOMENOL PHYTONUTRIENTS

So far, you've read about proteins, carbohydrates, fats, vitamins, and minerals and how these nutrients support your nutritional status. There is, however, another broad category of nutrients scientists recently have begun to study. For the most part, these nutrients simply have been called *phytochemicals*. "Phyto" means "plant", so phytochemicals simply means "plant-based chemicals."

Scientists know that 25,000 or more phytochemicals are spread across the immense variety and diversity of the plant kingdom. Nevertheless, scientists and lay people alike have applied more attention and research to vitamins and minerals, pretty well ignoring phytochemicals—until recently.

It's a bit paradoxical, then, that phytochemicals have been quite evident to you—even if you weren't aware of them. Have you ever appreciated the shiny red of a tomato, the deep blue of a blueberry, the rich purple of a grape, or the vibrant green of a parsley sprig? Perhaps you've salivated at the alluring scent of banana or pineapple or lemon—or popcorn. Or maybe you've associated autumn with the tart flavor of apples, Christmas with the tang of cranberry sauce, or a favorite drink with the subtle taste of lime. If you've noticed such colors, scents, and flavors, you've taken note of the wonderful world of phytochemicals.

But Mother Nature is not just beautiful, scented, and tasty; it turns out she's pretty smart, too. You see, phytochemicals are plants' main defenses against disease, insects, bacteria, viruses, and environmental stressors such as ultra-violet light, cold, heat, and pollution. In fact, scientists know that each plant type has "learned" to produce specific phytochemicals for particular defensive needs.

Research now shows that people who eat phytochemicals can be protected in much the same way that plants are protected (Carmia, 2004). In this regard, lay people may be ahead of science. Over time and through experiment, humans (as well as animals and insects) have learned to select foods on the basis of color, scent, and flavor. It seems lay people have known intuitively what experts have just begun to work out scientifically: the best nutrition tends to reside in those plants that appeal to sight, smell, and taste.

Unfortunately, many people also are attracted to packaged foods and junk foods, too—often because of their sweet or salty taste or seductive packaging. But think about it: A freshly picked, ripe strawberry from a certified organic grower doesn't need added sugar to make it sweet. A bright orange or red or yellow carrot (yes, carrots do come in all those colors) pulled fresh from nutrient-dense soil doesn't need artificial coloring to make it attractive or salt or chemical flavorings to make it delicious.

> **A SUPPLEMENTS SECRET**
>
> The Canadian and American Cancer Institutes recommend eating ten servings of fresh fruits and vegetables every day for cancer protection. If you can't or don't, look for a concentrated fruits and vegetables supplement to help fill this Nutritional Void.

Pick that strawberry before it's ripe, however, or grow that carrot in depleted soil and ship it hundreds of miles, and the plant that ends up on your dinner plate won't be the same as the plant you would pick in a local farmer's certified organic garden. And the phytochemical value won't be the same, either. Phytochemicals can be destroyed or diminished at any stage: cultivation, harvesting, storing, shipping, processing, or cooking. The result is loss of color, scent, and flavor—some of the qualities attributed to phytochemicals. The greater loss, however, is the nutrient loss associated with those qualities.

The immediate impact of eating plants diminished in their quantities of phytochemicals is the loss of vitamin-mineral potency in your cells. You see, it's important to combine vitamins, minerals, and phytochemicals for the same reason that you want to combine vitamins and minerals themselves: they all work synergistically. That is, vitamins, minerals, and phytochemicals work best in your body if you ingest them together. The best way to do that is to eat whole foods and whole food supplements derived from broad-spectrum, certified organic plants grown in nutrient-rich soils. Of course, these plants must be carefully harvested while at their nutritional peak, and they must be handled gently and efficiently so vital nutrients are not lost.

THE BEST OF NATURE

The evidence that phytochemicals are significant to human nutrition has become substantial enough that scientists are starting to refer to them as *phytonutrients*—plant "nutrients," not just plant "chemicals." Although science still is researching their many benefits, phytonutrients appear to be central to optimum human nutrition.

This means that, when you're spending money on supplements, you need to look for products containing vitamins and minerals *and* phytonutrients. Really, we should be changing the way we talk about supplements. There was a time when all anybody talked about was "taking your vitamins". Slowly, that has turned to "taking your vitamins and minerals". Now, it's time we started talking about "taking your vitamins, minerals, and phytonutrients." That is, you want to be taking the very best Mother Nature can provide.

A SUPPLEMENTS SECRET

Phytonutrient-rich fruit and vegetable supplements now are available. On their labels, some manufacturers will list the various plants that go into their product, but not the phytonutrients. If they're not listed, how can you know whether the delicate phytonutrients in the plants survived the manufacturing processes? To ensure your supplement actually contains phytonutrients, always choose a brand that tells you—specifically—which phytonutrients the product contains and at what levels.

And while we're changing our terminology, let's put those lab-produced supplements into perspective. Compared to natural, whole-food sources, they can't possibly contain much, if anything, in the way of phytonutrients. The sheer numbers of phytonutrients involved and the fact that they still are being discovered makes it impossible for laboratories to put them into a lab-produced product—no matter how good their scientists are. In the end, Mother Nature still is the world's best botanical chemist.

> **A SUPPLEMENTS SECRET**
>
> "…Phytochemicals induce apoptosis (programmed cell death) in cancer cells; they may have a potential role in…cancer therapy and may protect normal cells from the acute and long-term effects of free radicals produced in the course of treatment" (Borek, p.338).

With that in mind, let's have a look at two categories of phytonutrients that pretty much define some of North America's favorite plant foods. These two categories are *bioflavonoids* and *carotenoids*. They contribute to the protective quality, color, flavor, and scent of plants. As the food industry catches up with food science, you'll start seeing a whole range of bioflavonoids and carotenoids referred to on labels. Look for them. Knowing these names and their nutritional value will help ensure you get the best of nature in the supplements you choose.

BIOFLAVONOIDS

One of the groups of plant chemicals that determine the specific colors of plants is known as bioflavonoids. Sometimes, bioflavonoids simply are referred to as *flavonoids*. They are the same thing.

Bioflavonoids tend to be responsible for the blues, purples, emerald greens, and some reds of plants. They

> **A SUPPLEMENTS SECRET**
>
> A Vitamin C supplement that includes phytonutrients (such as bioflavonoids) provides dietary balance and enhanced nutrition.

also may be part of yellow and orange plants. Let's have a look at some of the specific bioflavonoids that make up the whole kaleidoscope. You'll want to know they're in the food supplements you purchase.

Epigallocatechin Gallate (EGCG)

Okay, so Epigallocatechin Gallate is a mouthful, but it's a wonderful nutrient. It's likely that you've heard of Epigallocatechin Gallate (EGCG) as a significant component of green tea. You'll also find it in supplements containing green tea extract.

EGCG is gaining a lot of notoriety largely because of its scientifically documented association with reductions in risk of chronic and age-related diseases (including cancer and cardiovascular disease). As well, EGCG is involved in a process called *thermogenesis*, in which the body uses calories to create energy and heat. That means EGCG may help your body maintain a proper weight by increasing fat burning (Boschmann). The apparent benefits of EGCG don't stop there, either. Independent studies (Wolfran, Vita) have linked this bioflavonoid to the treatment of diabetes and improved elasticity in major blood vessels.

Ellagic Acid

Ellagic acid is produced by various red fruits (such as raspberries, strawberries, and pomegranates) and nuts (such as pecans and walnuts). Ellagic acid protects the plants from microbiological infection and pests. In humans, it may help reduce the effects of free-radicals (as an antioxidant), reduce the advent of cancer by binding with cancer cells, and serve as an effective anti-viral compound (Yu M., et al). Like all other phytonutrients, however, it is not as effective on its own as it is in combination with other phytonutrients.

Quercetin

Quercetin is found in apples, onions, tea, and red wine. It's been shown to improve capillaries and connective tissues, to reduce varicose veins and edema (swelling), and to block the release of histamines.

Further, a convincing double-blind study (Shoskes, 1999) showed that quercetin had a significant effect in the treatment of chronic prostatitis (inflammation of the prostate gland). Some two million men of all ages suffer from this painful condition every year in the United States and Canada. Since it's not a bacterial problem, antibiotics cannot be used as a cure, and other pharmaceutical remedies have proven less than desirable.

Like all the phytonutrients, there is no recommended daily allowance for quercetin, but various studies suggest over-doses leading to toxicity are not a risk.

Hesperidin

The bioflavonoid hersperidin is found in citrus plants, especially in the pulp of lemons and oranges. It should be included in supplement formulations. Sweet oranges contain the highest concentration of this important flavonoid that combines with quercetin and other bioflavonoids, especially rutin, to assist in the absorption of Vitamin C. This is one excellent reason why your Vitamin C supplement should contain bioflavonoids.

A deficiency of hesperidin may show up as the weakening (leakiness) of capillaries, pain in the extremities, general weakness, and night leg cramps.

Given that most people tend to avoid the pulp of citrus fruits and tend to purchase the cheapest narrow-spectrum supplements available (especially Vitamin C in the form of ascorbic acid alone), it's no wonder such symptoms are commonplace.

Rutin

Rutin is an important bioflavonoid found in the same foods as hesperidin (mainly the rinds, pulp, and skins of citrus fruits). Grapes, cherries, plums, apples, peaches, apricots, and berries contain it as well. Rutin and hesperidin are also found in green and yellow peppers, tomatoes, onions, broccoli, and parsley. Their sources don't stop there: they are also found in honey, green and black tea, and buckwheat. In other words, if you're eating a diversity of fruits, vegetables, teas, and whole grains, you're likely ingesting a good supply of hesperidin and rutin (unless they have been processed out, of course).

Rutin is important largely because of its ability to strengthen and maintain the walls of blood vessels, including the small capillaries. It offers nutritional support to the capillaries in eyes and has been particularly useful in preventing recurrent bleeding caused by weakened blood vessels. This explains why a deficiency in rutin may manifest as frequent nose bleeds, bruising, periodontal bleeding, and even aneurism.

A SUPPLEMENTS SECRET

In many European countries, quercitin and rutin are used in combination for blood vessel protection.

In general, rutin can be effective in correcting poor circulation, high blood pressure, varicose veins, and much more. It also can serve as a toxin cleanser by chelating (removing) metal ions that come, in part, from breathing exhaust fumes or ingesting mercury, lead, cadmium, or other heavy metals in food or water.

In addition to its important role with blood vessels and chelation, rutin is known as a strong antioxidant. It literally scavenges certain extreme free radicals known as *superoxide radicals* from your body.

Benefits Of Bioflavonoids

Hesperidin, quercetin, rutin and their thousands of counterparts offer some very specific benefits on their own, as represented above. However, in combination with one another, they can:

- Serve as potent anti-inflammatory and anti-histamine agents

- Protect people at risk of heart disease

- Help relieve hemorrhoids, asthma, allergies, and menstrual problems

- Improve your skin and connective tissue

- Reduce the development of osteoporosis

Later, we'll look at two concepts (synergy and bioavailability) that help explain why these phytonutrients are so powerful in combination.

Meanwhile, let's look at just one more group of phytonutrients: carotenoids. If you've ever observed the magnificent color changes during the Fall season, you've observed carotenoids. At this time of year, the chlorophyll that makes leaves green recedes, and that makes the brilliant yellows, oranges, and reds of the carotenoids visible. When you look at a colorful autumn scene, you're looking at carotenoids.

CAROTENOIDS

The surface of the Earth is not a friendly place for living organisms not prepared for it. Anyone who has experienced skin cancer or developed serious asthma or disabling allergies is most keenly aware of that. And you might be aware of the myriad of living creatures that dwell in dark caves or at the dark bottom of the ocean, and even microbes that thrive deep beneath the earth's crust. Bring any of these to the sun-lit surface, and they die rather rapidly. They live deep down to avoid what is high up: searing sunlight, risky radiation, treacherous toxins, virulent viruses—in other words what you live in every day. How do you do it?

Humans are somehow adapted for life on Earth's surface, as are all the plants people depend upon for nutrients. Plants have evolved and survived by developing a system of defenses: the carotenoids. Without carotenoids, few plants would make it to noon of their first day!

The plants we humans eat manage to live while bathed in ultra-violet light and awash with toxin-laden air (from volcanic ash, meteoric activity, industrial by-products, sun-flashes, x-rays and air-borne bacteria). Protected by carotenoids, however, plants on Earth's surface have managed to thrive—and that's a good reason for you to eat them. Let's have a look at just a few.

A SUPPLEMENTS SECRET

Unless a qualified healthcare provider identifies that you have a problem converting beta-carotene to Vitamin A, always choose beta-carotene supplements over Vitamin A supplements. This way, your body will convert the beta-carotene to Vitamin A only as required—and your body will be doing the work it's supposed to do. Remember: A healthy body is a working body.

Beta-carotene

You likely have heard of beta-carotene because it's one of the most abundant nutrients in human bodies and human diets. It's found in carrots, peaches, apricots, spinach, and cantaloupes. You may know it as Vitamin A, but actually beta-carotene is a "precursor" to Vitamin A. In other words, once you ingest it, your body converts beta-carotene to Vitamin A. For more detail about this process, re-visit Chapter 9, *Vitamins for Vitality*.

Beta-carotene is known for its effectiveness in reducing various kinds of cancers and for protecting skin against the assault of ultra-violet light.

Lycopene

Lycopene, found in tomatoes, watermelon, and grapefruit (pink and red) is probably the single most effective anti-oxidant in your body. It's especially powerful against the most damaging free radical (singlet oxygen). As a result, lycopene may be particularly useful in lowering the risk of prostate cancer and stomach disease.

Lutein And Zeaxanthin

These two carotenoids are in spinach, red pepper, peas, kale, broccoli, and celery. They are responsible for yellows and reds. You see them most strikingly as autumn leaves reveal their colors.

Working in tandem, lutein and zeaxanthin conduct their most important work in your eyes, where they work to reduce the onset of age-related macular degeneration.

Benefits Of Carotenoids

Plants offer defenses against the unfriendly influences of the very environment human beings call home. Individually and—especially—in combination, carotenoids provide protection against a myriad of problems, including the following (Mason, 1995):

- Skin cancer

- Unnecessary aging and wrinkling

- The ravages of various oxidants

- Night blindness

- The consequences of LDL cholesterol (the Lousy kind)

- Allergies

- Cataracts

- Enlarged prostate gland

- Heart disease

It's an impressive list, but then, the list of carotenoids is impressive, too. After all, there are more than 600 of them researchers know about. That's right, this book just scratches the surface of all there is to know and say about carotenoids.

The list of benefits that carotenoids supply explains why you need to appreciate the benefits of ingesting totally terrific supplements rich in the whole family of carotenoids. For example, you may wish to supplement with a combination of bilberry and lutein (plus other ingredients) to help support eye health. Certainly, this can be a beneficial practice, but do it from a solid foundation comprised of a multi-supplement of vitamins, minerals, and phytonutrients as well as a concentrated phytonutrient supplement.

> **A SUPPLEMENTS SECRET**
>
> Healthcare professionals would like to see most North Americans increase their daily intake of carotenoids by four times. If that requires too much washing and cutting of carrots, peaches, apricots, spinach, and cantaloupes for you (or if you're not buying these fruits and vegetables from certified organic growers), then it's time to consider a natural source beta-carotene supplement in addition to your multi-supplement and phytonutrient supplement.

The reason is simple—like bioflavonoids, carotenoids have the power to work in combination with other food nutrients to provide remarkable nutritional benefits. Two concepts explain the power of these combinations. The concepts are *synergy* and *biovailability*.

SYNERGY

Other chapters have referred to the concept of synergy, but it's worth reminding you of it here. Simply put, synergy refers to the ability of two forces working together to yield, perhaps surprisingly, more than the sum of the two. It's like finding that, under certain circumstances, 1 + 1 = 3.

In nutritional science, such a concept can be very powerful. The synergistic effects of various combinations of vitamins, minerals, and phytonutrients can enable chemical reactions many thousands of times more effective as anything possible in a laboratory. It's likely that without synergistic interaction among food nutrients, you could not live.

Therefore, a lot of research is presently underway (with all the attendant debate one would expect) concerning the synergistic abilities of phytonutrients, particularly as anti-oxidant forces in the treatment of cancer.

While we cannot explore this issue here to any great degree, it's important to say that the research is pointing favorably to the fact that when phytochemicals are present in combination (especially in whole-plant mixtures), their anti-oxidant abilities are greater than the sum of the chemicals present. That certainly points to the reasonable expectation that we all should be eating food and food supplements rich in Nature's diversity.

BIOAVAILABILITY

Synergy is not the only benefit of ingesting a diversity of phytonutrients. If your body's cells cannot absorb nutrients at all, or in sufficient quantities, or in a timely manner, life-yielding synergistic chemical reactions may not happen in the first place.

The ability of a nutrient to be absorbed is called *bioavailability*. Think of bioavailability as a partner concept to synergy. The term bioavailability refers to the degree to which your body can actually absorb and retain the nutrients it takes in. The iron of a nail, for example, is not in a suitable form for your body to use. You need to get your iron from an animal or plant that has processed it into a form your body can use.

Recall the section on soil earlier in this book and the words of Dr. Gary Farr, who argues, "Minerals must first be consumed by earthworms and microscopic life and excreted as humus before they can be easily taken up by grazing animals." He's actually describing one process by which nutrients become bioavailable, and he's providing the parameters for purchasing supplements. They must be plant-based, and the plants must be grown in nutrient-dense soils rich in earthworms and microscopic life.

Another way to ensure bioavailability is to ensure you ingest nutrients in combination. For example, in nature, Vitamin C is teamed with bioflavonoids. Eating the whole fruit (or parts of the fruit, such as orange slices) means you also eat some of its pulp. This is where most of its phytonutrients are naturally contained. If you depend on processed juices for your Vitamin C, the fruit's pulp often is separated out and discarded. The result is a loss of bioflavonoids and all their combined benefits. Why does that matter?

A SUPPLEMENTS SECRET

To maintain dozens of elements in the soil, a totally terrific supplements company will own its own farms and focus on sustainable farming practices that protect and nourish the soil. In short, they will treat the soil as a living organism.

According to research published in the *American Journal of Clinical Nutrition*, phytonutrients may maximize the bioavailability of vitamins, including both initial absorption and retention (Vinson, J.A. and Bose, P; Concepción Sánchez-Moreno, et al, *American Journal of Clinical Nutrition*, Vol. 78, No. 3, 454-460, September 2003). Vitamin C, for example, is significantly more bioavailable in your body if you ingest the natural flavonoids with it (e.g. quercitin, hesperidin, rutin, and others). It's nutritionally better, therefore, to drink orange juice that includes the pulp, which contains the plant's phytonutrients.

The same is true of supplements—the Vitamin C tablet you buy should be processed from the whole plant, with all its attendant phytonutrients, or you risk taking in a vitamin with less bioavailability. If you're in serious need of Vitamin C (perhaps because you have a specific problem

Vitamin C may help resolve), it's even more important to include the plant's bioflavonoids in the supplement. Sometimes, though, deriving the tablet from natural sources alone will likely make the tablet too bulky. The alternative is to take additional supplements containing phytonutrients along with the isolated Vitamin C tablet.

Your best choice of multi-supplement will be derived from a whole array of plants: grasses such as alfalfa; vegetables such as asparagus and broccoli; fruits such as apples, blueberries, cranberries, grapes, pomegranates, and prunes; and herbs such as watercress, parsley, rosemary, sage, and oregano. Once you've found that, it would be wise to consider a supplement of concentrated fruitsvegetables to augment your intake of phytonutrients. Think color: acerola cherries, blueberries, broccoli, carrots, and spinach. Consider EGCG from green tea, hesperidin from oranges, ellagic acid from pomegranates, lutein from marigold, and lycopene from tomatoes.

A SUPPLEMENTS SECRET

A totally terrific multi-supplement or phytonutrient supplement not only will be made from an array of plants, it will be made from different plants as they ripen seasonally. This way, the plants that go into your supplements will be the freshest available, not something that has been stored for months. Remember: Storing depletes the phytonutrient content of plants. The plants in your supplements should be processed within hours of harvest.

In summary, optimal nutrition demands that you take in food and food supplements offering the widest possible variety of phytonutrients. Your goal is to enhance your cells' ability to absorb nutrients and to gain the considerable advantages offered by synergy.

THE BEST OF SCIENCE

For totally terrific supplements, look for those that team the very best Mother Nature can provide with the very best science can provide. For example, look for companies that:

- Use certified organic whole plants from nutrient-dense soils

- Harvest the right plants at the right time

- Process the plants shortly after harvest

- Employ whole teams of scientists dedicated to nutritional excellence

- Follow Good Manufacturing Practices (GMP)—from the soil to the seed to the supplement.

GMP helps maintain the quality of the delicate phytonutrients throughout the entire process of growing and manufacturing supplements. For this reason, it's important to understand a little more about just what GMP means.

A Big Secret: Pharmaceutical GMPs

Chapter 2 discussed GMP, referring to the dilemma supplement companies of integrity are faced with: they have no rigorous, fully-monitored GMP standards appropriate specifically to supplements.

Instead, they sit somewhere between food GMP and pharmaceutical GMP standards, neither of which are precisely appropriate to the manufacturing of their products.

That leaves lots of room for supplement companies to cut corners on the quality of their products. And it should leave you wondering whether the products you buy are as effective as you expect them to be. At worst, it should leave you in some measure of fear about the safety of the nutrients you and your family ingest.

It's worth making you a little more familiar with GMP issues, because if you can determine whether a company is fudging on standards and taking advantage of loop holes and poorly monitored processes, you can avoid it. On the other hand, if you can find companies that voluntarily comply with all the strictest standards appropriate to supplement manufacturing, then you can depend upon them.

Remember that GMP involves two sets of legal standards: one aimed at the food industry and the other at the pharmaceutical industry. The latter is the more rigorous and is intended to guarantee the prescription you receive is exactly as stated on the container, including dosage.

Because it's not required by law to adhere to pharmaceutical GMP standards with supplements (measuring all a plant's phytonutrient molecules is next to impossible, for example), only a small number of supplement manufacturers are likely to make the attempt—it's easier and cheaper to use lesser standards.

At the end of the next chapter, we'll provide you with the precise *totally terrific* question to ask your supplements provider about their commitment to the highest possible standards.

A SUPPLEMENTS SECRET

Buyer beware. Some companies who do claim adherence to GMP do not apply the standards at the raw materials stage. For example, a company that imports the produce it concentrates into supplements may claim it uses GMP for all its own processes, but it's not required to account for its suppliers' practices. As a result, you can end up with a final product with far less quality than you think. All the more important you ask the right questions.

Another Big Secret: ORAC Scores

Combinations of phytonutrients such as bioflavonoids and carotenoids provide considerable power to protect you, at the cellular level, from the ravages of environmental threats. It's a good bet that if you're buying and gently handling certified organic foods, you're getting the nutritional benefits you paid for, but what about supplements?

If you've been checking labels, you likely know references to popular phytonutrients (such as lutein and lycopene) and statements about antioxidants and free radicals appear on supplement packaging in every health food store today. The claim is either implied or stated directly that the supplement in question will slow aging, reduce inflammation, smooth wrinkling skin, protect against disease, or offer any number of other seductive benefits. These claims may be valid and they may not. How is one to know?

When talking about anti-oxidants, for example, it's not satisfactory to simply claim a product protects against free radicals. Scientists need a quantitative test to back up such statements—and so do you. That's why the Oxygen Radical Absorbance Capacity (ORAC) test was developed. An ORAC test score tells scientists what the antioxidant potential of specific food or food supplements is.

ORAC testing was an excellent development, as far as it went, but there are a couple of problems you need to know about. First, the marketing industry (never far behind science that can enhance sales) soon began to add ORAC scores to some of their advertising. As you know, advertising does not necessarily provide accurate nutition information. Second, ORAC scores don't tell the whole story and actually can be misleading. A product can have a high ORAC score relative to one designated free radical group, but it may

A SUPPLEMENTS SECRET

The secret to understanding whether a supplement truly protects against free radical damage is not to merely believe advertising claims about a high ORAC score. The real test is to find out how many groups of free radicals the product protects you from.

not protect against the whole range of free radicals. That one high ORAC score may lead you to believe you're getting something really good when it's just not necessarily true. ORAC scores are a little like test scores in school. If your child gets very high marks in English, but fails every other subject, he or she isn't doing very well overall.

The Free Radical Gang

Free radicals are a little like the members of a street gang. They do their worst damage when they combine their destructive forces, and they are in your body right now. Each group behaves a little differently from the others, and specific anti-oxidants are required to prevent them from causing considerable damage to your cells.

Here's a little information on each group of free radicals:

- *Peroxynitrite* radicals come from cigarette smoke and car exhaust. These free radicals contribute to atherosclerosis, chronic inflammation, lung disease, and neurological problems.

- *Superoxide* radicals come from exercising too vigorously; air pollution; UV light; cigarette smoke; viral, bacterial, or fungal infections; and even normal day-to-day cellular metabolism. These free radicals act as scavengers in your body, but if they run amok, they also can set up huge chain reactions in which more and more free radicals are formed. As you can imagine, this causes extensive cellular damage that can cause cancer, inflammatory diseases, atherosclerosis, and age-related diseases.

- *Hydroxyl* radicals also come from exercising too vigorously, air pollution, UV light, cigarette smoke, and cellular metabolism. These free radicals can damage pretty well all types of molecules, including carbohydrates, lipids (fats), and amino acids (building blocks of proteins). The only way to protect crucial cellular structures is to use anti-oxidants, such as phytonutrients and Vitamins A, C, and E.

- *Singlet oxygen* radicals come from cellular metabolism and UV light. They are a potent oxidizing agent the can be described as the worst of the free radical groups because they are the most reactive and, therefore, dangerous. They can be particularly harmful to proteins, lipids, and DNA, and they can have serious cardiovascular effects. Carotenoids can be especially beneficial in reducing singlet oxygen radicals to their non-toxic state.

One anti-oxidant will fight certain free radicals; another will fight others. In combination, they fight more effectively (synergy). You therefore need a variety of anti-oxidants to tackle the whole range of groups.

You need to be confident that you are getting, in your diet and in your supplements, the necessary combined power of the phytonutrient force. Your supplement company must therefore do the appropriate testing (because you certainly can't) and make the results available to you.

For such testing, a totally terrific supplement company will use ORAC analysis to investigate whether their supplement product can protect against multiple groups of free radicals. They will publish the results for the whole range, usually on their websites.

This additional analysis goes well beyond measuring anti-oxidant activity for single radicals or a narrow range of groups. Such analysis requires the use of high technology such as *Liquid Chromatography-Mass Spectrometry.* This powerful tool is used in the science of separating and identifying compounds such as the phytochemicals in a plant. If a company can actually chart the active compounds in a product, it's then in a position to make credible pronouncements about that products' potential. Otherwise, benefit statements are just guess work.

Once you know whether the supplements you're considering contain a complete, active, and effective phytonutrient component, you'll be well on your way to knowing whether you've found a totally terrific supplement. But there's a problem: The necessary technology is extremely expensive and few companies own the equipment to do the testing. We'll show you, in the last chapter, how to ask a company whether it has this capacity.

BOTTOM LINE SECRETS

THE COLOR OF A PLANT represents the particular groups of phytonutrients (bioflavonoids and carotenoids) it uses to protect itself against the environment and disease. Eating ten servings per day of diversely colored, certified organic plants will take you a long way toward protecting yourself against wide-ranging health threats.

TOTALLY TERRIFIC SUPPLEMENTS offer the same diversity of phytonutrients. In combination, such phytonutrients can provide considerable benefits

SYNERGY AND ENHANCED BIO-AVAILABILITY constitute two of the most significant advantages you gain from totally terrific supplements that provide the widest possible combination of phytonutrients.

PHARMACEUTICAL GRADE GMP STANDARDS are fundamental to the production of totally terrific supplements. Such standards are voluntary for supplements manufacturers (until 2009 in Canada), so not all companies strive to apply them. You want to find the companies who comply now and buy your supplements from them.

ORAC SCORES are determined with high-tech equipment. Few companies have such equipment, so you must find the ones that have it and that include the pertinent information on their labels or literature.

DANGEROUS FREE-RADICALS do damage at the cellular level. You want phytonutrient protection from a whole range of them.

THE NUTRITIONAL IMPORTANCE of phytonutrients, combined with their delicacy, explains why it's important to eat a variety of the freshest, most colorful, certified organic plants you can find. A diet consisting of just a few plants or a supplement product made from just a plant or two simply doesn't cut it—not if optimal nutritional status is your goal.

A ANECDOTE When I started studying cellular pathology, it became apparent that two critical elements of life were under stress: our soils were over-worked and depleted, and our plants seemed to be losing their nutrient potency. In effect, I realized the plants I was buying and eating might sustain me, but they no longer were sufficient on their own to ensure the quality of life I wanted, especially into my old age. Continuing trends in the rise of degenerative diseases alone told me I was right.

So I started a journey of exploration into the supplements industry, searching for the nutrient quality I felt was missing in my normal foods.

The question was where to start? Neither Canadian nor American regulatory bodies seemed very interested in supplements. These government bodies didn't hold the supplements industry to particularly high standards, and the standards that did exist were poorly regulated. I probably couldn't fight that particular battle, but I wondered whether there might be supplement manufacturers voluntarily subscribing to high standards. If so, how could I find them?

I decided to use all I knew about the factors influencing the nutrients in our foods. I started my search by asking various supplement companies a series of questions—based, in part, on all I'd learned back on my parents' farm. Why not look for a company that employed the same totally terrific standards my parents used? I'd buy my supplements from them in a heartbeat.

I contacted over 200 companies and asked about natural farming processes, about the soils, and about harvesting and processing. When the research was complete, I felt other people probably could use some guidance in asking the same hard questions. But I didn't want to merely hand people my research. I wanted them to do their own research and come to their own conclusions. With that in mind, I pulled together a list of pertinent questions and started teaching my clients how to query their supplements providers. As a follow-up, I developed a Wellness Program and began teaching in various countries around the world.

One of the most popular topics in all my talks is the one that deals with Questions to Ask Before You Buy a Dietary Supplement. These questions are the subject of this chapter. Do the questions work? Well, the good news is that I was able to determine that there **are** totally terrific supplements out there—this chapter will help you find them, too.

- Gloria

CHAPTER 13
HOW TO FIND TOTALLY TERRIFIC SUPPLEMENTS

In this chapter, we provide you with TEN TOTALLY TERRIFIC QUESTIONS that reflect all the content you learned in the previous chapters. These questions are intended to help you aggressively seek out the best supplements you can find. You'll have to read the questions carefully and understand the reasons you will want to pose them to your potential supplement provider, but the effort will be worth your while.

Having read the preceding chapters carefully, you'll understand why it's important to ask these questions. So let's review the important issues discussed throughout this book.

A REVIEW

Chapters 1 and 2 discussed how slowly society has moved to make the connection between food and health. Because conventional Western medicine features the relationship between food and disease, largely ignoring the relationship between food and health, North Americans have unwittingly contributed to the creation of a Nutritional Void that threatens the quality of their lives.

Next, Chapter 3 explored the operations and structure of the human cell, showing how every single cell in your body is nutrient-dependent and how the Nutritional Void threatens every single cell. In particular, we showed how critical quality nutrients are to your cells—especially enzymes, those little spark plugs of life.

In Chapters 4 through 7 (macronutrients) and Chapters 8 through 11 (micronutrients), we explored in some detail the essential nutrients that fuel, build, repair, and protect your body's cells. We emphasized that nutrients work best in combination with one another. We explained the nature of proteins and enzymes; all the various kinds of fats you need to either avoid or seek; and we detailed the vitamins, minerals, and phytonutrients your body requires for life and vitality.

The common theme that binds the chapters together is that national and global problems with food quality lead to a clear and historically unprecedented need for quality, plant-based supplements.

Chapter 13, the present one, concludes the discussion about nutrients and health by helping you sort through the myriad of supplement products available so you can identify only those that will give you a totally terrific start toward personalized, optimum nutritional status for the rest of your life. People tend to make their nutritional choices on the basis of emotion. The Ten Totally Terrific Questions will help you make your decisions more scientifically.

SO WHERE DO YOU START?

You don't start with supplements.

Some people do, though, reasoning (incorrectly) that they can maintain their fast-food, nutrient-depleted lifestyles as long as they're taking their vitamins. After reading the previous chapters, you know the road to optimal nutrition starts with rejecting foods from the Nutritional Void (in general, all those heavily refined junk foods and oxidized or synthetic fats) and replacing them with nutrient-dense foods—likely those you end up preparing yourself.

First, you need nutritious food on your plate. Then you start looking for the most totally terrific supplements you can find.

It is increasingly well known that a combination of nutrient-dense foods and totally terrific supplements is your best assurance for the kind of life you want to live. Ignore the quality of either the food or food supplements you eat, however, and you end up realizing few significant benefits from your supplementation regimen. In the end, you may become discouraged, resent the money you've spent, and return to your old disease-promoting lifestyle.

Here are the steps we consider important for you to follow, if you wish to achieve optimal nutritional status.

Step 1: Build A Nutritional Foundation

As we've said, the evidence is clear that eating well in combination with a multivitamin-mineral-phytonutrient supplement is the best insurance against poor health you can buy. We'll call such a blend of concentrated nutrients a *multi-supplement* for short.

In addition, and as you know from reading the chapters on fat (Chapters 6 and 7), most North Americans are not eating enough fish to ensure they have a sufficient supply of essential fatty acids. Chapter 12 showed that many people are also not eating enough fresh fruits and vegetables, which means they're not getting enough important phytonutrients. To make matters worse, many are eating diets high in sugars, fats, and additives that upset the ecology of the gut and weaken the body's natural immunity (*probiotics*, Chapter 5). So what should you do to launch yourself toward optimal supplementation? Read on.

Find A Totally Terrific Multi-Supplement

Selecting a high quality multi-supplement makes sense from a balanced nutritional perspective as well as a financial one. If there is only one thing you can afford to add to your diet, multi-supplements are the biggest nutritional bang for your buck—and your cells.

But if that is the only supplement product you're going to take, you must be very choosy about the brand you buy. It must meet all the quality demands you've discovered throughout this book. Our list of Ten Totally Terrific Questions will help you choose the right brand. And remember that, in the end, the most expensive supplements are the ones that don't work. They're the bad ones. We'll help you avoid those.

It's really very important to avoid bad supplements, but it's hard to do because the protection is simply not substantial enough. It's amazing, but manufacturers in the USA can legally put a variety of additives into their products without having to list these on the products' labels.

Manufacturers may, for example, include lactose and sodium benzoate as fillers and preservatives. These ingredients can cause allergic reactions. Some products, as we have said, contain heavy metals such as lead. Other ingredients that are, arguably, both unnecessary and potentially harmful include lubricants, flowing agents, glues, and various coloring agents that have less to do with nutrition and more to do with attractiveness for the emotional buyer. These truly are bad supplements and, ultimately, the most expensive.

The next most expensive are the supplements that are merely satisfactory, the "good" ones. These, at least, are assayed for toxins and their ingredients are honestly described on their package labels. Likely, they are supplements manufactured in a lab, not grown in a certified organic soil. Our Ten Totally Terrific Questions will not help you find those, because they're not the ones your cells are looking for. They are second best supplements. They simply don't offer enough for optimal nutritional status, and when it comes to matters concerning your body and the quality of your life, nothing less than optimal is sufficient.

The main difference between good supplements and totally terrific ones is this: a totally terrific supplement can be traced from…

…the broad-spectrum, phytonutrient-rich, certified organic soil

…that gave sustenance to the seed

…that became the plant

…that became the tablet

…that you put in your mouth.

That is a mouthful, indeed. And it's what you're looking for—and it's what you should demand.

Find Totally Terrific Essential Fatty Acids

As we discussed in Chapter 7 on EFAs, most people are not eating enough fish, the right kinds of fish, or fish free from the toxins that increasingly pollute our streams, lakes, and oceans. Ocean floors are the next-to-final resting place of heavy metals; the final resting place for these toxins may be the bodies of people who directly or indirectly eat fish contaminated with them.

As well, particularly in North America, many people are taking in too much Omega-6 compared to Omega-3. This imbalance can and does lead to disease.

The result is that virtually all North Americans are in need of high quality fish oil supplements that have been assayed for toxins and rendered safe. You will need to find a fish oil supplement company that conducts its fishing, processing, and distribution with the same quality safe-guards you are coming to expect from other forms of supplementation. Our Ten Totally Terrific Questions will help you with that.

Find Supplements that Feature Phytonutrients

Although we recommend that you search for a totally terrific multi-supplement that includes phytonutrients, you may want to enhance your intake of phytonutrients with a supplement that features them. There are no known side-effects of high doses of phytonutrients. Indeed, there are no recommendations whatsoever for what constitutes a suitable daily intake. New research, however, is showing phytonutrients such as bioflavonoids and carotenoids can offer significant benefits, particularly when it comes to protecting you from common diseases (Chapter 12).

In light of fast-food lifestyles; the continuing influx of toxins into the air, water, and food supply; and heightened stress levels, it is prudent to ensure an enhanced supply of phytonutrients in your diet. To do that, you need to identify a totally terrific phytonutrient supplement. After all, healthcare professionals now recommend that each of us eat about ten servings of fruits and vegetables every day. If you can't or don't eat that many servings of fresh, certified-organic plants, consider a supplement of certified organic fruits and vegetables.

So there are the basics for Step 1: When you're starting a supplementation regimen to optimize your nutritional status, consider starting with a nutrient-rich diet enhanced by the following **Foundational Supplements**:

1. A totally terrific multi-supplement that contains vitamins, minerals, and phytonutrients

2. A totally terrific EFA supplement

3. A totally terrific supplement that features phytonutrients.

Of course, if you have health problems that require supplements to target specific diseases or ailments, or if you require higher doses than are provided in multi-supplements, you should consult with your healthcare provider.

Step 2: Know Yourself

While just a few totally terrific supplement products may meet the needs of some individuals for most of their lives, other individuals have unique needs. In fact, some people—whether women, men, seniors, or youth— may experience the need for specific supplements either not included in those described above (especially the multi-supplement), or which are required in much higher doses than a multi-supplement can provide.

Let's have a look at what those specific supplements might be before we get to the Ten Totally Terrific Questions. A word of caution, though: These lists are not intended to describe a remedy for any ailment or disease, nor are these lists intended to be all-inclusive. Rather, they are offered as starting points to help you learn about supplementation and to help you consider your own unique needs. As always, you should consult with your healthcare provider before you adopt a supplement regimen as a possible remedy for specific health issues. Finally, these lists do not account for any genetic predispositions that DNA testing might reveal and which would provide you with a recommendation for personalized supplementation regimens.

Women

In addition to the **Foundational Supplements** already described, women might well add the following to their nutritional program:

*   A Vitamin B-complex (see Chapter 9)

- Vitamin D3 with iproflavone (see Chapter 10)

- A Calcium-Magnesium-Vitamin D complex that also contains Vitamin C, copper, manganese, and zinc to help prevent osteoporosis (see Chapter 11)

- Vitamin C with bioflavonoids (see Chapters 8 and 12)

- CoQ10 (See Chapters 3 and 4)

- GLA (see Chapter 7)

Men

Men need many of the same supplements women tend to use, but they have specific needs as well, especially related to prostate and heart disease. In addition to the **Foundational Supplements**, men may wish to consider:

- A Saw Palmetto complex with saw palmetto, nettle root, and bioflavonoids for prostate and urinary health (see Chapter 6 regarding the use of olive oil as a supplement "carrier")

- Vitamin C with bioflavonoids (see Chapters 8 and 12)

- Vitamin D3 with iproflavone (see Chapter 10)

- A Vitamin B complex (see Chapter 9)

- CoQ10 (see Chapters 3 and 4)

Seniors

Again, seniors need many of the same **Foundational Supplements** as their younger counterparts, but they may need special support—particularly if they experience symptoms or have particular genetic predispositions:

- Vitamin B-complex, plus extra Vitamin B-12 (see Chapter 9)

- Vitamin C with bioflavonoids (see Chapter 8)

- Siberian Ginseng/Gingko Biloba to increase oxygen flow to the brain

- CoQ10 (see Chapters 3 and 4)

- A Calcium-Magnesium-Vitamin D complex that also contains Vitamin C, copper, manganese, and zinc to help prevent osteoporosis (see Chapter 11)

- Saw Palmetto, for men experiencing prostate symptoms or for those wishing to take preventative measures

- Black Cohosh, for women experiencing menopausal or post-menopausal symptoms

- Soluble Fiber, to help maintain good bowel function without laxatives. Taking a soluble fiber supplement together with probiotics can be especially helpful in promoting both healthy bowel function and a strong immune system (see Chapter 4)

Youth

Youth, both male and female, are building bone mass and hormone structure and leading a very dynamic lifestyle. Therefore, they have some specific supplementation needs. Of course, youth will benefit from the same **Foundational Supplements** their parents use (so supplementing can be a family thing), but some teens need special help with regard to lifestyle and dietary issues.

First, start building their nutritional foundation with a totally terrific **multi-supplement** and a **phytonutrient supplement**, as we have discussed. Then, consider strengthening that foundation with an **Omega-3 EFA supplement**—but, make sure it's DHA-dominant. Finally, **probiotics** likely are a good idea to shore up their nutritional foundation because probiotics will help compensate for challenging junk food diets (although they can't make up for a poor diet) . Finally, here are a few more supplements to consider:

- Vitamin B-complex (see Chapter 9)

- Vitamin C with bioflavonoids (see Chapters 8 and 12)

- A Calcium-Magnesium-Vitamin D complex that also contains Vitamin C, copper, manganese, and zinc to help prevent osteoporosis (see Chapter 11)

- GLA for females with PMS issues (see Chapter 7)

Children

This book is not intended to address the specific and complex needs of children. When it comes to children in the age group infant to pre-teen, we want you to work with your healthcare providers on questions specifically concerning young children. Nevertheless, one warning is appropriate in your search for children's supplements (flavorful, chewable forms of Vitamin C, for example): Don't be seduced by marketing trickery. Read the label for sugar content, colorants, additives, and other non-nutritional ingredients.

The tablets might look like friendly animals, cartoon characters, or space aliens all designed to appeal to a child, but the standards of excellence that hold for you hold for your children. Our Ten Totally Terrific Questions will help you and your healthcare provider find the right supplement products for your children, too.

Frequently Used Supplements

Along with all the supplements listed above for specific groups of people, it might help you to know some of the most popular choices for nutrition-enhancing supplements:

- A probiotic supplement to support healthy gut flora and, consequently, the immune system (see Chapter 5 for some details). In fact, you might be wise to use a probiotic as a foundational supplement in addition to the multi, EFA, and phytonutrient supplements already recommended for a strong, nutritional foundation. Remember: Your gut is the largest part of your immune system and needs to be healthy

- A broad spectrum digestive enzyme product and a totally terrific fiber product, both to help keep the gut healthy

After that, you might consider:

- For bones: Calcium Magnesium, including zinc and copper, and Vitamins C and D3

- For blood sugar: Chromium

- For occasions when heavy carbohydrate meals are unavoidable: A carb blocker

- For the brain: EFAs that are DHA-dominant

- For emotions: B-Vitamin complex

- For eyes: Specialized formulations combining bilberry, citrus bioflavonoids, and lutein

- For the GI tract: Soluble fiber

- For poor digestion: A Digestive Enzyme complex

- For the heart: Co-enzyme Q10 with Vitamin E

- For immune system support: Echinacea

- For prevention of colds when you feel one coming on: Echinacea, Vitamin C, and Garlic

- For inflammation and discomfort: cetylated esters and EFAs that are EPA-dominant

- For joints: Glucosamine complex with bioflavonoids and boswellia

- For the liver: Botanical formulations of dandelion and milkthistle

- For pregnancy: Folic acid and Iron with Vitamin C

- For sleep: Valerian root

In addition, don't forget free radical fighters, including the very powerful Vitamin E with selenium, Beta-Carotene, and all-important Vitamin C.

This list is not intended to be complete, of course, but it may prove helpful if you suffer from ailments for which you have thought only pharmaceutical drugs were appropriate and when you are consulting with your healthcare provider.

Step 3:
Determine Genetic Predisposition

We talked briefly in Chapter 3 about the newest frontier of nutrition and health: the ability of scientists to determine whether you have genes that increase your predisposition to specific diseases. This ability emerges out of the incredible Human Genome Project that, after decades of remarkably difficult and diligent work, mapped out the genetic code of a human being. With the DNA code now in hand, scientists are able to identify the role that each gene plays in putting you at risk of everything from heart disease to cancer.

More than that, a new field of health has emerged—Nutrigenomics, the science of linking or targeting specific nutrients to people with specific gene problems. Targeting nutrients is not new (the American Heart Association has long recommended fish-oil supplements to those at risk of heart disease). What is new is the increasing precision and confidence with which nutrients and potential health problems can be linked.

Companies such as Interleukin Genetics Inc. are already providing health advice based on their testing of an individual's DNA, and the costs are surprisingly low, even at this early stage of nutrigenomics. And it's easy—you request a test package from the company, a kit arrives at your home, you swab your own mouth for DNA material, and mail the package back. In a reasonably short time, results of your DNA test are sent to you along with advice about nutritional supplements you may require if a genetic fault was revealed. It's almost like being part of a CSI television show.

The concept requires a bit of elaboration, though. Just because a genetic fault may be found in your DNA sample does not mean you will get the disease linked to the particular fault (such a fault is called a SNP and pronounced SNIP—short for *Single Nucleotide Polymorphisms*). The point is that DNA is not the only influence on your well-being. Once you know you have a potential for a given disease, you can alter your diet and lifestyle to mitigate the risks. You can also nutritionally optimize both your food and supplements intake. The goal of acquiring such precise information about your DNA is to take achievable, proactive measures against known risks. Remember, your DNA is the gun; your diet and lifestyle can pull the trigger.

The combination of the science of nutrigenomics and the science underlying the production of outstanding food supplements may well mark a beginning of wonderful things to come for those interested in optimal well-being.

Step 4:
Identify The Totally Terrific Brands

Armed with knowledge about supplements that will meet your personal needs, you can now begin your search for the best brands. Unfortunately, there are a lot of bad supplements on the market, for all the reasons imaginable, including a national system of regulations in the United States that continues to be less than satisfactory. Even in Canada, where GMP regulations recognize supplements as distinct from food, more attention is paid to safety than to optimization of health benefits. More concern is shown for manufacturing than for the quality of the raw materials or the quality of the soil from which raw materials come. Nevertheless, companies do exist that reflect public concerns for quality and exceed government standards: these companies make good supplements.

But why accept merely good supplements, when, with a bit of discernment and critical questioning, you can find some totally terrific supplements? Remember: the most expensive supplements are those that do not work optimally or that do not work at all or even cause you harm.

The best thing to arm yourself with as you conduct your shopping is a set of clear questions you can pose to shop owners, distributors, and supplement manufacturers. If you can get all these questions answered satisfactorily, you will have found yourself a totally terrific source of food supplements. Terrific!

TEN TOTALLY TERRIFIC QUESTIONS

In the name of making choices based on science, not emotion, we recommend you ask these carefully considered, proven questions whenever you shop. Be forthright with the persons from whom you're considering purchasing health products. Pose the following questions to them right at the start. That will alert them to the fact you're not merely a passive customer and that you take your nutritional needs most seriously.

If they won't accept your questions or can't answer each and every one, their products are not for you. By the way, when you encounter sellers or manufacturers who can't or won't answer these questions, you're directly in touch with the Nutritional Void.

Here are the questions we recommend to help you identify the totally terrific supplements you're looking for. We've provided a short version at the end of the chapter for you to take along on your supplement shopping trip. Every question on this list should be answered with "yes."

If not, you haven't found a totally terrific product.

QUESTION 1

Is your multi-supplement primarily a plant-based product that includes vitamins, minerals and phytonutrients?

UNDERLYING PRINCIPLES

First, only whole plants can provide all the nutrients your body demands.

Second, it's reasonable for a company to complement a plant-based multi-supplement with lab-produced nutrients for a number of practical reasons (to avoid producing huge tablets, for example, or to ensure precise dosage), but its product line must feature whole-plant compounds for their synergistic and bioavailability qualities. There is no "work-around" on this issue (see Chapter 2).

Third, it's not enough to include merely vitamins and minerals. That's the old standard, but recent research shows how important it is to have phytonutrients included in your multi-supplement (see Chapter 12).

QUESTION 2

If the multi-supplement is plant-based, is it derived from a variety of plants?

UNDERLYING PRINCIPLE

Phytonutrients vary from plant to plant, so you need a supplement that provides Nature's diversity (see Chapter 12). If we only needed one plant source, Mother Nature would have designed only one. Variety is her hallmark for some very good reasons; it should be yours, too.

QUESTION 3

If the multi-supplement is plant-based and derived from a variety of plants, does the manufacturer own its own land and grow, harvest, and concentrate its own plants?

UNDERLYING PRINCIPLE

A rich, broad-spectrum soil is required to produce healthy plants, and you want to ensure the plants in your supplements came from such soil (see Chapter 2). The more a company out-sources its products (does not produce them itself), the greater the chances of loss of nutrients and quality control.

Neither Canadian nor American GMP standards refer to the soil from which a company's raw materials come. In both countries, it's up to you to promote the need for certified organic soils and all the goodness that comes from them.

Help organic farmers by insisting on their products: visit farmers' markets, buy from health food stores, ask your local food stores to include certified organics in their inventory, and insist (of course) on certified organic food supplements.

QUESTION 4

Does the Vitamin C supplement contain the whole-plant concentrate, including associated phytonutrients?

UNDERLYING PRINCIPLE

Vitamins and minerals and phytonutrients work in partnerships with one another. That's why you want a whole-plant source for just about everything (see "synergy" in Chapters 8 – 12).

Your Vitamin C supplement should contain more than just ascorbic acid. There are times when you may require more of the Vitamin C molecule itself (ascorbic acid) than your whole-plant multi-supplement provides. In those cases, phytonutrient content may have to be diminished, but it shouldn't be eliminated.

QUESTION 5

Are the supplements certified organic from the soil and seed up?

UNDERLYING PRINCIPLE

Sometimes, a product can be certified just from manufacturing onward and not from the soil and seed where processing of a totally terrific supplement really begins. Beginnings are where things typically go wrong in all aspects of our lives. If the seed is not certified organic or if the company out-sources its seeds without insisting on certified organic origins for them, then all that follows is less than it should be. And if a company is going to cut corners at this point, you can expect them to be less scrutinous throughout their operations than you need them to be.

QUESTION 6
Is the disintegration time on the tablet 30 minutes or less?

UNDERLYING PRINCIPLE

You should think of vitamins, minerals, and phytonutrients as food. For optimum digestion, they must be broken down and prepared in the stomach, just as food is, before they are passed into the small bowel for interaction with specific and various enzymes and for absorption. The U.S. Pharmacopoeia's (USP) standard is 15 – 30 minutes.

QUESTION 7
Does the manufacturer *voluntarily* adhere to Good Manufacturing Practices from seed to end product and to the The Council for Responsible Nutrition for its fish oil products?

UNDERLYING PRINCIPLE

This question and the previous one relate to the concept of Good Manufacturing Practices, or GMP (see Chapters 2 and 7). Only companies voluntarily adhering to the standards of GMP (from seed to tablet) are in control of their supplements' quality.

For now, assume that manufacturers not prepared to

identify the GMP guidelines they follow do not deserve your consumer loyalty.

As well, standards of quality for fish oils developed by The Council for Responsible Nutrition's "Omega-3 Monograph" are the base line for toxin-free, safe products. The standards cover raw materials, manufacturing, packaging, and nutrition. Make sure your potential fish oil provider is one of the voluntary members of the CRN and that they comply with its standards. You can usually find this information on the company websites.

QUESTION 8

Does the manufacturer assay its entire line for heavy metals, microbiological contaminants and pollutants, and desirable nutrient compounds?

UNDERLYING PRINCIPLE:

It bears repeating here what we said earlier: Information obtained from the FDA in May 2007 states that a company "does not have to provide FDA with the evidence it relies on to substantiate safety or effectiveness before or after it markets its products." Recall, too that *Consumerlab.com* reported finding contamination with toxins such as lead, mercury, and PCBs in supplements.

QUESTION 9

Does the manufacturer have *published* Bio-Assays that I can easily access?

UNDERLYING PRINCIPLE

Toxins are common-place in our environment and can overwhelm any goodness present in organic compounds. Companies must be ethical and held accountable in demonstrating they are not including known toxins in their products.

QUESTION 10

Does the manufacturer publish an ORAC score on its anti-oxidants that is based on a wide range of Free Radical groups?

UNDERLYING PRINCIPLE

ORAC (Oxygen Radical Absorbance Capacity) is a measuring standard for quantifying how effective a product is at dealing with free radicals. A totally terrific supplement will also identify the specific Free Radical groups it protects against (see Chapter 12).

So there you are: our Ten Totally Terrific Questions designed to help you achieve optimal supplementation. Every single question on this list should be answered with "Yes." If the answer is "No" or ambiguous, look for another brand, because you have not found a totally terrific product.

The last page of this chapter has all these questions laid out so you can either cut them out or photocopy them to take along with you on your next supplements shopping trip.

Try it out—you might be uncomfortable the first time or so that you ask a retailer such detailed and direct questions about his or her products, but you'll get past the discomfort soon enough. Then you'll simply enjoy the experience of knowing you're filling your Nutritional Void.

BOTTOM LINE SECRETS

A MULTI-SUPPLEMENT consisting of vitamins, minerals, and phytonutrients (not just vitamins and minerals) is the best bang for your nutritional buck. Add an Essential Fatty Acid (EFA) and a phytonutrient supplement and you're well on your way to building a solid nutritional foundation.

WOMEN, MEN, SENIORS, YOUTH, AND CHILDREN have characteristics or experience circumstances unique to their respective age groups. They may require the assistance of particular supplements not necessarily found in multi-supplement blends alone. For example, women may need GLA for menopause issues or calcium-magnesium with Vitamin D and other nutrients to help protect against osteoporosis, men may need saw palmetto with nettle root for prostate and urinary problems, seniors may want ginseng with gingko biloba to help increase oxygen flow to the brain or cetylated esters for inflammatory conditions, and youth may require probiotics to help compensate their junk food diets.

A TOTALLY TERRIFIC MULTI- or phytonutrient supplement can be traced from the broad-spectrum, certified organic soil that gave sustenance to the seed that became the plant that the company concentrated into the tablet that you put in your mouth. A bad, or even a (merely) good supplement, has no such history.

ESSENTIAL FATTY ACIDS (EFAs) should be subjected to the same rigor of standards as other supplements. Purchase from companies that voluntarily comply with The Council for Responsible Nutrition's Omega-3 Monograph.

YOUR DNA CAN BE ASSESSED for SNPs (pronounced SNIPS, standing for Single Nucleotide Polymorphisms) that may put you at risk for particular diseases.

MANUFACTURERS OF FOOD SUPPLEMENTS may or may not voluntarily comply with the highest food production standards (GMP and CRN), especially in the USA. The Ten Totally Terrific Questions will provide an insurmountable challenge for non-compliant companies to answer. That makes these questions very powerful shopping and research tools to help you identify only the totally terrific food supplements.

TEN TOTALLY TERRIFIC QUESTIONS are tailored to help sort out the good, the bad, and the totally terrific supplement companies. After all, there *are* totally terrific companies out there, and you will find them willing and able to answer your questions.

YOU'RE DONE! NOW WHAT?

If you're reading this page, you're either one of those who like reading the last page of a book first, or you've read the whole book in order. Perhaps you've only read those chapters that seem to speak directly to YOU and left the others to another day.

We're happy with however you got here, because just having our book in your hands indicates you're likely to challenge yourself, your family, your supplements providers, your doctor, and your government to raise standards of quality concerning, at least, the production of food supplements. If you've already read the entire book, you know why this is so important.

When you challenge manufacturers and retailers with the Ten Totally Terrific Questions, you are, in effect, speaking for all of us. The greatest power in our countries belongs to those who speak the loudest, the smartest, with the most persistance, and with the strongest convictions. By learning what you need to know to truly look after yourself, and by acting on that knowledge, you evoke the power of all of us who are doing the same thing at the same time.

Can you imagine what would happen if millions of people demanded "Yes" answers to each of the totally terrific questions before buying their supplements?

Sound a little idealistic?

Exactly!

We invite you, now, to turn the page and note we have put the Ten Totally Terrific Questions all together for you. Copy them and try them out. We wish you good shopping and optimal health.

Gloria Askew

Jerre Paquette

TEN TOTALLY TERRIFIC QUESTIONS

1. Is your multi-supplement a plant-based product that includes vitamins, minerals, and phytonutrients?

2. If the multi-supplement is plant-based, is it derived from a variety of plants?

3. If the multi-supplement is plant based and derived from a variety of plants, does the manufacturer own its own land and grow, harvest, and concentrate its plants?

4. Does the Vitamin C supplement contain the whole-plant concentrate, including associated phytonutrients?

5. Are the supplements certified organic from the soil and seed up?

6. Is the disintegration time on the tablet 30 minutes or less?

7. Does the manufacturer *voluntarily* adhere to Good Manufacturing Practices from seed to end product and to The Council for Responsible Nutrition for its fish oil products?

8. Does the manufacturer assay its entire line for heavy metals, microbiological contaminants and pollutants, and desirable nutrient compounds?

9. Does the manufacturer have published Bio-Assays that I can easily access?

10. Does the manufacturer publish an ORAC score on its anti-oxidants that is based on a wide range of Free Radical groups?

A FINAL WORD

While reading this book, you may have looked for specific instructions about which supplements to take and in what doses. In a book designed for general information and eduation, we can't provide that information.

As we have indicated throughout, we want you to gain the advice of qualified healthcare professionals who know you as a unique individual and who are fully trained in the fields of nutrition and supplementation.

When you consult with your healthcare professional, though, take along your Ten Totally Terrific Questions. We think you'll find that some healthcare providers have not adequately researched supplements and supplements quality. You may even know more than some healthcare professionals when it comes to finding Totally Terrific Supplements.

In the end, you have to take responsibility for your own nutritional status and your own journey out of the Nutritional Void. We expect this book will help you do that.

Gloria Askew

Jerre Paquette

REFERENCES

"Association between serum concentrations of 25-hydroxyvitamin D and gingival inflammation," American Journal of Clinical Nutrition . September 2005; 82 (3): 575-580.

"Canadian Cancer Society announces Vitamin D recommendation." 2007. Canadian Cancer Society. http://www.cancer.ca/ccs/internet/ mediareleaselist/0,3208,3225_235480453_1997623427_langId-en,00. html . June 8.

"Chromium picolinate supplementation attenuates body weight gain and increases insulin sensitivity in subjects with type 2 diabetes." Diabetes Care. 2006 29: 1826 – 1832.

"Chromium supplementation shortens QTc interval duration in patients with type 2 diabetes mellitus." American Heart Journal 2005; 149(4): 632 – 636.

"Coconut Palm: From Island Myth to Deadly Diet or Healing Miracle? The Importance of Coconut Oil, The." Http://www.coconut-connections.com/ res1.htm. Accessed March, 2006.

"Effect of Vitamin E and Beta Carotene on the incidence of lung cancer and other cancers in male smokers, The." 1994. The Alpha-Tocopherol, Beta Carotene Cancer Prevention Study Group. New England J Medicine, 330:1029-1035.

"Higher dose vitamin D prevents first osteoporotic fracture." JAMA 2005; 293:2257 – 64.

"Minerals." Linus Pauling Institute. Oregon State University. Micronutrient Information Center. http://lpi.oregonstate.edu/infocenter/minerals/html . Accessed February 10, 2007 and February 17, 2007.

"Osteoporosis: A debilitating disease that can be prevented and treated." 2006. www.nof.org. January 26.

"Prenatal Multivitamin Supplementation and Rates of Pediatric Cancers: A Meta-Analysis." Clinical Pharmacology & Therapeutics (2007) 81, 685–691. doi:10.1038/sj.clpt.6100100; published online 21 February 2007

"Proteins and enzymes." http://universe-review.ca/F11-monocell. htm#proteins accessed March 15, 2006.

"Randomized clinical trials of fish oil supplementation in high risk pregnancies." British Journal of Obstetrics and Gynecology. 2000. Vol.107 pp. 382 – 395. March.

"Study Indicates Omega 3 Fatty Acids Influence Mood, Impulsivity And Personality," University of Pittsburgh Medical Center. http://www.upmc. com. Posted: March 4, 2006.

"What is the glycemic index?" http://www.glycemicindex.com/ . Home of the Glycemic Index. University of Sydney. Accessed March 17, 2006.

Agency for Toxic Substances and Disease Registry, Department of Health and Human Services, Centers for Disease Control. "Case studies in environmental studies (csem): lead toxicity." http://www.atsdr.cdc.gov/ HEC/CSEM/lead/cover.html#alert. Accessed June 17, 2007.

American Diabetes Association. "Diabetes Statistics." http://www.diabetes. org/diabetes-statistics.jsp. Accessed March 22, 2006.

American Heart Association and American Stroke Association. "Heart Disease and Stroke Statistics—2006 Update." www.americanheart.org. Accessed March 22, 2006.

Anne M. Lewis, Sheelu Varghese, Hui Xu and H. Richard Alexander. "Interleukin-1 and cancer progression: the emerging role of interleukin-1 receptor antagonist as a novel therapeutic agent in cancer treatment." 2006. http://www.translational-medicine.com/content/4/1/48. November 10.

Attention deficit disorder: Facts, prevention and treatment strategies. http:// www.healingwithnutrition.com/adisease/add-adhd/add-adhd.html. March 2, 2006.

Australian Academy of Science. "When bugs have you on the run: Chemicals in Food." 2006. http://www.science.org.au. January 28.

Barrow, C.J.. Land degradation: Development and breakdown of terrestrial environments. 1991. Cambridge: Cambridge University Press.

Batmanghelidj, F., MD. Your body's many cries for water. 1995. Vienna, Virgina: Global Health Solutions Inc..

BBC News. "Heart disease and stroke: The facts." http://news.bbc.co.uk/ hi/english/static/in_depth/health/2000/heart_disease/default.stm . Accessed March 21, 2007.

Beach, Rex. "Modern Medical Men." A review of the work of Dr. Charles Northen, reprinted from Cosmopolitan Magazine. 1936. Senate Document #264, 74th Congress 2nd Edition. U.S. Printing Office, Washington DC.

Beck, Leslie. Interview on CTV Television. March 21, 2007.

Bennett, Peter, ND, RAc, DHANP. Coenzyme Q10 and the human energy crisis. 2005. Alive Magazine. No 267. January.

Berkson, D. Lindsey. Healthy digestion the natural way. 2000. New York, New York: John Wiley & Sons, Inc. 2000.

Better Life Institute. Antioxidants and plant nutrients. 2002. Grand Rapids, MI: Better Life Unlimited.

Better Life Institute. Why supplement? 2005. Grand Rapids, MI.: Better Life Unlimited.

Birch EE, D.G. Birch, D.R. Hoffman, R. Uauy. Dietary essential fatty acid supply and visual acuity development. Investigative Ophthalmology & Visual Science. 1992 October 33(11):3242 – 53.

Blanchard, Ken, M.D., Ph.D. with Marietta Abrams Brill. What your doctor may not tell you about hypothyroidism: A simple plan for extraordinary results. 2004. New York, New York: Warner Books.

Boschmann, Michael, Ph.D. Presentation on ECGC fat oxidation. 2006. Quoted in http://www.medicalnewstoday.com/articles/53704.php October 6.

Borek, CarmiaDietary, Ph.D. "Antioxidants and human cancer." 2004. Integr Cancer Ther 2004; 3; 333. http://ict.sagepub.com/cgi/content/ abstract/3/4/333. Accessed March 26, 2006.

Bowen P., L. Chen, M. Stacewicz-Sapuntzakis, C. Duncan, R. Sharifi, L. Ghosh, H.S. Kim, K. Christov-Tzelkov, R. van Breemen. "Tomato sauce supplementation and prostate cancer: lycopene accumulation and modulation of biomarkers of carcinogenesis." 2002. http://www. ebmonline.org/cgi/content/abstract/227/10/886

Bretherton-Watt, D., R Given-Wilson, J. L. Mansi, V Thomas, N Carter and K W Colston. "Vitamin D receptor gene polymorphisms are associated with breast cancer risk in a UK Caucasian population." British Journal of Cancer. 2001; 85:171 – 175.

Bryhn, Morten, MD, Ph D. "Marine omega-3 fatty acids are the preferred source of epa and dha in humans." http://www.omega-3.ch/essential_n-3_FA.htm. Accessed March 2006.

Canadian Association of Naturopathic Doctors. "Position paper: Avian flu." 2006. www.cand.ca. February 17.

Canadian Association of Naturopathic Doctors. "Position paper: Flu vaccines." 2006. www.cand.ca. February 17.

Canadian Association of Naturopathic Doctors. "Position paper: severe acute respiratory syndrome (SARS)." 2006. www.cand.ca. February 17.

Canadian Association of Naturopathic Doctors. "Position paper: West nile virus." 2006. www.cand.ca. February 17.

Carper, Jean. Your miracle brain. 2000. New York, New York: Harper Collins Publishers.

Carpi, Anthony, Ph.D. "Carbohydrates." http://www.visionlearning.com/library/module_viewer.php?mid=61 accessed March 4, 2006.

Carpi, Anthony, Ph.D. "Fats and Proteins." 2006. http://www.visionlearning.com/library/module_viewer.php?mid=62&l=&c3 March 2.

Chang, Adrian Q.S. 2004. Innovative Engineering. Honolulu, Hawaii. Interview with Author. November.

Chichoke, Anthony J., DC, PhD. Enzymes: The sparks of life. 2002. Burnaby, British Columbia: Alive Books.

Clese Erikson, MPAff; Edward Salsberg, MPA; Gaetano Forte, BA; Suanna Bruinooge, BA; Michael Goldstein, MD. 2007. "Future supply and demand for oncologists: Challenges to assuring access to oncology Services." 2007. Journal of Oncology Practice, Vol. 3, No. 2, March 2007: 79 – 86.

Colgan, Michael. The new nutrition: Medicine for the millenium. 1995. Vancouver, BC: Apple Publishing.

Conklin, Sarah, Ph.D. Quoted in http://www.upmc.com. Accessed March, 2006.

Cooperman, Todd, M.D., William Obermeyer, Ph.D., and Denikse Webb, R.D. Ph.D, eds. Guide to buying vitamins supplements: What's really in the bottle? 2003. White Plains, New York: ConsumerLab.com.com, LLP.

Cooperman, Todd, MD. "No more mass confusion in the vitamin aisle: What you need to know when buying vitamins and other natural remedies." 2005. Reprinted from Daily Health News. http://www.bottomlinesecrets.com/blpnet/article.html?article_id=37297. September 29.

Cranton, Elmer M., MD. "Modern bread, The Broken Staff Of Life." 2004. http://drcranton.com/nutrition/bread.htm . April.

Crook, William G., M.D., and Marjorie Hurt Jones, R.N. 1989. The yeast connection cookbook: a guide to good nutrition and better health. Jackson, Tennessee: Professional Books.

CSPI's guide to food additives. 2006. http://www.cspinet.org/reports/hemcuisine.htm#Alphabetical . February 2.

Davies, C.L, M. Loizidou , A.J. Cooper , et al. "Effect of gamma-linolenic acid on cellular uptake of structurally related anthracyclines in human drug sensitive and multidrug resistant bladder and breast cancer cell lines." Eur J Cancer, 1999. 35:1534-1540.

Dean, Carolyn, M.D., N.D.. The magnesium miracle : discover the essential nutrient that will lower therisk of heart disease, prevent stroke and obesity, treat diabetes, and improve mood and memory. 2007. New York: Ballantine Books.

Dolecek, Therese. Epidemiological evidence of relationships between dietary poly-unsaturated fatty acids and mortality in the multiple risk factor intervention trial. Proceedings of the Society for Experimental Biology & Medicine 1992; 200(2):177 – 82.

Dufty, William. Sugar blues. 1975. New York, New York: Warner Books Inc.

Enig, M.G., PhD and Sally Fallon. 1998. The Oiling of America. Nexus Magazine 6, no.1.

Enig, M.G., PhD and Sally Fallon.. "The Skinny on Fats," 1999. http://www.westonaprice.org/knowyourfats/skinny.html. Accessed August 2005.

Enig, M.G., PhD. Know your fats: The complete primer for understanding the nutrition of fats, oils, and cholesterol. 2000. Bethesda Press.

Enig, M.G., PhD. Trans fatty acids in the food supply: A comprehensive report covering 60 years of research. 1995. 2nd Edition. Silver Spring, MD: Enig Associates, Inc.

Enig, Mary, Ph.D. "Gamma-Linolenic Acid," Winter 2004. Appearing in The quarterly Magazine of the Weston A. Price Foundation. http://www. westonaprice.org/knowyourfats/gamma-linolenic.html.

Enzyme Essentials, LLC. "The Main Food Substrates: Proteins." 2002. http:// www.enzymeessentials.com/HTML/substrates.html.

Erb, John E. and T. Michelle Erb. The slow poisoning of america. www. spofamerica.com

Erasumus, Udo. Fats that heal, fats that kill. 1994. Burnaby, B.C. Alive Books.

Eswaran, H., Lal, R., and P.F. Reich, P.F. "Land degradation: An overview," 2006. http://soils.usda.gov/use/worldsoils/papers/land-degradation-overview.html February 20.

Ewaschuk, JB and LA Dieleman. "Probiotics and prebiotics in chronic inflammatory bowel diseases." World J Gastroenterol 12, no. 37(2006): 5941 – 5950.

Fallon, Sally, and M.G. Enig, PhD. Diet and Heart Disease—Not What You Think. 1996. Consumers' Research. July 15 – 19.

Fallon, Sally, with M.G. Enig, PhD. Nourishing Traditions: The Cookbook that Challenges Politically Correct Nutrition and the Diet Dictocrats. 1999. 2nd Edition, New Trends Publishing, Inc.

Farr, Gary Dr. "Nutrition/Soil, Grass and Cancer Editorial review." 2002. http:// www.becomehealthynow.com/article/contactusmeet/525 .

FDA (Food and Drug Act). "Diabetes information," www.FDA.gov/diabetes/ food.htm#61 . Accessed May 2, 2007.

Framingham Heart Study. "National Heart, Blood, and Lung Institute." http:// www.framingham.com/heart/. Retrieved June 12, 2005.

Ghandi, Mahatma. Quoted in "The Art of Eating." http://www.artofeating. co.uk/P4_importance%20_of_chewing.html . Accessed August 11, 2007.

German, J.B., and C.J. Dillard. "Saturated fats: what dietary intake?" Am. J. Clinical Nutrition 2004 80: 550-559.

Geusens, Piet, MD, PhD, Carine Wouters, Jos Nijs, Yebin Jiang, Jan Dequeker. "Long-term effect of omega-3 fatty acids supplementation in active rheumatoid arthritis." Arthritis & Rheumatism Volume 37, Number 6, June 1994, pp 824 – 829.

Goebel, Lynne, MD. and Henry Driscoll, MD. "Scurvy." 2005. www.emedicine. com/med/topic2086.html .

Goyer, R.A. "Lead toxicity: from overt to subclinical to subtle health effects." Environmental health perspectives 1990 Jun; 86:177-81.

Harmon, D, et al. J Am Geriatrics Soc, 1976, 24:1: 292 – 8.

Harvard School of Public Health. "Vitamins." http://www.hsph.harvard.edu/ nutritionsource/vitamins.html. Accessed March 30, 2006.

Health Canada. "Drugs and health products." 2007. http://www.hc-sc.gc. ca/dhp-mps/prodnatur/index_e.html . May 1.

Higdon, Jane, Ph.D. "Biotin." Linus Pauling Institute, Micronutrient Information Center. Oregon State University. http://lpi.oregonstate.edu/infocenter/ vitamins/biotin/index.html. Accessed April 21, 2006.

Hoffer, Abram, M.D., PhD, FRCP (C). Hoffer's laws of natural nutrition. 2001. Kingston, Ontario: Quarry Press Inc.

Hoffer, Abram, MD., PhD, FRCP (C). Dr. Hoffer's ABC of natural nutrition for children. 1999. Kingston, Ontario: Quarry Press Inc.

Hull, Dr. Janet, PhD, MESc. www.sweetpoison.com. January 2005.

Hunter, Ian, Stephen A Green, Thomas M. MacDonald, Andrew D Morris. "Prevalence of Aietiology of Hypothyroidism in the Young." Arch Dis Child 2000; 83:207-210 (September). http://adc.bmj.com/cgi/content/ abstract/83/3/207. Accessed March 7, 2007.

Ingram, Dr. Cass. Nutrition tests for better health. 2004. Buffalo Grove, IL.: Knowledge House.

Institute of Medicine. "Dietary reference intakes for folate and other B vitamins." http://www.iom.edu/CMS/3788/4015.aspx . Accessed June 17, 2007.

Johnson, Carol. "A case for C." 2006. http://researchmag.asu.edu/articles/vitaminc.html . January.

Kris-Etherton; M. Penny, PhD, RD; William S. Harris, PhD; Lawrence J. Appel, MD, MPH. "Fish consumption, fish oil, omega-3 fatty acids, and cardiovascular disease." Circulation. 2002;106: 2747-2757.

Kunin, Richard A., MD. "Coenzyme Q10: A Miracle Vitamin." 2000. http://www.healthy.net/scr/column.asp?ColumnId=26&Id=543

Lapinskas, P. "Omega-6 fatty acids - What, why, where and how?" 2000. Conference paper presented at *A fitter future for fats?, Leatherhead Food Research Association,* Leatherhead, England. http://www.lapinskas.com/publications/3548.html . June 6.

Lichtenstein, A.H. and R.M. Russell. "Essential nutrients: Food or supplements? Where should the emphasis be?" JAMA. 2005;294:351-358.

Liebman, Michael, Ph.D. "The Truth About Oxalate: Answers to Frequently Asked Questions." Reprinted from *The Vulvar Pain Newsletter,* Number 22, Summer/Fall 2002

Linginger, Schuyler W., Jr., DC; Allan R. Gaby, MD; Steve Austin, ND; Donald J. Brown, ND; Jonathan V. Wright, MD; Alice Duncan, DC, CCH. The natural pharmacy: Healthnotes. 1999. Random House Inc.

Lipscombe L.L and J.E Hux . "Trends in diabetes prevalence, incidence, and mortality in Ontario, Canada 1995–2005: a population-based study," Lancet , Vol. 369, Issue 9563, 03 March 2007, Pages 750-756.

Long, Cheryl and Lynn Keiley. "Agribusiness and the decline of nutritious food," Mother Earth News. Republished on Organic Consumers Association, February 20, 2006 http://www.organicconsumers.org/corp/nutrition061304.cfm.

Lopez, D.A., MD; R.M. Williams, MD, PhD; K. Miehlke, MD. 1994. Enzyme: The fountain of life. Munchen, Germany: The Neville Press, Inc.

Lori Lipinski. "Milk: It does a body good?" The Weston A. Price Foundation. http://www.westonaprice.org/transition/dairy.html . Accessed February 18, 2007.

Lyon, Dr. Michael, MD.; Dr. Laurell, G. Christine, PhD. 2002. Is your child's brain starving? Food not drugs for life and learning. Canada: Mind Publishing Inc.

Maccaro, Janet, PhD, C.N.C. 2003. Natural health remedies. Lake Mary, Florida: Siloam, a Strang Company.

Mason, Pamela. Handbook of dietary supplements. 1995. Blackwell Science.

Mayo Clinic Staff. "Periodonitis." 2006. http://www.mayoclinic.com/health/periodontitis/DS00369 . November 21.

Mayo Clinic Staff. "Rickets." 2006. http://www.mayoclinic.com/health/rickets/DS00813 . November 7.

Merck Manuals Online Medical Library. "Introduction: Overview of Nutrition." http://www.merck.com/mmhe/sec12/ch152/ch152a.html#sec12-ch152-ch152a-5m . Accessed March 31, 2006.

Miller, J.W., R Green, MI Ramos, LH Allen, DM Mungas, WJ Jagust, MN Haan, JW Miller. "Homocysteine and cognitive function in the Sacramento area Latino study on aging." American Journal of Clinical Nutrition 78, no. 3 (2003): 441 – 447.

Mindell, Earl, R.Ph., Ph.D. 1994. Food as medicine. New York, New York: Pocket Books, a division of Simon & Schuster, Inc.

Mirkin, Gabe, M.D. "How do the bone-strengthening medications work?" 2006. http://www.drmirkin.com/joints/bone_drugs.html. January 8.

Moro G, et al. "A mixture of prebiotic oligosaccharides reduces the incidence of atopic dermatitis during the first six months of age." Arch Dis Child 91, no.10 (2006): 814 – 9.

Mother Earth News. http://www.motherearthnews.com/ reprinted at: http://www.organicconsumers.org/organic/momearth072805.cfm .

Murphy, J. M., Maria E. Pagano, Joan Nachmani, et al. "The Relationship of School Breakfast to Psychosocial and Academic Functioning." 1998. Archives of Pediatric and Adolescent Medicine, Hell152:899-907. September.

Murray, Michael T., ND. Supporting evidence: Top ten clinical research studies of 2004. 2005. Alive Magazine. January.

National Cancer Institute. "Cancer stat fact sheets: Cancer of all sites." http://seer.cancer.gov/statfacts/html/all.html?statfacts_page=all. html&x=14&y=17. accessed March 22, 2006.

National Center for Chronic Disease Prevention and Health Promotion. "Arthritis." http://www.cdc.gov/arthritis . Accessed March 21, 2007.

National Center for Chronic Disease Prevention and Health Promotion. "Healthy youth! Asthma." http://www.cdc.gov/HealthyYouth/asthma/index.htm . Accessed March 21, 2007.

National Centre for Complementary and Alternative Medicine, National Institutes of Health. "What's in the bottle? An introduction to dietary supplements." 2006. http://nccam.nih.gov/health/bottle/ . February 16.

National Institutes of Health Osteoporosis and Related Bone Diseases— National Resource Centre. "Osteoporosis overview." 2006. www.osteo.org. February 6.

National Institutes of Health. Office of Dietary Supplements. http://ods.od.nih.gov. Accessed February 10, 2007.

Oak Ridge National Laboratory. "Human Genome Project Information. http://www.ornl.gov/sci/techresources/Human_Genome/home.shtml.

Omenn, GS. et al. "Effects of a combination of Beta Carotene and Vitamin A on lung cancer and cardiovascular disease." 1996. New England J Medicine, 334:1150-1155.

Pauling, Linus. How to live longer and feel better. 1986. New York, New York: Harper Collins Publishers Inc.

Pelton, Ross. R. Ph. and James LaValle, B. R. Ph. The nutritional cost of prescription drugs: how to maintain good nutrition while using prescription drugs. 2000. Inglewood, CO: Morton Publishing Company.

Perricone, Nicholas, MD. The Wrinkle Cure. 2000. New York, NY: Warner Books.

Ronco, A., E. De Stefani, P. Boffetta, H. Deneo-Pellegrini, M. Mendilaharsu, and F. Leborgne. Vegetables, fruits, and related nutrients and risk of breast cancer: a case-control study in Uruguay. 1999. Nutr. Cancer 35: 111-119.

Sanda, Bill, MS, MBA. "The Double Danger of High Fructose Corn Syrup." http://www.westonaprice.org/modernfood/highfructose.html#author. Accessed March 15, 2006.

Shomon, Mary J. Living well with chronic fatigue syndrome and fibromyalgia: What your doctor doesn't tell you that you need to know. 2004. New York, New York: Harper Collins.

Shomon, Mary J.. "Autoimmune hypothyroidism. A mind-body exploration with Drs. Richard and Karilee Shames." http://www.thyroid-info.com/articles/shamesautoimm.htm . Accessed March 7/07.

Shoskes, D. Use of bioflavonoid quercetin in patients with long-standing chronic prostatitis. J Am Neutraceut Assoc 1999; 2:18-21.

Sikk, Gunn. "The G files: Distilled water." 2004. Video presentation and interview on Balance TV. August 3.

Slattery, M.L., J. Benson, K. Curtin, K.-N. Ma, D. Schaeffer, and J. D Potter. 2000. Carotenoids and colon cancer. Am J Clin Nutr 71:575-582.

Smith, Timothy J., MD. Renewal: Learn how to rejuvenate your cells, turn back the clock, and.... 1999. New York, New York: St. Martin's Press.

Smith, Timothy J., MD. "Why supplements are necessary—and introducing the optimum daily allowances." 2006. http://www.chiro.org/nutrition/FULL/Why Supplements Are Necessary.html. February 13.

St. Armand, R. Paul, M.D., Claudia Craig Marek,. What your doctor may not tell you about fibromyalgia fatigue. 2003. New York, New York: Warner Books.

Sundram, K., Tilakavati Karupaiah, and KC Hayes. Stearic acid-rich interesterified fat and trans-rich fat raise the LDL/HDL ratio and plasma glucose relative to palm olein in humans. Nutrition and Metabolism. 2007. http://nutritionandmetabolism.com/content/pdf/1743-7075-4-3.pdf . Accessed March 2007

Tarnopolsky, M. A., S. A. Atkinson, J. D. MacDougall, A. Chesley, S. Phillips, and H. P. Schwarcz. Evaluation of protein requirements for trained strength athletes. 1992. J Appl Physiol, Nov 1992; 73: 767-775.

Tavani, A., et al. Beta Carotene intake and risk of nonfatal acute myocardial infarction in women. 1997. Eur. J. Epidemiol. 13:631-637.

Taylor, Dr. Carl, B.Sc., Prof. Eng., MD, LMCC. "Diabetes: Strategies that Work." 2002. Audio tape series. Stony Plain, Alberta: Eden's Best Inc..

Thompson, Jenny (Ed.). "Bring on the Team." 2007. Health Sciences Institute. HSI e-alert. January 25.

Thompson, Jenny (Ed.). "Heart of gold." 2006. Health Sciences Institute e-Alert, International Edition. March 22.

Thompson, Jenny (Ed.). "The Multi-Tasker." 2006. Health Sciences Institute. HSI e-alert. December 28.

Thompson, Jenny (Ed.). "The Way of K." 2006. Health Sciences Institute e-Alert. September 12.

Thompson, Jenny (Ed.). "Fresh coat of paint." 2006. Health Sciences Institute e-Alert, International Edition. May 22.

Thompson, Jenny (Ed.). "Keeping it unreal." 2006. Health Sciences Institute e-Alert, International Edition. May 30.

Thompson, Jenny (Ed.). "Plant Life." 2006. Health Sciences Institute e-Alert. International Edition. August 21.

Thompson, Jenny (Ed.). "Secret protector." 2006. Health Sciences Institute e-Alert. February 9.

Thompson, Jenny (Ed.). "Trouble in the tunnel." 2006. Health Sciences Institute e-Alert. March 2.

U.S. Department of Health and Human Services, Centers for Disease Control and Prevention, National Center for Health Statistics, Hyattsville, MD. "Heart disease." http://www.cdc.gov/nchs/fastats/heart.htm . Accessed March 21, 2007.

U.S. National Institutes of Health, National Institute on Aging. "General Information." http://www.nia.nih.gov/Alzheimers/AlzheimersInformation/GeneralInfo/#howmany. Accessed April 26, 2006.

U.S. National Institutes of Health, Office of Dietary Supplements. "Dietary Supplement Fact Sheet: Vitamin B6." http://ods.od.nih.gov/factsheets/vitaminb6.asp. Accessed April 26, 2006.

U.S. National Institutes of Health, Office of Dietary Supplements. "Dietary Supplement Fact Sheet: Vitamin B12." http://dietary-supplements.info. nih.gov/factsheets/vitaminb12.asp#h11l . Accessed April 26, 2006.

University of Maryland Health Center. "Endocrinology health guide." http:// www.umm.edu/endocrin/index.htm. Accessed February 22, 2007.

Vanderhaeghe, Lorna and Patrick Bouic, J.D., Ph.D. The Immune System Cure: Nature's Way to Super-Powered Health. 1999. Scarborough, Canada: Prentice-Hall..

Vegetables without vitamins. Life Extension Magazine. 2001. http://www.sfsu. edu/~holistic/document/Down/Food_Health/vegetables.html

Verhoef, P., M.J. Stampfer, J.E. Buring, J.M. Gaziano, R.H. Allen, S.P. Stabler, R.D. Reynolds, F.J. Kok, C.H. Hennekens, W.C. Willett. Homocysteine metabolism and risk of myocardial infarction: Relation with vitamins B-6, B-12, and folate. 1996. American Journal of Epidemiology 143: 9:845 – 859. May 1.

Vinson, J.A. and P. Bose. Comparative bioavailability to humans of ascorbic acid alone or in a citrus extract. American Journal of Clinical Nutrition 1988;48:601 – 4.

Vita, Joseph A. Tea Consumption and Cardiovascular Disease: Effects on Endothelial Function. 2003. J. Nutr. 133:3293S-3297S, October.

Voisin, Andre. Soil, grass and cancer. 1959. New York 16, N. Y.

Weil, Andrew, M.D. Natural health, natural medicine. New York, New York: Houghton Mifflin Company. 1998.

Wentzler, Rich. The vitamin book. 1979. Garden City, NY.: Double Day & Company.

Weston, S et al. Effects of probiotics on atopic dermatitis: a randomized controlled trial. Archives of Disease in Childhood 2005 90: 892 – 897.

Whiting, Dr. Steven E. Trace minerals and learning disabilities--a third opinion. 2006. Booklet, Institute of Nutritional Science. San Diego, California. Summarized in http://www.healingwithnutrition.com/adisease/ add-adhd/add-adhd.html

Wikipedia. "Trans fat." 2006. http://en.wikipedia.org/wiki/Partially_ hydrogenated_vegetable_oil. Accessed March 22.

Willett, W.C., et al. Am J Clin Nutr, June 1995, 61(6S):1402S – 1406S

Willett, W.C., F Sacks, A Trichopoulou, G Drescher, A Ferro-Luzzi, E Helsing, and D Trichopoulos. Mediterranean diet pyramid: a cultural model for healthy eating. Am. J. Clinical Nutrition. June 1995; 61: 1402 – 1406.

Wolfram, S., D. Raederstorff, Y. Wang, S.R. Teixeira, V. Elste, P. Weber. TEAVIGO (epigallocatechin gallate) supplementation prevents obesity in rodents by reducing adipose tissue mass. Ann Nutr Metab. 49, 1:54-63, 2005.

Wolfram, S., Daniel Raederstorff, Mareike Preller, Ying Wang, Sandra R. Teixeira, Christoph Riegger and Peter Weber. Epigallocatechin gallate supplementation alleviates diabetes in rodents. American Society for Nutrition J. Nutr. 136:2512-2518, October 2006.

Wood, Shelly. "Interesterified fats poised to replace trans fats, but specter of CVD risk factor effects looms here, too." 2007. Interview w.ith K.C. Hayes. http://www.theheart.org/article/765927.do. January 19.

Yu YM, Chang WC, Wu CH, Chiang SY. Reduction of Oxidative Stress and Apoptosis in Hyperlipidemic Rabbits by Ellagic Acid. Journal of Nutritional Biochemistry. 2005 Nov; 16(11):675-81. Epub 2005 Aug 2.

INDEX